European Economic Integration
and the United States

⫸ LAWRENCE B. KRAUSE ⫷

European Economic Integration
and the United States

THE BROOKINGS INSTITUTION
Washington, D.C.

THE BROOKINGS INSTITUTION is an independent organization devoted to nonpartisan research, education, and publication in economics, government, foreign policy, and the social sciences generally. Its principal purposes are to aid in the development of sound public policies and to promote public understanding of issues of national importance.

The Institution was founded on December 8, 1927, to merge the activities of the Institute for Government Research, founded in 1916, the Institute of Economics, founded in 1922, and the Robert Brookings Graduate School of Economics and Government, founded in 1924.

The general administration of the Institution is the responsibility of a self-perpetuating Board of Trustees. The trustees are likewise charged with maintaining the independence of the staff and fostering the most favorable conditions for creative research and education. The immediate direction of the policies, program, and staff of the Institution is vested in the President, assisted by an advisory council chosen from the staff of the Institution.

In publishing a study, the Institution presents it as a competent treatment of a subject worthy of public consideration. The interpretations and conclusions in such publications are those of the author or authors and do not purport to represent the views of the other staff members, officers, or trustees of the Brookings Institution.

Foreword

SINCE THE END of the Second World War, economic integration has played an increasingly important role in the evolution of the European economy. The formation of the European Economic Community and the European Free Trade Association has affected international trade in manufactured products and agricultural goods, direct investment flows, and other international transactions.

In this book Lawrence B. Krause, a member of the Brookings Senior Staff, explores the consequences for the United States of the formation of the two organizations, for nearly every economic event occurring in them has an effect on major interests of the United States, and sufficient time has elapsed since the establishment of the EEC and EFTA to permit a comprehensive appraisal. In addition, new customs unions, based in part on the European model, are being formed in other areas such as Latin America, and these are of significance to the United States.

In making this assessment of the EEC and EFTA and their impact on the United States, the author has addressed himself to the general reader interested in economic integration, although, because of the nature of the subject, some technical issues are discussed.

The author acknowledges with gratitude the cooperation he has received from representatives of the EEC and EFTA in both Brussels and Geneva and from their representatives in Washington. He is also indebted to many officials of the member governments and to U.S. government officials for the many conversations he had with them. The author has benefited from the incisive comments he received from Richard Cooper, William Diebold, Jr., and Ronald McKinnon. Walter S. Salant made an important contribution by reviewing the entire manuscript. Joseph A. Pechman, Director of the Economic Studies Program, and William M. Capron were helpful advisers throughout. The statistical work could not have been accomplished without the assistance of Ilse Higgins, Lillian B. Buck, and especially Monica Rubens. Suzanne Conti and Joell Thomas typed the manuscript in its many drafts. The manuscript was edited by Rosalie Epstein, and the index was prepared by Florence Robinson.

The study was financed in part by the general support grant from the Ford Foundation and in part by Brookings Institution funds.

The views expressed in this book are those of the author and are not presented as the views of the staff members, officers, or trustees of the Brookings Institution or of the Ford Foundation.

KERMIT GORDON
President

October 1967
Washington, D.C.

Contents

CHARTS

APPENDIX TABLES

Introduction

IN JUNE 1955, the Foreign Ministers of France, Italy, the Federal Republic of Germany, Netherlands, Belgium, and Luxembourg met at Messina, Italy, to discuss the possibility of forming a united Europe. Their efforts led to the creation of the European Economic Community and thereby radically altered the economic structure of Europe. The implications of the EEC for the rest of the world have been profound. To establish a countervailing power, other European countries banded together to form the European Free Trade Association. The Latin American countries formed two separate common markets in the hope that the successful European formula for economic integration was transferable. Asia and Africa felt the impact of the changes in traditional commercial relations. And in the United States there was both hope for the political success of the union and fear that the United States might suffer economic loss.

The drawing of lines dividing member from nonmember countries has accentuated a trend toward regional economic integration that began after the war. At the same time a more general tendency toward closer economic relations among all countries has continued. The liberalization of international trade and the freeing of capital movements that have occurred since the recovery from the Second World War have brought all countries closer together in an economic sense.

It is against this background that the economic interest of the United States in European integration should be viewed. The economies of the United States and Europe are closely linked. If they were not, then the United States could take a detached and disinterested view of economic developments on the Continent. But, on the contrary, important interests of the United States are affected by practically every economic event occurring in the EEC and EFTA. The implications for the United States of both these regional arrangements need examination. Sufficient time has

1

now elapsed since their establishment to permit a comprehensive appraisal.

The primary purpose of this study is to provide such an appraisal. It examines both the European Economic Community and the European Free Trade Association and the impact of each upon the United States. Their effects on the international trade of manufactured products are considered in Chapter 2 and on agricultural goods in Chapter 3. The economic consequences of the EEC and EFTA for direct and indirect investment relationships are considered in Chapter 4. Chapter 5 deals with unresolved internal issues and Chapter 6 deals with the external relations of the Communities. Throughout the study, the implications for the United States are drawn in economic terms, but political factors are also discussed where appropriate.

The conclusions of this study were derived primarily with existing economic policies in mind. Important changes, such as the successful completion of the Kennedy Round of tariff negotiations or possible British accession to the Rome Treaty, will affect these results. The Kennedy Round is examined in the concluding chapter, as is the question of British membership, but other policy changes not currently anticipated could be of equal importance.

In appraising the economic consequences of European integration for the United States, it is desirable to have in mind some standard of performance against which actual events can be measured. The United States can reasonably expect the restrictions and difficulties it must face as a result of the formation of the EEC and EFTA to be no more burdensome than the sum of the restrictions previously imposed by the member countries. Since the EEC is the largest trading unit in the world and EFTA the second, it also seems reasonable to expect the EEC and EFTA to recognize the responsibility that each of them has in continuing progress toward the liberalization of world commerce. This expectation is formalized in the General Agreement on Tariffs and Trade (GATT), which recognizes customs unions and free trade areas as permissible exceptions to the general prohibition against discriminatory trading arrangements. The exceptions are based on the premise that, when countries are prepared to accept the obligations of membership in a full-fledged customs union or free trade area, they will also recognize their responsibilities to nonmember countries and correct injustices if they should arise.

Most of the important conclusions that can be derived from a study of this nature involve estimates of values. The impact of economic integration on nonmembers can never be measured with precision. But if the probable direction of change and an approximation of magnitudes can be established, then the attempt will have been worthwhile. Conclusions based on estimated effects must explicitly recognize the uncertainty involved. What makes this most difficult is the inability to estimate the degree of uncertainty or, in statisticians' language, the standard error of estimate.

In view of this, the many attempts to estimate dollar values in this study need some comment. Dollar estimates are most frequently misused when they are cited without due regard for the assumptions and quality of the statistics upon which they are based. To guard against misusing the estimates, one should ask the question, "How much different would the estimates have to be before the conclusion is reversed?" If the difference is not very great, then little confidence should be put in the conclusion.

The detailed methods used differ from chapter to chapter, depending on the subject matter. Clearly, the methods appropriate for analyzing the trade of manufactured products, where market factors predominate, will be inadequate for agricultural developments, where governmental interference is the rule. Nor will the methods employed for goods be adequate for capital movements.

Throughout, an attempt has been made to avoid two naive errors frequently made in analyzing economic integration. The first is to attribute all economic change since the formation of a customs union or a free trade area to economic integration without recognizing other contributing factors. The second error is to attribute certain economic effects to integration as a process, when they may be uniquely attributable either to the particular form of integration practiced by the EEC and EFTA or to the particular policies they have adopted. The European experience does have many valuable lessons for other areas, but much care is needed in translation.

CHAPTER ONE

Origins and Development of European Integration

To GAIN SOME UNDERSTANDING of the process of economic integration in Europe and of its effects, one must begin with an examination of the origins of the European Economic Community. In the early 1950's, many European statesmen believed that the development of an integrated Western Europe through new institutions was necessary to provide for the economic health of the area, to guarantee external security, and to ensure internal political stability. In addition, they believed that an integrated Europe could play a greater political role in the world.

The economic gains to be derived from European integration were recognized long before the postwar era, but post-World War II developments made them greater and more visible. The benefits come from expanding the size of the market open to producers. They are thus able to obtain the economies of scale resulting from mass production and specialization, and the economy as a whole can gain from the effects of greater competition. The advantages of integration assumed greater importance in the 1950's because technological developments that occurred during and after the war increased the size of the market necessary to support efficient industry. Competition from large U.S. business firms seemed insurmountable to European firms faced with small, fragmented markets and equipped with obsolete machinery. Larger markets and protection from the competition of U.S. products were thought necessary to sustain rapid European growth. Both could be obtained through economic integration.

The political gains from integration seemed at the time to be even more important than the economic ones. The destructive war in Europe was not followed by peace but by cold war. Under Joseph Stalin, the Soviet Union threatened the very existence of European governments. Germany was divided and faced a powerful Russian army on its frontier. Italy and France both experienced great uncertainties from having large Communist minorities within their borders. In this situation, only the military power of the United States maintained security. But the Europeans felt that they had to make an important contribution to their own defense, both to avoid being totally dependent on the United States, and to prepare for the day when U.S military forces would be removed from European soil. Integration through supranational institutions was thought to be both a means of ensuring efficient expenditure of the resources Europeans felt they could devote to security, and a way of downgrading independent military establishments. In Germany, particularly, integration was viewed as a means of providing sufficient strength in the West to convince the Soviet Union that nothing could be gained from a continued division of Germany, in the hope that reunification would eventually be permitted.

In addition to the military threat from the East, there were fears that peace could still be disturbed from within Western Europe. A recurrence of the war catastrophe was the concern uppermost in the minds of European statesmen, and therefore interest centered particularly on the future of Germany. A resurgence of German economic power was recognized as inevitable and also important to the well-being of Western Europe. But Germany's neighbors wanted a guarantee that this power would not be turned again to aggressive military uses. One solution was to integrate the German economy by institutional means with the rest of Europe to such a degree that an independent economic base for military action would no longer exist.

In addition to reinforcing the feeling of security of the other European governments, this solution had the advantage of being desirable from Germany's point of view. While waiting for reunification, Germany had to live as a divided country. Some of the frustration of this condition could be relieved by playing an equal role in a larger European enterprise, a role Germany could fill with honor.

Integration was also viewed as a means of giving Europe a greater voice in world political developments. The postwar scene was dominated by two powers, the United States and the Soviet Union. Small countries, even comparatively wealthy ones, could not expect to have much influence. In countries whose history and tradition had emphasized leadership in world affairs, such a change in fortunes could not be viewed with equanimity. The impotence of European initiatives was graphically demonstrated by the Suez crisis, during which the United States and the Soviet Union forced a reversal of the British and French actions. The only apparent way the European countries could escape being "a footnote to history" was to combine their national powers in an integrated European system.

Jean Monnet and the other founding fathers of the "European idea" had a definite use in mind for the political power that would be created by the unification of Europe. That power would be used in conjunction with the United States to promote the goals of the Atlantic Alliance. Europe and the United States would form a partnership based on their common ideals and would share decision-making authority.

It was possible to concur in the advisability of creating a unified Europe without agreeing to the Monnet conception of the purpose to which the power thus created would be used. General Charles de Gaulle found himself in such a position. De Gaulle conceived of Europe as a truly independent or "third force" in the world, not subservient to either the United States or the Soviet Union, and, in its larger conception, even including the Soviet Union. The "third force" conception, while a minority view, was shared by others in France and in other Continental countries.

With the passage of time, some of the original motivations for an institutionally integrated Europe have remained compelling, but others have become less so. The implications of these changes have been important for the continued development of the European Economic Community. During the last five or ten years, technological developments in industry, such as computers and supersonic aircraft, have underscored the value of large markets and financially strong enterprises, thereby reinforcing the desirability of economic integration. On the other hand, internal and external political developments have tended to reduce the need and desire for integration. The military threat of the Soviet Union has receded, particularly since the Cuban missile crisis, thereby reducing the force a common enemy provides to bind nations together. Also, the threat of internal instability has declined. France and Germany have signed a treaty of friendship described as the seal marking the end of Franco-German conflicts. While the concrete results of this pact are hard to discover, the very existence of the treaty and the frequent intergovernmental conferences involved are reassuring from the European point of view.

While the defensive motives for political integration were becoming less influential, the advantages of greater unity in European policies to provide more political independence from the United States were more widely recognized. Many Europeans agree with de Gaulle that a lessening of American dominance over the policies of the non-Communist world would be highly desirable, despite misgivings concerning de Gaulle's methods and ultimate objectives. The fear of being drawn into an Asian conflict has plagued political leaders in Europe, and has been an important force strengthening de Gaulle's position. Another dimension of the desire for greater European independence is the belief that the United States is preoccupied with Asian problems, and is therefore less interested in European developments and less able to provide imaginative leadership in Europe.

Conflicts over the goals of European unity and over the degree of supranationality of its institutions have marked the European movement during the postwar period. Indeed, the most far-reaching attempts to institutionalize unity through the European Defense Community (EDC) and the companion European Political Community (EPC) foundered on issues directly related to these conflicts. In order to circumvent this problem, the promoters of the "European idea" decided to concentrate their efforts on economic integration. European governments (France in particular) could enter into agreements in the economic sphere, as demonstrated by the formation and continued existence of the European Coal and Steel Community (ECSC), but were not prepared to accept a direct attack on national sovereignty, as shown by the defeat of the EDC proposal. Thus, the Rome Treaty establishing the EEC is devoid of provisions for political integration. However, political motives were paramount, and the ultimate objective of the EEC is still political unity. As frequently stated by Walter Hallstein, the long-tenured first president of the EEC, "The EEC is in politics, not in business." But, because of the limitations of the EEC, the desired political ends can be achieved only through economic means.

Institutions of the EEC
and Their Effects on Policy

The Treaty of Rome provided for a number of separate institutions for the EEC, including the Council of Ministers, the Commission, the Court of

Justice, and the European Parliament. These and other institutions have already been examined in great detail in existing literature and little remains to be added. It is important, however, to identify the centers of power in order to understand the influential factors in policymaking. The member governments reserved to themselves the power to decide policy issues not already codified in the treaty. The formulation of new policies occurs in the Council of Ministers, where the ministers function as representatives of the member governments. During most of the twelve-year transition period specified in the treaty, all important decisions in the Council require a unanimous vote. There are many difficulties inherent in such a requirement, since many decisions involve welfare transfers among members. Countries are loath to agree to a policy which results in some welfare loss for them, and they will be likely to block it until they are satisfied that other issues will be settled in a way to provide offsetting benefits. For purposes of balancing, unrelated issues get coupled together and this tends both to delay agreement and to promote "least common denominator" solutions. Since the process itself is cumbersome and painful, decisions once made are not easily reversed.

Nonmember countries have an interest in this system since they are affected by the decisions taken. With so many conflicting positions to reconcile, there is little room to accommodate the needs of countries not represented at the bargaining table. For example, little weight is given to the demands of American, Canadian, or Danish farmers in an EEC dispute over agricultural policy, since there are so many member farming groups to satisfy. Furthermore, countries bargaining with the Common Market for tariff concessions, or even membership, confront the reluctance of the EEC to reopen issues once settled. These characteristics of the EEC stem directly from the form of the decision-making machinery.

According to the treaty, unanimous decisions are to be replaced, in time, by majority voting on most issues, with the votes weighted roughly in proportion to the size of the country. Without the power of veto, an individual country would no longer be able to impose its will upon the others, and it would be forced to become more accommodating. It then might be possible to find solutions to problems involving the welfare of the Community as a whole, taking into account at the same time the legitimate interests of nonmember countries. Since majority voting has not yet occurred, its consequences cannot be appraised. However, it is difficult to envision a situation in which the vital interests of a country would be sacrificed without causing intolerable frictions within the group. During the constitutional crisis of 1965-66, the French proposed that the treaty be amended to ensure that this could not happen. While the treaty has not been changed, the dangers of majority voting have been dramatized, and if majority voting is to be used at all, it will be with a great deal of caution.

The executive functions of the EEC are performed by the Commission. While constitutionally devoid of much power, in practice the Commission has a very significant influence on policy. It directs a large staff of experts who, through their own research and by collating studies from the member countries, can support policy recommendations. There is no comparable group of experts whose testimony can be used as a counterweight to a Commission proposal. The Commission alone has the right to propose measures for the consideration of the Council of Ministers. The Council can obviously reject a Commission initiative, but in order to substitute a member-country-sponsored alternative, unanimous agreement is required. The Commission gains considerable power from its role as honest broker between the conflicting positions of member countries and from its ability to steer compromises in particular directions. The Commission's ability to direct the attention of the Council to subjects of its choosing is of some importance. Furthermore, the Commission is charged with the responsibility of representing the EEC in negotiations with other countries, and this adds to its stature. While limited by the negotiating mandate supplied by the Council, the Commission, through its own lobbying activities, and indirectly through its contacts with other governments, has a great deal of influence in the formulation of the mandate.

The Commission is the most supranationalistic institution in the EEC. Its members are nominated by member governments, but they are not country representatives. In the discharge of their duties, commissioners are supposed to have only the welfare of the Community as a whole in mind, and most evidence suggests that this is the case. Nonmember countries can turn to the Commission to obtain a sympathetic hearing of the problems involved in dealing with the Community. But the Commission, quite understandably, is concerned primarily with strengthening the Community, and particularly the supranational elements within it. When faced with a choice between pressing a divisive issue upon the member countries or allowing an injustice to be perpetrated upon a nonmember country, the latter course will be likely to be more attractive. It can be argued that, in the long run, the Community can become more responsible if it develops greater internal unity, but nonmember countries may suffer until this occurs. Fortunately, the interests of nonmembers can sometimes be accommodated without creating internal difficulties for the Community, and the Commission frequently takes the initiative in bringing this about.

The Treaty of Rome itself put into operation most of the measures needed to form a customs union. In the treaty, the member countries agreed to remove internal tariff and quota barriers and to equalize their external tariffs according to an established time schedule. While some decisions were made in the direction of speeding up the schedule, removal of governmental obstacles to internal trade proceeded at the predetermined rate. This was not the case in other areas—agriculture and antitrust policy, for example. The treaty indicated the necessity of formulating a policy in these and other fields, but provided for the actual policy to be worked out through the operations of the Community. Some of the unfinished policy issues are of such great importance that failure to reach agreement would seriously curtail, if not destroy, the EEC.

The Commission initiates studies of subjects on which the need for a common policy has been indicated by the treaty, and brings forward proposals to be considered by the Council. If a proposed policy is of some significance, differences of opinion develop among the member countries, and action by the Council is deferred. Because decisions require unanimous agreement, the Council frequently has not been able to take action. Commission proposals tend to build up in a backlog awaiting Council disposition. Decisions are delayed as long as possible. Action will finally be taken when the delay causes a crisis for one or more of the member countries or for the Community as a whole, but issues that can be delayed indefinitely are seldom settled. Problem solving under crisis conditions does not necessarily lead to poor solutions, but there are dangers. A solution is often a compromise between opposing positions, and while the original positions may have been investigated in detail, the full implications of the compromise may not be examined at all.

Some attempts have been made to improve the efficiency of the decision-making machinery. At times the Commission has taken an active hand in pressing for settlement of issues. By keeping pressure on the permanent delegates, by presentations to the European Parliament and to the public, and by lobbying in the capitals of the member governments, the Commission can highlight the importance of an issue so that failure to reach agreement would be disturbing to the entire Community. While this ensures that the issue will get serious consideration by the Council, the procedure cannot be repeated too frequently because of the risks of failure and because the goodwill which member governments feel toward the

Commission can be overtaxed. A second method of speeding decisions is the setting of arbitrary deadlines. If the Council is within sight of a solution, it can sometimes be induced to set a date by which an agreement will be reached. Having done this, the Council must either meet the commitment or be prevented from considering other problems. While deadlines set by the Council are frequently not honored, they are important in centering attention on the most crucial issues.

There is a lesson in all this for nonmember countries dealing with the Community. No matter how important a problem may be to a nonmember country, unless it is crucial for a member country no action will be taken. Furthermore, in negotiations with the EEC, it is very important to have deadlines by which progress must be made in order to have any hope of successful completion. This became obvious during the Kennedy Round of tariff negotiations under the General Agreement on Tariffs and Trade (GATT) and also in the efforts of many countries to conclude association agreements with the EEC.

Ideologies and EEC Policy

Since the first sitting of the Council of Ministers, the policy decisions of the EEC have been watched to see if a consistent pattern was emerging. Two separate but related questions have been posed for examination. First, are the internal policies closer to those advocated by a "Manchester" liberal or by a "dirigiste" central planner? Second, in its dealings with the outside world, is the EEC outward-looking or inward-looking? The answer to the first question bears upon the second one. Unless the Community accepts the discipline of the market place advocated by liberals, goods from nonmember countries will not be given easy access to the EEC. The second question concerns nonmember countries directly, since the Community could accept competition among producers within the EEC but be protectionist vis-à-vis outsiders.

The discussion of the Rome Treaty at the time of its inception left its ideological orientation very much in doubt. Those who hoped for a liberal Community could take comfort from the fact that the formation of a customs union implied a desire for more efficient markets. Furthermore, the treaty advocated free movement of capital and labor as well as goods. The inclusion of provisions for antitrust investigation and enforcement also pointed in a liberal direction. This side of the EEC was emphasized in the United States, and was important in mobilizing American support for the venture. However, another aspect of the Rome Treaty was emphasized in Europe. Aware that Socialist opposition in France was a major cause of the defeat of the European Defense Community proposal, the promoters of the EEC went out of their way to play down the free enterprise characteristics of the treaty and emphasized that the Community would be perfectly compatible with national planning of the French type, state ownership of selected industries, and advanced social legislation. It was argued that, with an expanded market, economic planning could be even more efficient, leading perhaps to a Community-wide French style economic plan. This line of argument was persuasive, and all the Socialist parties in the member countries supported ratification of the treaty. This view was also publicized in Britain in order to win Labour Party acceptance of the EEC. The EEC thus stood for different things for different people.

In the early years of operation, decisions taken by the EEC have reflected both sides of this ideological dispute. On the one hand, internal free trade of goods has been pursued with vigor, intramember movements of capital and labor have been liberalized, some antitrust regulations have been promulgated, and a few antirestraint directives issued. On the other hand, government management will remain paramount under the Common Agricultural Policy, horizontal mergers between firms have been universally permitted, and in some cases independent firms have been encouraged and even forced to merge. While Community-wide planning has not developed, the statistical groundwork is being laid for such an exercise. Of course, a mixed economy characterizes all of the advanced Western countries and there is no reason to expect or desire a purely competitive system for the EEC. The concern, however, is for the future development of some critical EEC economic policies. Since there is no known ideological framework, there is little basis for predicting future policy trends.

The attitude of the EEC toward external economic relations would be quite clear if words alone were considered. The Rome Treaty is explicit and the Commission spokesmen have been eloquent in proclaiming how outward-looking the Community is in economic dealings with the rest of the world. But in action, the picture is mixed. The Community did generalize the early rounds of internal tariff reductions to nonmember countries where conditions permitted, they did offer relatively generous tariff reductions in the Dillon Round of GATT negotiations, and they have brought the Kennedy Round of negotiations to a successful conclusion. But the Common Agricultural Policy is recognized even by Europeans as highly protectionist, and the EEC has been consistently insensitive to the problems created for European countries who are not members.

Reactions to the Formation of the EEC

Because of the economic importance of the EEC, nonmember countries were forced to consider the possible deleterious consequences which its formation might bring. If membership in a customs union gives economic benefits to a country, then exclusion implies the possibility of an economic loss. As member countries reduce their tariffs on products coming from other member countries and maintain levies on nonmember country products, traditional trading patterns can be undermined and economic losses can occur. This differentiation in tariff treatment can be considered "passive discrimination," in the sense that the system is not designed to hurt nonmember countries but may do so in bringing to member countries the benefits of free trade.

In the United States, most observers were sanguine about the prospects. Nonmember countries in Europe, however, were apprehensive. The EEC countries were major if not dominant trading partners for all of the European nonmember countries, and a loss of even a small percentage of the EEC market would be noticed. It was generally believed that a large part of the European recovery from the war was due to the liberalization of intra-European commerce promoted by the Organization for European Economic Cooperation (OEEC) and the Marshall Plan. It was inconceivable to many that governments would consciously segment the European market whose unity was thought essential to economic well-being. Thus, coming to terms with the EEC to prevent a market division within Europe became the major concern of many governments.

The limiting of the EEC to six Continental countries resulted from the choices of those not joining rather than from exclusionary policies of the members. This explains the cool reception the EEC has given most suggestions for healing the European trading breach. Sweden and Switzerland felt that their political neutrality prevented them from joining such a tight economic group, especially since political integration was anticipated. Austria was in a similar position, except that its neutrality was imposed by the Soviet Union in the Austrian State Treaty rather than self-selected. Denmark and Norway were wary of joining a customs union which, through the requirement of a uniform external tariff, might reverse traditional low-tariff policies, especially for raw materials, upon which their economies were built. Furthermore, they could not consider joining a customs union that did not include the other Scandinavian countries and the United Kingdom.

The United Kingdom has been most important in determining European regional developments. Britain emerged from the war as the strongest European country, having been neither defeated nor occupied. The sense of desperation that pervaded the Continent and the search for new institutions did not occur to the same extent across the English Channel. Britain recognized no economic necessity which would justify the compromise of national sovereignty that would result from joining a customs union. Furthermore, Britain wanted independence in order to fulfill its role as leader of the Commonwealth and to maintain its special relationship with the United States. Since there were no overriding political interests, the British rejected membership in the Common Market on the technical economic grounds of the difficulty it would cause for sterling and the investment position of the City of London, and because convincing economic arguments could not be made for membership.

It may well be that Britain never expected the Continental countries to succeed in forming a customs union, and would have been happy if they had not. Without Britain to mediate the differences between France and Germany, the proposed customs union was expected to go the way of the European Defense Community. When Britain finally realized that the Messina powers were going to be successful, a plan was devised to prevent intra-European trade discrimination. The British proposed a free trade area for Europe, with the EEC as one of its members. The proposal covered only industrial products, thus avoiding the difficulties of integrating British agriculture with Continental agriculture; demanded no coordination of external tariffs, leaving the British free to maintain Commonwealth preferences; and did not provide for a central executive authority or give any hint of political unification, leaving intact British independent foreign policy. After the proposal was submitted to the OEEC, it was remanded to a committee for investigation and negotiation under the chairmanship of Reginald Maudling, the British delegate.

It is understandable that the British initiative was greeted with suspicion by the EEC countries. The previous British position, and the content of the proposal, which seemed to satisfy all of Britain's requirements without regard for the interests of other countries, caused even some of the Anglophile Continentals to question British motives. The ardent supporters of the "European idea" were fearful that the supranational characteristics of the EEC would lose significance in the wider free trade area and their efforts would lead to nothing more than a commercial venture. They viewed free trade as an inducement to countries to accept constraints on their national sovereignty, and they did not want to grant the benefits of free trade without the obligations of supranationality. No doubt the coolness of the United States to the proposal was a reflection of this thinking. Nevertheless great effort went into the negotiations, and the many technical problems that were unearthed resulted in major changes in the proposal. But the French governmental crisis prevented further political discussions, and with the ascent of General de Gaulle to the leadership of the French government, the proposal was doomed. De Gaulle promptly terminated the negotiations, with the endorsement of the EEC Commission, in the name of maintaining the integrity of the Rome Treaty.

Creation of the
European Free Trade Association

Following the collapse of the free trade area negotiations, the British were reluctant to recognize the need for a rival trade bloc to the EEC. In fact, it was the Swedish government that took the initiative in calling for the discussions which led to the European Free Trade Association. Three important motives pushed the governments of Sweden, Great Britain, Norway, Denmark, Austria, Switzerland, and Portugal in this direction. First, there was great concern over the economic loss which would result from being excluded from the EEC and a belief that some relief could be obtained by free trade among themselves. Second, there was the hope that, through unity, they would have greater strength in negotiating with the EEC. None of the EFTA countries wanted a permanent division of Europe into rival groups, and they thought that EFTA provided the best strategy for preventing this. Third, there was the desire to prove that the free trade area was a viable concept despite the technical problem of trade deflection, that is, the importation of nonmember country products into low-tariff member countries and their subsequent reexportation to high-tariff member countries. And they wanted to show that this could be done with a minimum of centralized administrative machinery.

Once the EFTA negotiations were begun, agreement was reached rather easily, and in January 1960 the Stockholm Convention was signed. Very little administrative machinery was specified, since the provisions for trade liberalization were self-enforcing. The executive function was assigned to a Council, on which sat representatives of the member countries. The Council was to be serviced by a Secretariat, headed by a Secretary General, but no elaborate bureaucracy was envisioned, nor has it developed. EFTA in this respect is much closer to GATT than to the EEC. While many problems were recognized as possibly requiring joint action in the future, the only decision-making machinery thought necessary was the Council, in which member countries could negotiate solutions.

Overview of the EFTA Experience

Some of the characteristics of the EFTA countries are favorable for a free trade area. The United Kingdom has had traditional trade ties with the Scandinavian countries and Portugal upon which to build closer relations. Within the Scandinavian group, similarity in language and culture and common borders have already yielded much experience in economic cooperation. But some other factors are less favorable. Geographically, EFTA is dispersed around the Common Market and members on one side are quite far from those on the other. Austria and Switzerland in particular are isolated, and although they are neighboring countries, they have little trade with each other. Also, EFTA is greatly unbalanced. The United Kingdom alone accounts for half of the total population of EFTA and more than half of its gross national product, industrial production, and external trade. Thus, EFTA does not have the advantage of large equal members, so that an inadequate economic performance by one country is not counterbalanced by the others. Finally, Portugal is at a substantially different level of economic development from the other members, and requires constant attention to special adjustment problems.

Yet by most standards EFTA has been very successful. Not only have the countries adhered to the internal tariff reductions negotiated in Stockholm; they have speeded up the schedule, and internal free trade for industrial products was completed on January 1, 1967. EFTA accomplished this eighteen months before the EEC target date, despite the fact that the EEC had an eighteen-month headstart.

As seen in Table 1-1, these tariff reductions have had an impact on trade. Over the six-year period 1958-59 to 1965, intra-EFTA imports increased at a compound annual rate of 11.3 percent, compared to a 7.6 percent rate for EFTA imports from nonmember countries. Furthermore, the differential in rates in favor of intra-EFTA trade took place for every

TABLE 1-1

Growth of EFTA Imports and Exports, Selected Years, 1953–65[a]

(Dollar amounts in billions)

Type of Trade	1953	1958–59	1965	Compound Annual Rate of Increase (Percent)	
				1953 to 1958–59	1958–59 to 1965
Total imports	$15.4	$20.2	$33.8	5.2	8.3
From members	2.7	3.6	7.2	5.5	11.3
From nonmembers	12.8	16.6	26.7	4.9	7.6
Total exports	12.9	17.4	28.0	5.6	7.6
To members	2.5	3.4	6.8	5.4	11.5
To nonmembers	10.4	14.0	21.1	5.7	6.6

Sources: European Free Trade Association, *EFTA Trade 1959–64* (Geneva, 1966); International Monetary Fund-International Bank for Reconstruction and Development, *Direction of Trade, Annual 1961–65* (Washington, D.C., 1966); United Nations, *Commodity Trade Statistics*, Statistical Papers, Series D, Vol. III, No. 4 (New York, 1954).

[a] See App. A, p. 235, for discussion of choice of time periods. Detail may not add to totals because of rounding.

member country. (See Appendix A for country detail.) When measured by export growth, the contrast is even greater. Intra-EFTA trade grew at a compound annual rate of 11.5 percent and by only 6.6 percent to the rest of the world. The experience in the later period compared very favorably with that of the previous six years, when export trade among these countries grew at a compound annual rate of only 5.4 percent. Notably, other EFTA countries replaced the EEC as the most dynamic trading partners for EFTA members.

Another aspect of intra-EFTA trade is shown in Table 1-2. Between 1959 and 1965, intra-EFTA imports as a share of total member country imports increased from 17.6 percent to 21.2 percent. There was very little increase in these trade shares from 1953 to 1959. But the size of intra-EFTA trade shares is not large, and is even quite small for some of the member countries. In 1965, after six years of EFTA operation, only 15 percent of the imports of Austria and Switzerland came from other member countries. These shares had grown from about 12 percent in 1959, but the dependence of these two countries on the EEC for imports and for export markets was not reduced. In addition, Portugal, Sweden, and the

TABLE 1-2

EFTA Trade, by Member and Nonmember Shares, Selected Years, 1953–65

(In percentages)

Type of Trade	1953	1959	1965
Total imports	100.0	100.0	100.0
From members	17.4	17.6	21.2
From nonmembers	82.6	82.4	78.8
EEC countries	20.9	28.1	31.0
United States	8.0	9.0	9.6
Others	53.7	45.3	38.2
Total exports	100.0	100.0	100.0
To members	19.7	19.7	24.4
To nonmembers	80.3	80.3	75.6
EEC countries	20.6	23.4	26.5
United States	7.7	9.9	9.0
Others	52.0	47.0	40.1

Sources: EFTA, *EFTA Trade 1959–64*; IMF-IBRD, *Direction of Trade, Annual 1961–65;* U.N., *Commodity Trade Statistics,* Vol. III.

United Kingdom obtained more of their imports from the EEC than from EFTA countries, but the differential narrowed.

The most dramatic evidence of closer integration among the EFTA countries is in the Nordic area (Scandinavia plus Finland, an associate of EFTA). Among this subgroup of EFTA countries, trade has been expanding at a remarkable 17 percent annual rate. This rate of growth is much above that for EFTA as a whole, and above that achieved by these countries before EFTA. It also compares favorably with the Common Market's experience. The Nordic area trade has been particularly important to these countries in their efforts to diversify exports from traditional raw materials and slightly processed goods to more advanced forms of manufactured products. Ironically, it took the vision of a larger European association to persuade these countries to integrate their economies, a goal that was resisted when only a small Nordic customs union was proposed.

The very fact that EFTA still exists in its original form, however, indicates that it has failed in its aim of creating a single Western European market. The inability to come to terms with the Common Market has not been due to lack of effort. The unsuccessful free trade area negotiations clearly demonstrated that the Common Market would not grant the benefits of membership without its obligations. Even when the obligations are accepted, membership is not always granted. In 1961, Britain applied for full membership in the EEC, and the other EFTA countries, with the exception of Portugal, followed suit and submitted applications for membership or associate status. Not much can be added to what has been written on the subject of Britain's first attempt to become a full member of the EEC and the January 1963 de Gaulle veto. The negotiation was complicated by many technical issues over which reasonable men could and did differ, and errors of judgment on strategy and substance were by no means confined to one side, but one can still conclude that the British were "more sinned against than sinning." When de Gaulle finally had to face the issue of whether to admit a country that would threaten continued French political domination of the Community, he decided in the negative. The EFTA countries did not interpret the veto as closing the door to all possible ways of building a bridge between the two organizations, and numerous attempts to begin a dialogue have originated in EFTA, but the EEC has not responded positively to these overtures. In May 1967, the British once again applied for full membership in the EEC, but the outcome is uncertain.

Other crises have struck EFTA, the most important of which was the temporary 15 percent British surtax on imports imposed in November 1964 for balance-of-payments reasons. The surtax was applied to imports from all countries and only food and certain raw materials were exempted. The other members of EFTA were disappointed, if not outraged, by the British action. Being the largest country in EFTA, Britain was expected to be the most responsible member, but instead it forced part of its burden of adjustment onto other members. Denmark was particularly critical of this action, pointing out that the surtax violated the spirit of the EFTA agreement (as well as GATT commitments) and made the removal of the tax a necessary condition for the continued existence of EFTA. The British were somewhat surprised by the degree of hostility aroused, and responded by promising an early end to the tax. By the end of 1965, the tax was reduced to 10 percent and was eliminated completely on December 1, 1966.

A fundamental factor inhibits the closer integration of the EFTA countries. Despite its successes, there is an underlying feeling that EFTA is not a permanent organization. This feeling is shared by businessmen and governments of member and nonmember countries alike. Whether justified or not, the impact is very real. Business firms of member countries, with the exception of the Nordic area, have not made the investments needed for market penetration of other countries. American firms also have not invested in EFTA countries so that they could serve the entire EFTA market, as they have done in the EEC, although they continue to set up facilities to serve individual national markets. The bureaucracies of the member governments have not been reorganized to recognize EFTA, except in a superficial manner, and this failure has led to policy errors such as the British surtaxes. As long as member countries continue to limit their long-run commitments to EFTA, it will provide little more than a means for granting tariff preferences.

Overview of the EEC Experience

Having been launched with high hopes and substantial political commitments, the Common Market was "condemned to succeed," and it has succeeded, but not without setbacks and disappointments. The EEC should be judged primarily on its economic achievements, and they have been substantial. The conditions requisite for a successful customs union are all present: the members are advanced countries at an almost equivalent level of industrialization; they have long been major trading partners and have common geographical borders; they are all heavily engaged in international trade; and some of them had high tariffs originally, allowing much scope for rationalization. Furthermore, the EEC began during a period of economic prosperity, which made the required economic adjustments easier. In turn, because the EEC was successful, economic prosperity was prolonged and enhanced. Thus there has occurred an interaction between income growth and international trade in a "virtuous circle" often sought but seldom achieved.

The growth of trade of the EEC countries is shown in Table 1-3. Intra-

EEC trade, as measured by imports, grew at a truly remarkable compound annual rate of 17.0 percent between 1958-59 and 1965. This is almost double the growth rate of 9.2 percent for EEC imports from nonmember countries during the period. The contrast is somewhat greater when measured on the export side—a 17.1 percent annual rate of growth for intra-EEC trade compared to an 8.0 percent growth rate for exports to nonmember countries. While the trend toward closer trading ties among

TABLE 1-3

Growth of EEC Imports and Exports, Selected Years, 1953–65[a]

(Dollar amounts in billions)

Type of Trade	1953	1958–59	1965	Compound Annual Rate of Increase (Percent)	
				1953 to 1958–59	*1958–59 to 1965*
Total imports	$15.1	$23.7	$49.0	*8.5*	*12.0*
From members	4.0	7.4	20.4	*12.2*	*17.0*
From nonmembers	11.2	16.2	28.6	*7.1*	*9.2*
Total exports	14.3	24.0	47.9	*10.0*	*11.3*
To members	4.0	7.5	20.8	*12.3*	*17.1*
To nonmembers	10.3	16.5	27.1	*9.0*	*8.0*

Sources: U.N., *Commodity Trade Statistics*, Vol. III; IMF-IBRD, *Direction of Trade, Annual 1958–62* (Washington, D.C., 1963), and *Annual 1961–65*.
[a] Detail may not add to totals because of rounding.

these countries preceded the EEC, the growth rate of imports from members in the previous period, 1953 to 1958-59, was only 12.2 percent, substantially less than after the establishment of the EEC. Without exception, the growth of every member's intra-EEC trade has been noticeably greater than that with nonmembers. (See Appendix A for country detail.) The Benelux countries (Belgium, Luxembourg, and the Netherlands) have not had quite as high a rate of growth in imports from the EEC as the other members, but this was to be expected. Benelux, itself a customs union, has been in existence since 1948.

One of the most striking characteristics of the Common Market, and one that distinguishes it from EFTA, is seen in the data on shares of trade presented in Table 1-4. Between 1958 and 1965, the percentage of total

EEC imports coming from member countries increased from 29.5 to 41.7. Recognizing that a substantial portion of the goods imported from the outside world is raw materials and foodstuffs not available within the EEC, the increase in intra-EEC shares is clearly extraordinary. There is little doubt that the Common Market is mainly responsible for this development. Each of the member countries imports at least 30 percent of its needs from within the group, and this figure is over 50 percent for the Benelux countries. The largest increase in intra-EEC shares between

TABLE 1-4

EEC Trade, by Member and Nonmember Shares, Selected Years, 1953–65

(In percentages)

Type of Trade	1953	1958	1965
Total imports	100.0	100.0	100.0
From members	26.2	29.5	41.7
From nonmembers	73.8	70.5	58.3
EFTA countries	17.4	16.8	15.1
United States	10.4	12.2	11.6
Others	46.0	41.5	31.6
Total exports	100.0	100.0	100.0
To members	27.9	30.1	43.5
To nonmembers	72.1	69.9	56.5
EFTA countries	23.3	22.7	21.1
United States	7.2	7.3	7.2
Others	41.6	39.9	28.2

Sources: IMF-IBRD, *Direction of Trade, Annual 1958–62*, and *Annual 1961–65*; U.N., *Commodity Trade Statistics*, Vol. III.

1958 and 1965 was for France, where it nearly doubled; however, very large increases also occurred for Germany and Italy. The Common Market is now overwhelmingly important for all members, even though they carry on a brisk trade with the outside world.

Going beyond increases in trade, the Common Market has become more important to the well-being of the member countries because it now encompasses agricultural as well as industrial products. Agriculture has been a major factor in determining overall economic growth, not only because it still provides employment for close to 20 percent of the population, but also because it has been the principal source of new industrial workers within recent years. With the inclusion of agriculture, all of the essential segments of the economy have been brought within the single market mechanism of the EEC, and meaningful economic policy for the whole area can be devised.

The economic achievements of the Common Market have not been easily attained. Its history has been marked by a series of conflicts leading to crises, followed by compromise solutions which ushered in periods of rapid development until new conflicts arose to start the cycle over again. Counting only the major confrontations, there has been the agricultural crisis of December 1961, the United Kingdom veto crisis of January 1963, and the agricultural-constitutional crisis of June 1965 to January 1966. The resolution of each of these crises changed the Common Market in a fundamental way. An interesting question is which, if any, of these events marked the "point of no return" for the EEC as an institution. Walter Hallstein noted in the spring of 1962 that the member countries, in agreeing to integrate agriculture, had passed over the watershed point and that the future of the Common Market was assured. Similar statements, however, were also made after the two subsequent crises. In any event, the cohesiveness of the EEC has successfully withstood numerous challenges and presumably can meet similar ones in the future.

Many of the original advocates of the EEC have been disappointed, however, because there has been very little progress toward political integration. Economic integration was expected to lead automatically to this goal. It was believed that, as internal barriers to trade were removed and the economies of the member countries became more closely integrated, the need for coordination of national monetary and fiscal policies would become obvious, and institutions would develop to perform this essentially political function. The process was expected to occur through small incremental steps, possibly beginning with conferences of lower-level technical representatives of the member governments to discuss problems of mutual interest. Subsequently, such meetings could become routinized, administrative and technical staffs would naturally be added, and a new institution would have been created. Member governments, unable to deny the functional need for the institution, would be forced to ratify its existence. This process, however, has not developed very far.

Political integration has not progressed because of a basic disagreement within the Community over the form it should take. On one side stand Jean Monnet, Walter Hallstein, and others who view European federalism with supranational institutions as the ultimate goal of political integration. On the other side are found General de Gaulle and others who recognize only national states as effective political units and foresee political integration coming only as a result of agreement among national states to coordinate their policies. Such coordination could be continuous, but national governments alone would remain responsible for political actions. France has blocked all efforts to strengthen the supranational elements in the EEC Commission and the European Parliament, and de Gaulle has insisted that French delegates to Brussels meetings be clearly instructed so as to prevent any unintended political integration. The other five countries in turn have refused to go along with French suggestions for national policy coordination (as might have been possible via the "Fouchet" approach) and thus a deadlock has developed.

Another reason why political integration has not developed as expected may be that the theory that economic integration will necessitate political integration is defective. Economic integration requires coordination of many economic policies and this involves essentially political decisions, but formal political institutions may not be needed to bring this about. Governments do not need to be told, for instance, that excessive inflation in an open economy quickly leads to difficulties for themselves and their trading partners. They can see for themselves the rapidly deteriorating balance of payments, and pressures immediately arise for corrective actions. A "hidden hand" toward policy coordination is directed by the market mechanism and it has proven to be very effective with the EEC. Better balance of economic policies among the member countries might be obtained if there were conscious coordination (although this is not certain), but its absence is far from critical. What is certain is that political integration will occur only as a result of a positive political decision to bring it about, not as a result of economic pressures alone.

Before January 1963, political integration as originally intended appeared to be a feasible goal. A kind of euphoria surrounded those early days of the Common Market. There were problems, of course, but they were being met with a sense of responsibility. Member governments appeared ready to sacrifice some national interests for the good of the Community as a whole. This attitude stemmed from a universal desire to see the Community succeed, from an awareness that all members must make sacrifices for the general good, and also from a belief that concessions made today would be matched immediately or in the future by the others. While no direct political progress was made, this appeared to result more from the fact that economic issues were all-absorbing than from an inability to agree.

This phase of the Common Market ended abruptly with the de Gaulle veto of the British application for membership. The change of atmosphere in the Community resulted as much from the form of the French action as its substance. Up to that point, essential decisions had been taken through the give-and-take of bargaining, with each member country and the EEC Commission taking part. In contrast, the veto was a unilateral French action, taken without prior consultation, and announced at a press conference completely outside Community institutions. Given the importance of the veto, the paralysis of the Community that followed was rather short-lived. However, when business was resumed, the implicit ground rules were changed. The keynote was struck by the then Foreign Minister of Germany, Gerhard Schroeder. He insisted that the Community proceed on a basis of "synchronization" in which there would be a careful balancing of national interests in every round of decisions. No longer was the Community welfare regarded as the primary goal. Now member delegates were prone to ask, "What has the Community done for us lately?" Thus the supranationalistic elements of the Community were overwhelmed by traditional nationalistic forces.

The European environment may be even less conducive to political development in the future than it was in the past. An extended period of peace and prosperity is bound to weaken European concerns over external and internal threats to security. Without these threats, many European governments will be reluctant to take drastic steps toward political integration. As opportunities develop for expanded contacts with Eastern Europe, support will lessen for a tightly knit Western Europe. This has important implications for the Common Market (as well as for the North Atlantic Treaty Organization). The economic gains of the customs union are real, and are appreciated in all of the member countries. Members will go to great lengths to protect the degree of economic integration already achieved, but the step from economics to politics is a great one, and will not be taken unless new motivation is forthcoming.

The United States and European Integration

The United States has been an ardent advocate of European integration in the postwar period. This policy was expressed in the Marshall Plan which was designed to force the European countries both to view their separate economies as part of an integrated European whole and to cooperate in the formulation of economic policies. The creation of the European Coal and Steel Community gained U. S. support, although it comprised only six of the European countries, because it was felt to be a step in the proper direction, and its exclusiveness was not thought to be permanent. Formation of the EEC and the European Atomic Energy Community (Euratom) as companion organizations to the Coal and Steel Community was also supported by the United States. While regretting the economic split within Europe, the United States did not support dilution of the Rome Treaty through the creation of a larger free trade area, but did advocate Britain's subsequent attempt to enter the Common Market with her EFTA partners. On grounds of consistency, U. S. policy has been unassailable.

This policy has been based primarily upon politico-military considerations. Having been drawn into two European conflicts, the United States was as interested as any European power in a lasting Franco-German rapprochement, and economic integration was thought to be a good starting point. Also, broader integration of the military establishments of the Atlantic nations was believed to be the best way of organizing Western military defenses. While the United States was prepared to station American troops on the European continent as long as necessary to guarantee Western security, it desired an efficient organization of all allied military forces in Europe and a foundation for an eventual replacement of American troops by Europeans. To these ends, the North Atlantic Treaty Organization (NATO) was created, uniting Western Europe and North America. The Atlantic Alliance, however, was believed to have more than a traditional military dimension. The members were thought to have a unity of interest in economic and political as well as in military matters. One difficulty with the alliance, which was designed to be an association among equals, was the imbalance of U. S. power relative to that of Europe. If Europe could strengthen itself through economic integration and unify itself through political integration, then a partnership between equals could be formed.

Americans were captivated by the arguments of Jean Monnet and his followers. These ideas were bold, imaginative, and creative. They seemed to meet the needs of postwar Europe and appeared to require only political determination and American support for their success. The federalist solution quite naturally appealed to Americans because of their own experience with such a system. A federation seemed so superior to small independent nation states that to argue against it was thought almost equivalent to denying the obvious. Some observers noted the long history of independent European countries, but this was recognized as an additional challenge rather than a reason for rejecting federation. Thus, the United States supported the Common Market in its totality, including both economic and political aspects. In contrast, EFTA never aroused much enthusiasm among Americans. While considered a necessity under the circumstances, EFTA was recognized as a temporary expedient of economic but not political importance.

The economic implications of the Common Market for the United States were examined, although given very little weight. The discrimination against nonmember countries inherent in a customs union and a free trade area was not expected to cause difficulties for the United States. After being conditioned by many years of a dollar shortage, factors tending to weaken the balance of payments of the United States were taken quite lightly. Furthermore, the United States expected to benefit from the overall expansion of the European market which economic integration was to promote. Even if there were some economic risk to the United States from European economic integration, many observers thought the risk worth taking if the EEC (and EFTA) could prevent the mistakes of the interwar period and the economic losses involved in the disintegration of the international economy. Furthermore, it was recognized that total U. S. exports were only about 4 percent of American gross national product, and exports to Europe alone less than 1 percent, implying negligible economic consequences for the United States, in real terms, of even a drastic contraction of trade.

The United States is particularly interested in British membership in the Common Market and in arrangements that might be made for the other EFTA countries. The ending of the economic split in Western Europe has been desired by the United States, however, solely for the political purpose of strengthening the Atlantic Alliance. But many of the presumptions upon which this support is based are open to serious question. First, it was assumed that a unified Western Europe would necessarily have an identity of interest with the United States on major political issues and that the Atlantic Alliance could take the form of an equal partnership. But an identity of interest cannot be assumed in the face of much evidence to the contrary. There are substantial differences in the views of the United States and many Western European countries on such crucial issues as relations with the Soviet Union and Eastern Europe, attitudes toward China and the other Asian communist states, and the problems of less developed countries in Asia, Africa, and Latin America. The United States might better be able to maximize its leadership position by dealing with a group of disunited European states than by having to confront in the Atlantic Alliance an equal partner with very different policy goals.

A second assumption underlying the American position is that Western Europe can only fulfill its partnership role if it is united, and along federalist lines. But expanding the EEC to include all or most of Western Europe is certain to undermine the prospects for a European federation. Opposition to European federalism is deeply ingrained in political thinking in Great Britain, and this is unlikely to change with membership in the Common Market. Furthermore, France may well extract from its EEC partners a commitment against supranational development as a condition of British entry. It thus appears that the U. S. position is out of touch with political developments in Europe. It may well be that the United States properly desires British entry into the Common Market, but for the wrong reasons.

Finally, the United States has been willing to devote substantial political and economic resources to support the unification of Western Europe because Europe has traditionally been of primary importance to American foreign policy. The Soviet Union was the focal point around which United States policy revolved and the European continent was the most strategic area involved. But to an increasing extent, the Soviet Union is sharing its position as the focus of U. S. policymaking with China, and the Soviet Union is now of more importance to the United States because of its power in Asia than its status in Europe. A continuation of existing trends will find Japan and the countries represented at the 1966 Manila Conference occupying the positions of importance to the United States once reserved for Western Europe. As U. S. attention is more and more drawn to the Pacific, its relative interest in the Atlantic Alliance will of necessity abate. Even if the United States continues to desire the integration of Western Europe, it may be less willing to devote its own energies to bringing it about.

Thus, as European integration gains in economic importance to the United States, it appears to be receding in political importance. This suggests that, in the formulation of United States policy toward European integration in the future, more weight should be attached to economic factors than has been true in the past.

United States Exports

The substantive analysis of this study concerns the economic impact of European integration on the United States. Since trade in goods is most directly affected, an overview of the experience of the United States as an exporter to the EEC and the EFTA is required. In Table 1-5, the growth of U. S. exports to the EEC and EFTA before and after the start of these organizations is shown. At first glance, it appears that U. S. exports have been stimulated by European integration, since the growth of exports to the EEC was at a compound annual rate of 11.8 percent after integration

TABLE 1-5

Growth of United States Exports, Selected Years, 1953–65

(Dollar amounts in millions)

Destination of Exports	1953	1958–59	1965	Compound Annual Rate of Increase (Percent)	
				1953 to 1958–59	*1958–59 to 1965*
Total exports	$15,626	$17,775	$27,400	2.4	7.0
EEC countries	1,447	2,427	4,974	10.0	11.8
EFTA countries	1,024	1,549	2,800	7.9	9.6
Others	13,155	13,799	19,626	0.9	5.7

Sources: IMF-IBRD, *Direction of Trade, Annual 1958–62*, and *Annual 1961–65;* U.N., *Commodity Trade Statistics*, Vol. III.

began, compared to a 10.0 percent rate in the earlier period. Also, U. S. exports to EFTA increased at a faster rate after integration (9.6 percent) than before (7.9 percent). However, U. S. export performance resulted primarily from the faster growth of income in the EEC and EFTA countries in the later period, and unless all of this growth can be attributed to economic integration, the United States might have exported as much or more without the Common Market and EFTA. This question is examined in subsequent chapters.

Another view of U. S. export performance is seen in Chart 1, in which shares of trade are presented. From the early 1950's to 1958-59, the United States was able to increase its penetration of the European

CHART 1

U.S., EEC, and EFTA Shares of Trade, Selected Years, 1953–65

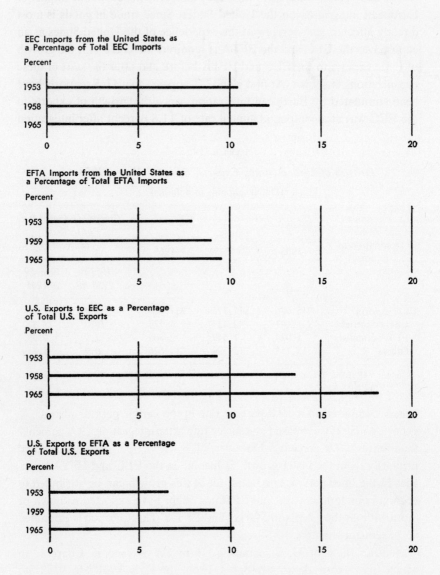

EEC Imports from the United States as
a Percentage of Total EEC Imports

EFTA Imports from the United States as
a Percentage of Total EFTA Imports

U.S. Exports to EEC as a Percentage
of Total U.S. Exports

U.S. Exports to EFTA as a Percentage
of Total U.S. Exports

Sources: U.N., *Commodity Trade Statistics*, Vol. III; IMF-IBRD, *Direction of Trade, Annual 1958-62* and *Annual 1961-65.*

market. The U. S. share of EEC imports increased from 10.4 percent in 1953 to 12.2 percent in 1958, and the United States share of EFTA imports increased from 8.0 percent in 1953 to 9.0 percent in 1959. This trend can be attributed to the gradual relaxation of European "dollar-shortage" restrictions against United States products and came at a time when U. S. products were less competitive in world markets. In the period following the introduction of the EEC and EFTA, the trend was reversed for the EEC. The U. S. share of EEC imports declined to 11.6 percent in 1965, and this occurred despite the improvement of U. S price competitiveness relative to most industrial countries, and particularly in relation to Germany, the major competitor of the United States within the Community. In EFTA markets, the U.S. share continued to rise and reached 9.6 percent in 1965.

However, when U. S. export sales to Europe are viewed as a share of U. S. exports to all areas, the results are somewhat different. From 9.3 percent of total U. S. exports in 1953, sales to the EEC rose to 13.6 percent by 1958 and increased further to 18.2 percent in 1965. Similarly, the EFTA share of total U. S. exports increased from 6.6 percent in 1953 to 9.2 percent in 1959 and to 10.2 percent in 1965.

Taken together, these shares of trade data present a mixed picture. The United States lost some of its position in the EEC market, but exports to these countries remained a most dynamic element in U. S. export growth. Only detailed analysis can establish which portion of the loss of EEC markets can be attributed to the formation of the Common Market. With respect to EFTA markets, U. S. exports continued to progress, but it is still possible that EFTA discrimination kept U. S. exports below what they might have been. Again, further analysis is necessary to determine this.

CHAPTER TWO

Manufactured Products

ECONOMIC INTEGRATION most directly affects the trade of goods, and the degree of its success quite naturally has been measured by changes in this trade. Nonmember countries have looked at their exports to the European Economic Community and the European Free Trade Association to assess the trade consequences of European integration. Aggregate trade flows are difficult to analyze, however, because manufactured products and agricultural products are subject to substantially different economic influences. Therefore, separate analyses have been undertaken for these two types of products. In this chapter, manufactured products are discussed.

Both the Rome Treaty and the Stockholm Convention provide for the gradual removal of all barriers to the trade of manufactured products among member countries. In the case of the Common Market, provision is also made for forming a unified tariff wall against the outside world (common external tariff, or CXT); the members of EFTA are free to determine their own trade barriers to nonmember countries. Nonmember countries feel the effects of these tariff changes on both their patterns of trade and their levels of national income, usually called static and dynamic effects.

In theoretical discussions of the static and dynamic effects of integration, most economists agree that, while nonmember countries may suffer as a result of shifts in the patterns of trade, they are likely to gain from the higher levels of income in the member countries.[1] But there is no consensus on the magnitude of these two effects and therefore no agreement on

[1] Bela Balassa, *The Theory of Economic Integration* (Richard D. Irwin, 1961).

32

which of them will be larger in any particular situation. The net direction of change is thus in doubt. The question can be resolved only by measurement.

An overall view of the growth of imports of manufactured products by the EEC and EFTA is given in Table 2-1. It indicates that there was an acceleration of intra-EEC trade after integration. Imports rose at a compound annual rate of 18.4 percent from 1958-59 to 1965, compared to a

TABLE 2-1

Growth of Imports of Manufactured Products by the EEC and EFTA Countries, Before and After Integration[a]

Source of Imports	Compound Annual Rate of Increase (Percent)	
	1953 to 1958–59	1958–59 to 1965
Total imports of EEC	13.4	16.1
From members	15.3	18.4
From nonmembers	11.6	13.3
EFTA countries	9.7	11.7
United States	13.0	14.3
Total imports of EFTA	10.1	12.6
From members	7.2	13.5
From nonmembers	11.1	12.3
EEC countries	12.5	11.1
United States	9.3	15.0

Source: United Nations, *Commodity Trade Statistics*, Statistical Papers Series D, Vol. III (New York, 1954), Vol. VIII (1959), Vol. IX (1960), and Vol. XV (1966).
[a] Manufactured products are defined as Standard International Trade Classifications 5, 6, 7, and 8.

growth rate of 15.3 percent between 1953 and 1958-59. Furthermore, the pattern as well as the volume of trade was affected. While imports from member countries grew faster than from nonmembers in both periods, the difference was more marked after integration. It would have been even greater if allowance were made for a disproportionate spurt of trade among members from 1953 to 1955, reflecting intra-European trade liberalization sponsored by the Organization for European Economic Cooperation (OEEC).

The impact of the EEC on member country imports of manufactured products can also be seen in Table 2-2, where data on shares of trade are presented. Between 1953 and 1958, there was only a small rise in intra-

EEC shares, and it was concentrated in the earlier part of the period. From 1958 to 1965, intra-EEC imports increased from 50 percent of the total to 58 percent. The EEC thus appears to have had some effect upon these trade flows.

The same conclusion applies to EFTA. Intra-EFTA imports of manu-factured products also showed an accelerated rate of growth, changing

TABLE 2-2

EEC and EFTA Imports of Manufactured Products, by Member and Nonmember Shares, Selected years, 1953–65

(Dollar amounts in millions)

Source of Imports	Value			Trade Shares (*Percent*)		
	1953	*1958*[a]	*1965*	*1953*	*1958*[a]	*1965*
Total imports of EEC	$4,841	$8,910	$25,138	*100.0*	*100.0*	*100.0*
Imports from members	2,270	4,455	14,645	*46.9*	*50.0*	*58.3*
Imports from nonmembers	2,571	4,455	10,493	*53.1*	*50.0*	*41.7*
EFTA countries	1,385	2,174	4,680	*28.6*	*24.4*	*18.6*
United States	620	1,132	2,850	*12.8*	*12.7*	*11.3*
Others	566	1,149	2,963	*11.7*	*12.9*	*11.8*
Total imports of EFTA	4,792	8,555	17,385	*100.0*	*100.0*	*100.0*
Imports from members	1,270	1,933	4,213	*26.5*	*22.6*	*24.2*
Imports from nonmembers	3,522	6,622	13,172	*73.5*	*77.4*	*75.8*
EEC countries	2,022	4,047	7,589	*42.2*	*47.3*	*43.7*
United States	508	864	2,032	*10.6*	*10.1*	*11.7*
Others	992	1,711	3,551	*20.7*	*20.0*	*20.4*

Source: U.N., *Commodity Trade Statistics*, Vols. III, VIII, IX, and XV.
1959 for EFTA data.

from a compound annual rate of 7.2 percent between 1953 and 1958-59 to a 13.5 percent annual rise from 1958-59 to 1965. Further, the intra-EFTA growth rate after 1958-59 was greater than that of imports from nonmembers, and this reversed the relationship that had existed in the pre-EFTA period. As a result, the member country share of EFTA im-ports increased from 22.6 percent in 1959 to 24.2 percent in 1965. It is worth noting, however, that this share in 1965 had not yet reached its 1953 level. The EFTA figures are dominated by the United Kingdom, and reflect Britain's smaller share of world markets for manufactured products, a trend that has been only partially offset by EFTA.

When EEC and EFTA imports of manufactured products from the United States are examined, a mixed picture emerges. Table 2-1 indicates that the rates of growth of EEC and EFTA imports from the United States were greater after integration than in the previous period. This suggests that U. S. exports have benefited from the formation of the EEC and EFTA. However, it may be that EEC imports from the United States grew less than intra-EEC imports because tariff discrimination against the United States (and other nonmember countries) hindered U. S. trade with the EEC. This is not true of EFTA; imports from the United States grew in relation to intra-EFTA imports. This may imply that the United States gained as a result of EFTA, but what complicates the question is the shift in competitive positions of countries over time and, in particular, the improvement of the U. S. position vis-à-vis its European competitors. To determine the likely course of events in the absence of the EEC and EFTA, an examination is required of the income effects as distinct from the trade-pattern effects of economic integration. Only then can the U. S. experience be appraised.

Income Effects of Integration

The major factor determining the growth of trade of manufactured goods is not a change in the tariff level, but real income growth. Most of the growth of imports of manufactured products is explained by the rapid increase of national income in the EEC and EFTA countries. Only part of this income growth can be attributed to the formation of the EEC and EFTA. It is necessary, though difficult, to quantify the effect of economic integration on the growth of national income.

There are four reasons why economic integration would lead to higher levels of income in member countries. First, the reduction of tariffs among members would enlarge the market open to producers within the group, allowing them to capture the economies of scale that come with greater output. Second, with the removal of trade barriers, countries would tend to specialize in those products in which they have a comparative advantage, and thereby gain the benefits of a greater division of labor. Third, with an opening of the borders to goods of other member countries, a spirit of enterprise can be kindled and a greater degree of competition can be created, which would lead to greater efficiency and more growth. Finally, growth might be stimulated through improved terms of trade because the group would be in a stronger position when it traded with nonmember countries.

These factors influence growth in two ways. They increase the desire of business firms to invest, and thereby raise the proportion of gross domestic product (GDP) going into investment. They also are expected to increase the efficiency of the economy. Since the provisions of the Rome Treaty and the Stockholm Convention were implemented gradually, rather than at a single point of time, the growth stimulus should continue for the duration of the transition period.

Analysis of the stimulus to the growth of income resulting from integration can begin with an examination of actual rates of growth of member countries over time. Table 2-3 presents data on the growth of the real gross domestic product of the EEC and EFTA countries and the United States. In the period 1958-59 to 1964, reflecting the consequences of economic integration, the growth rates of all member countries were quite high and compared very favorably with that of the United States, with the possible exception of the United Kingdom. The average annual rate of growth of the EEC countries was close to 6 percent, almost 50 percent more than growth in the United States in the same period. One cannot conclude from this evidence, however, that economic integration has had an impact on economic growth. Even before integration, all of these countries were growing at a faster rate than the United States.[2]

What is more significant is the contrast between growth rates after economic integration and those in the earlier period. As shown in Table 2-3, all the EEC and EFTA countries (other than Austria) had higher growth rates after integration than during the 1953 to 1958-59 period. This evidence gives some indication that integration has been stimulating, but it is by no means conclusive. Many factors other than economic integration influence growth, and they are likely to be much more important.[3] The point can be illustrated by a comparison of European and U.S. experience. The U.S. rate of growth also increased between the two periods, and by a larger amount than in most European countries, despite the fact that the United States was not a party to economic integration, and may have suffered because of it. There is, however, a fundamental difference be-

[2] Alexander Lamfalussy, "Europe's Progress: Due to Common Market?" reprinted in Lawrence B. Krause (ed.), *The Common Market: Progress and Controversy* (Prentice-Hall, 1964).

[3] Edward F. Denison, assisted by Jean-Pierre Poullier, *Why Growth Rates Differ: Postwar Experience in Nine Western Countries* (Brookings Institution, 1967).

TABLE 2-3

Growth of Gross Domestic Product of the EEC and EFTA Countries and the United States, Before and After Integration, in 1958 Prices[a]

(In percentages)

Country	Compound Annual Rate of Increase		Change in Growth Rates
	1953 to 1958–59	1958–59 to 1964	
EEC			
Belgium-Luxembourg	2.7	5.1	2.4
France[b]	4.7	5.6	0.9
Germany	6.9	7.1	0.2
Italy	5.2	6.0	0.8
Netherlands	4.5	5.6	1.1
EFTA			
Austria	6.7	4.8	−1.9
Denmark	2.9	5.8	2.9
Norway	2.9	5.3	2.4
Portugal	4.0	6.7	2.7
Sweden	3.9	5.1	1.2
Switzerland	4.6[c]	5.7	1.1
United Kingdom	2.4	3.8	1.4
United States	2.1	4.1	2.0

Sources: Organization for Economic Cooperation and Development, *Statistics of National Income Accounts, 1950–61* (Paris, 1963), and *National Accounts Statistics, 1955–64* (Paris, 1966).
[a] At factor costs.
[b] At market prices.
[c] 1954 to 1958–59.

tween the United States and Europe. The United States had growth rates below its historical average in the earlier period, and much of the change reflects a return to normal. In contrast, the European countries had high growth rates in the earlier period. The fact that they were able to increase them even further suggests that an especially strong stimulating force was in operation.[4]

Estimating the Effect of Increased Business Investment

The first step in estimating the income effect of economic integration is the examination of business investment in the member countries, since

---

[4] The Austrian situation is unique because the extremely high growth rate in the 1953 to 1958-59 period reflected the ending of occupation, a factor that other European countries experienced earlier.

part of the stimulation was expected to come from this source. The relationship between investment and growth is not a direct one, however. Following the method developed by Edward Denison,[5] business investment is assumed to influence growth rates by increasing the capital stock of productive enterprises. This assumption arises from viewing growth of income as resulting from an increase in the supply of factors of production. The contribution to the growth rate of an increase in the capital stock can be evaluated by multiplying the percentage increase in capital stock (nonresidential structures and equipment) during the period under review by the share of national income earned by this factor.

The rationale for this procedure is as follows: In an economy that is not subject to aggregate economies of scale and is fully utilizing its resources over time, a 1 percent increase in all factor inputs would lead to a 1 percent increase in output. But what fraction of the increase in output would come from a 1 percent increase in only one of the factors? The answer depends on the contribution that the factor is making to total output. Thus, if labor is responsible for 80 percent of total output, a 1 percent increase in labor inputs would yield an increase in output of 0.8 of 1 percent. How is a factor's contribution to output measured? According to marginal productivity analysis, the earnings (prices) of the various factors of production are proportional to the value of their marginal products, if economic units combine factors in such a way as to minimize their total costs. Thus, a factor's marginal contribution to output can be roughly measured by the ratio of the total earnings of the increasing factor to the earnings of all factors combined. Denison recognizes the possibility that the various assumptions may not hold exactly, but he believes that this will not cause a serious error in measurement.[6]

The relevant ratios of business investment to gross domestic product for each member country of the EEC and EFTA are shown in Table 2-4. Every member has experienced an increase in investment ratios since integration began, which strongly suggests that economic integration has been very important in determining business behavior. Qualitative observations by many analysts of the European economy support this generalization. Faced with new competitive pressures, business firms invested in new plant and equipment to reduce costs and increase capacities.Within EFTA, the countries receiving the most stimulus, Denmark and Portugal,

[5] Denison, *Why Growth Rates Differ*. See also App. B. of the present study.
[6] Denison, *Why Growth Rates Differ*, Chap. 4.

had relatively low ratios in the earlier period. Norway, showing only a small rise, had an investment ratio which was already very high. It is assumed that these higher investment ratios will be maintained only until the adjustment to economic integration is completed.

TABLE 2-4

Ratios of Business Investment to Gross Domestic Product of the EEC and EFTA Countries, 1955–57 and 1960–64[a]

(In percentages)

Country	Ratios[b]		Increment in Ratios[d]
	1955–57 (1)	1960–64[c] (2)	(3)
EEC			
Belgium-Luxembourg	14.7	16.1	1.4
France	13.1	15.2	2.1
Germany	16.9	19.7	2.8
Italy	16.8	19.6	2.8
Netherlands	22.0	23.3	1.3
EFTA			
Austria	19.8	22.9	3.1
Denmark	15.1	20.0	4.9
Norway	28.8	29.0	0.2
Portugal	12.3	16.1	3.8
Sweden[e]	16.2	18.9	2.7
Switzerland[f]	23.7	27.1	3.4
United Kingdom	13.1	16.0	2.9

Source: OECD, *National Accounts Statistics, 1955–64.*
[a] Business investment is defined as nonresidential construction plus machinery and equipment.
[b] Ratios at 1958 prices.
[c] For EFTA, 1961–64.
[d] Col. 2 minus col. 1.
[e] Ratios at current prices, 1955–57.
[f] Ratios of gross capital formation (includes residential construction) to gross domestic product.

Because of previous differences in investment experience, an increment in the ratio of investment to gross domestic product will not yield the same percentage increases in the capital stock of different countries. An adjustment was made for this influence (see Appendix B). Estimates of the increment in growth rates during the transition period due to greater business investment are shown in Table 2-5. Within the Common Market, Germany and Italy appear to have been most influenced by this factor; Denmark and Portugal were most affected among the EFTA countries.

TABLE 2-5

Integration-Induced Increments to Gross Domestic Product from Business Investment, EEC and EFTA Countries, During Transition Period

Country	Annual Increment to Gross Domestic Product[a]
EEC	
Belgium-Luxembourg	0.041
France	0.076
Germany	0.151
Italy	0.094
Netherlands	0.044
EFTA	
Austria	0.093
Denmark	0.187
Norway	0.005
Portugal	0.124
Sweden	0.097
Switzerland	0.066
United Kingdom	0.082

Source: App. Table B-1.
[a] Compound annual rate in percent.

Estimating the Effect of Increased Efficiency

The other part of the integration-induced increment of growth, increased efficiency, is more difficult to estimate. Economic integration increases efficiency by removing some of the protective barriers to international trade that sustain inefficient production. With integration, the export industries of a member country will expand, because other member countries are eliminating their tariffs and other trade barriers, and imports will also increase, because of the country's own tariff reductions. Thus, the resources of the country will be attracted into the efficient export industries, and away from the inefficient import-competing industries, and real income will be higher after the transition has been completed.

The estimate of the increase in income during the transition period resulting from greater efficiency was also calculated by Denison's method. This requires measuring the increase in international trade, evaluating the reduction in costs (or, as an alternative, the increase of output from given inputs) attributable to the expansion of the foreign sector, and converting the increase in income into an equivalent increase in annual growth rates, based on the length of time elapsed.

The increase in international trade due to economic integration was estimated by calculating the change in the ratios of imports to gross domestic product from the base period 1957-59 to 1964, measured in constant prices, for each member country of the EEC and EFTA. (The differences in the corresponding export ratios were similarly calculated.)[7] It is possible for these measures to indicate that international trade was not stimulated by economic integration, even though trade with member countries rose in relation to gross domestic product if there was a corresponding decline in trade with nonmember countries. Clearly, the real output of a member country will not increase, and may decline, if foreign trade is merely redirected from nonmember to member countries, leaving the aggregate unaffected. For integration to be the major causative factor, however, the increase in total imports in relation to gross domestic product must be mainly due to the growth of intra-Community trade.[8] The calculated ratios are shown in Table 2-6. The foreign trade sector of every member country of the EEC and EFTA appears to have been increased by economic integration, but by differing amounts.

There is no fully satisfactory way of measuring the cost savings accruing to a country from reallocating resources from inefficient to efficient industries as a result of the expansion of international trade. One could measure the decrease in inefficiency coming from larger imports, or the increase in efficiency from larger exports, or a combination of the two with an adjustment to avoid double counting. The data for measuring the decrease in inefficiency are more readily available, however, and the measurement will be confined to the import side (see Appendix B for discussion). Denison used average tariff rates, arbitrarily adjusted for excess protection, to indicate the per-unit cost of inefficiency (and thus cost savings from larger imports), although recognizing the shortcomings of the measure. The difficulty comes from two sources of bias inherent in the traditional measurement of average tariffs, that is, dividing value of duties collected by value of dutiable imports. First, if a tariff rate is so high as to completely bar all imports, it will not influence the measurement of average tariffs, which are weighted by actual value of imports, and thus domestic inefficiency will be underestimated. Second, a tariff rate may be higher than necessary to prevent a substantial flow of imports and thus the method

[7] This analysis assumes that, in the absence of economic integration, these ratios would have been unchanged, an assumption which seems reasonable in view of their stability in the mid-1950's (with the possible exception of Austria).

[8] This issue is examined further in App. B.

will overestimate domestic inefficiency. But even if every single tariff rate contained excess protection, the average of these rates may not be biased upward because of the downward bias introduced by the weighting sys-

TABLE 2-6

Ratios of Imports and Exports of Manufactured Products to Gross Domestic Product, EEC and EFTA Countries, 1957–59 and 1964

(In percentages)

Country	Ratios of Imports to Gross Domestic Product[a]		Increment in Import/ GDP Ratios[b]	Ratios of Exports to Gross Domestic Product[a]		Increment in Export/ GDP Ratios[c]
	1957–59	1964		1957–59	1964	
	(1)	(2)	(3)	(4)	(5)	(6)
EEC						
Belgium-						
Luxembourg	17.5	28.0	10.5	26.1	35.3	9.2
France	3.3	7.2	3.9	7.3	9.4	2.1
Germany	5.0	7.1	2.1	14.2	15.3	1.1
Italy	4.6	9.9	5.3	7.5	14.1	6.6
Netherlands	23.2	32.5	9.3	19.0	25.2	6.2
EFTA						
Austria	13.6	19.2	5.6	15.0	17.6	2.6
Denmark	18.3	24.6	6.3	8.9	12.5	3.6
Norway	25.2	26.1	0.9	12.4	15.9	3.5
Portugal	14.8	15.3	0.5	7.3	10.9	3.6
Sweden	15.3	18.5	3.2	13.3	17.7	4.4
Switzerland	16.1[d]	21.8	5.7	20.6[d]	21.1	0.5
United Kingdom	4.7	7.4	2.7	13.6	13.0	−0.6

Sources: U.N., *Commodity Trade Statistics*, Vols. VI, VII, VIII, and XIII; OECD, *National Accounts Statistics 1955–64;* U.N., *Monthly Bulletin of Statistics*, Vol. 20 (June 1966).
  [a] Ratios at 1958 prices.
  [b] Col. 2 minus col. 1.
  [c] Col. 5 minus col. 4.
  [d] 1959 only.

tem. Fortunately the two sources of bias are in opposite directions and, in the absence of other information, will be assumed to be offsetting. Thus, the average of manufactured goods import tariffs of a member country in the base period was used to estimate the costs saved by greater imports. (See Appendix Table B-4.)

For the EEC countries, France and Italy had the highest import tariffs and Germany the lowest. For the EFTA countries, Portugal, the United

Kingdom, and Austria had high import tariffs, and Sweden and especially Denmark had low import tariffs. The increments to growth obtained from removing these internal barriers are shown in Table 2-7. The estimates indicate that, among the Common Market countries, Belgium and the Netherlands have gained the most from increases in efficiency, and Austria (possibly overestimated), Switzerland, and the United Kingdom have gained the most among the EFTA countries.

TABLE 2-7

Integration-Induced Increments to Gross Domestic Product from Greater Efficiency, EEC and EFTA Countries, During Transition Period

Country	Annual Increment to Gross Domestic Product[a]
EEC	
Belgium-Luxembourg	0.173
France	0.112
Germany	0.029
Italy	0.127
Netherlands	0.152
EFTA	
Austria	0.139
Denmark	0.064
Norway	0.019
Portugal	0.025
Sweden	0.042
Switzerland	0.089
United Kingdom	0.077

Source: App. Table B-4.
[a] Compound annual rate in percent.

Total Income Effect

By adding together the stimulus caused by higher business investment and that stemming from greater efficiency, estimates of the total increment to income attributable to economic integration are obtained.[9] These estimates are shown in Table 2-8. According to these results, every member of the EEC and EFTA experienced some income stimulation from economic integration. There are, however, important differences between the two groups. Common Market members received somewhat more in-

[9] There is a minute interaction effect between the two income stimulants that is disregarded.

come stimulus than EFTA countries. The median increase for the Common Market was at a compound annual rate of 0.19 percent (Netherlands and France) while the median for EFTA was 0.16 percent (Switzerland and the United Kingdom). The lowest estimate for an EEC country was above the EFTA median. If the two organizations were identical in other respects, one would have expected the EFTA estimates to be larger, be-

TABLE 2-8

Annual Income Increments Induced by Economic Integration, EEC and EFTA Countries, During Transition Period

(Compound annual rate in percentages)

Country	Annual Investment Increment[a] (1)	Annual Efficiency Increment[b] (2)	Annual Income Increment[c] (3)
EEC			
Belgium-Luxembourg	0.04	0.17	0.21
France	0.08	0.11	0.19
Germany	0.15	0.03	0.18
Italy	0.09	0.13	0.22
Netherlands	0.04	0.15	0.19
EFTA			
Austria	0.09	0.14	0.23
Denmark	0.19	0.06	0.25
Norway	0.01	0.02	0.03
Portugal	0.12	0.03	0.15
Sweden	0.10	0.04	0.14
Switzerland	0.07	0.09	0.16
United Kingdom	0.08	0.08	0.16

[a] From table 2-5.
[b] From table 2-7.
[c] Col. 1 plus col. 2.

cause the shorter transition period required quicker adjustments; obviously other things were not equal.

The difference in the EEC and EFTA experience is due entirely to the gains in efficiency in the Common Market. The EFTA countries gained more from expansion of business investment. For the Common Market, gains from greater efficiency were more important than gains from business investment, while in EFTA they were less important. Within the EEC, Italy had the highest overall increment to income, with Belgium-Luxembourg close behind. The increments to income of the Netherlands and France were almost as high, followed by Germany. Denmark received the greatest overall stimulation. Austria was next, but is probably overestimated. Among other EFTA countries, the United Kingdom, Switzerland, Portugal, and Sweden showed smaller effects, with Norway trailing significantly.

Underlying Reasons

It is not difficult to deduce a rationale for the observed pattern of these estimates. The degree to which a country can benefit from the income stimuli previously discussed depends upon the following characteristics: (a) the size of the country relative to other member countries; (b) the pre-integration degree of inefficiency of a country protected by trade barriers; (c) the degree to which the natural markets of a country were closed by trade barriers; (d) the geographical position of a country relative to other member countries; (e) the general or aggregate economic conditions of a country before integration; and (f) the subjective beliefs of decision makers as to the firmness of the commitment of a country to the integration process.

The most important characteristic of the EEC countries for determining increments of income appears to be the size of the country; to a lesser extent, this is also true of EFTA. A small country experiences a substantial increase in market potential when joining a customs union, while for a large country the increase is relatively small. The size of the market for the Benelux countries and Italy grew relatively more than for France and Germany. There is some evidence of an inverse correlation between the ranking of EEC countries by value of gross domestic product in 1958 and a ranking by the estimated increments of income coming from economic integration, but in general the variance is very small. In EFTA, the size disparities are even greater. The United Kingdom so dominates EFTA that the increase in markets opened to British exporters through integration is relatively small. This helps to explain the small increment to British income. However, from the size factor alone, one would have expected larger income increments for Norway and Portugal than were obtained.

Since much of the income stimulus of economic integration comes from improving the efficiency of an economy, the countries that were the most inefficient at the start of the integrative process have the most scope for improvement. Thus, the countries with the highest tariff rates in 1958 would be the ones to gain the most from removing these barriers to intra-Community trade. Italy and France had the most to gain from reducing their tariffs within the Common Market while Germany had the least to gain.[10] The EFTA situation is confused, but the low level of tariffs existing in some EFTA countries suggests that there was little room for improvement.

A similar effect occurs with respect to the tariff levels of a country's natural trading partners. If economic integration is to enlarge a country's export markets, and thereby encourage economies of scale, high foreign tariffs must have closed or limited these markets before integration. Thus, Belgium may have gained a great deal because of its proximity to the formerly highly-protected French market, while the Netherlands gained less in achieving access to the relatively free German market. It is noteworthy that one of the most dynamic segments of intra-EEC trade has been the bilateral exchange between France and Italy, the two high-tariff members of the EEC. Likewise, Denmark may have gained much through freer entry into the protected British market.

One of the most noticeable features distinguishing the EEC from EFTA is the contiguity of its members. Transportation costs discourage trade with distant countries. The EEC is likely to be more stimulating than EFTA, on the average, because serving the large market opened by integration in the EEC does not involve wasteful transportation expenses. The separation of Austria and Switzerland from the major EFTA markets, plus the great distance from Portugal to Scandinavia, suggest that the natural transportation barriers that remain in EFTA are probably as important as man-made tariff barriers in preventing trade. This is illustrated by the fact that the most dynamic segment of EFTA is made up of the neighboring Scandinavian countries.

An additional factor that may help to explain the observed pattern of income stimuli is the aggregate state of the economy of each member country on the eve of integration. Economic integration can increase growth by inducing both a better allocation of productive resources and a fuller use of them. More credit, possibly, should be given to integration for its allocative function than for its role in expanding the utilization of resources, since other politically acceptable tools are available for the latter task; however, the two cannot easily be disentangled in measuring the causes of actual income growth. The scope for expanded utilization of resources can be approximated by the amount of unemployment, which

[10] See App. Table B-4.

suggests that Italy and Belgium were particularly in need of such expansion. Portugal should be considered a special case, since by 1959 it had not reached a stage of economic development that permitted it to respond fully to the stimuli provided by economic integration.

Another factor which may have affected the degree to which individual countries reacted to the income stimuli coming from the EEC and EFTA is the psychological reaction of the business community to the new arrangements. For income to be changed, business investment decisions have to be affected. But the investment decisions needed to penetrate markets are based on a rather long time-horizon. If businessmen feel that integration arrangements are permanent, then investment decisions will be based on expectation of expansion in an identifiable market. If the arrangements are thought to be temporary, however, this will not be the case, and little income stimulation can be expected. There is little question that from the outset, the EEC was viewed as a permanent institution and EFTA as only a temporary expedient. Thus, one would have expected the EEC to be, on the average, more stimulating than EFTA. It can be argued that EFTA was thought to be temporary only because it was to be replaced by wider European integration and therefore businessmen still could plan for expansion. But expecting a larger market without being certain of it, and without knowing where it may be, creates severe difficulties. The investments required for market penetration, such as market research and distribution outlets, cannot be made, since they depend on the location of customers.

Increments to Income and Nonmember Trade

With a higher level of income in the EEC and EFTA, imports are stimulated from both member and nonmember countries, and this rise in imports will continue as long as the stimulus lasts. It is assumed here that there is such a stimulus for the entire transition period, which covers from 1958 to mid-1968 for the EEC countries, and from mid-1960 to 1967 for the EFTA countries. In terms of the economic variables involved, this assumption implies that business investment as a percent of gross domestic product will remain at a higher integration-induced level until the transition period is over and then drop to its previous level. Imports (and exports) as a percent of gross domestic product will continue to rise at the observed rate until the transition period is over and then remain at the higher level.

The total value of imports from nonmember countries attributable to the income-stimulating effects of integration depends on the estimated annual increment to income, the length of the transition period, and the ratio of imports from nonmember countries to income before integration. The stimulus to U. S. trade was estimated by assuming that the United States

TABLE 2-9

Increments of Imports of Manufactured Products from Nonmember Countries as a Result of Integration-Induced Growth, EEC, 1958–68, and EFTA, 1960–67

(Millions of dollars, 1958 prices)

Importing Country	Source of Imports				
	All Non-members	United States	EFTA	EEC	Other
Total EEC	428	111	206	—	111
Belgium-Luxembourg	72	15	35	—	22
France	85	33	34	—	18
Germany	149	30	70	—	49
Italy	61	19	31	—	11
Netherlands	61	14	36	—	11
Total EFTA	231	31	—	145	55
Austria	29	2	—	25	2
Denmark	28	2	—	22	4
Norway	4	a	—	3	1
Portugal	7	1	—	6	0
Sweden	36	6	—	27	3
Switzerland	39	5	—	31	3
United Kingdom	88	15	—	31	42

Source: App. Table B-5.
a Less than $1 million.

would maintain its base-year share of nonmember trade. The results of the calculations are shown in Table 2-9.

Economic integration has apparently increased the national incomes of the member countries, and has thereby expanded their imports from nonmembers. If this were the only effect of integration, the EEC would have increased its imports of manufactured goods from nonmember countries by $428 million (1958 prices) during its transition period, equal to 10 percent of 1958 imports from these countries. The United States would have been expected to share proportionately in this growth and to increase its exports to the EEC by $111 million. The corresponding figures for EFTA are $231 million in imports from all nonmembers (4 percent of 1958 trade) and $31 million from the United States.

However, the effects of economic integration on trade patterns alone would be expected to work against the interests of nonmember countries because of the tariff discrimination inherent in a customs union or free-trade area, and the total result will reflect both consequences. This will be discussed in the following section.

Trade-Pattern Effects of Integration

Trade in manufactured products is influenced by three conceptually separate effects of the tariff changes accompanying the formation of a common market.[11] Two relate to the overall level of trade, through their impact on the price of imports relative to domestic substitutes; the third concerns the division of import shares between members and nonmembers through differential price effects on the two sources of imports.

The first effect comes from the formation of the common external tariff, and thus concerns only the EEC. Trade will be likely to expand for any product if this tariff is, on the average, lower than the previously existing national tariffs, since this is equivalent to a price reduction of imports; trade will contract if the common external tariff is higher. As long as the member countries have negative price elasticities of demand for imports, reduction of their average tariff levels will increase the value of their imports, since the effective price reduction of imports is not at the expense of the receipts of exporters.

The second effect on patterns of trade is a result of the removal of all tariffs between member countries. Because the removal of tariffs reduces the effective price of imports from member countries, it expands total trade and therefore can be considered purely trade-creating.[12]

The third effect concerns the share of member country imports provided by nonmembers, and arises from the loss of market position of nonmembers whose exports are subject to the common external tariff (and

[11] Harry G. Johnson, "The International Competitive Position of the United States and the Balance of Payments Prospect for 1968," *Review of Economics and Statistics,* Vol. 46 (February 1964), pp. 14-32.
[12] Jacob Viner, *The Customs Union Issue* (Carnegie Endowment, 1950).

are in competition with member countries in the markets of other members). This effect is deleterious to nonmembers and approximates pure trade diversion.

By adding the three price effects for each product, and then adding these sums for all manufactured products, a total trade-pattern effect can be approximated.[13]

Three approaches were used to estimate the effects of the formation of the EEC and EFTA on the trade patterns of nonmember countries. The first is a direct approach based on the expected consequences of tariff changes. Empirical values were estimated for the equation just noted. While the equation was conceptually divided into three parts, all three were calculated simultaneously. This yielded estimates of the expected percentage loss of imports of manufactured products from nonmembers as a result of the tariff changes.[14] These estimates were converted to dollar values by multiplying them by the value of nonmember imports in 1958, the year before internal tariff reductions were begun in the EEC. The second approach is a variant of the first and dependent upon it for input data, but, in addition, it utilizes the actual shifts in trade shares that have occurred. The third approach is an indirect one, analyzing actual shifts in trade patterns and measuring the effects of economic integration as a residual.

[13] Formally, the three effects of the tariff changes are as follows:
Let

X_{ij} = imports from nonmember countries of product i by member country j in 1958.
$\dot{x}_{ij}$ = proportional change in imports of X_{ij} due to economic integration.
η_{xi} = elasticity of import demand for product i from all sources.
t_{ij} = old national tariff on product i by country j.
T_i = CXT on product i.
S_{ij} = nonmember country share of product i imports by country j.
E_{Sij} = share elasticity of nonmember imports of product i by country j.
Y = Value of trade-pattern-effect loss of nonmember countries.

A dot over a variable indicates the proportional change in the variable due to economic integration. Then

$$(1) \qquad \dot{x}_{ij} = \eta_{xi}\frac{t_{ij} - T_i}{1 + t_{ij}} + \eta_{xi}\frac{T_i(1 - S_{ij})}{1 + t_{ij}} - E_{Sij}T_i;$$

$$(2) \qquad Y = \sum_{ij} X_{ij}\dot{x}_{ij}.$$

Adapted from Johnson, in *Review of Economics and Statistics.*

[14] The products are 61 three-digit SITC classes taken from the major SITC headings 5, 6, 7, and 8. These are essentially all of the 1958 three-digit classes, except for base metals. See App. C.

First Direct Approach to EEC Estimates

For the Common Market countries, imports of manufactured products amounted to $9 billion in 1958. Half of these imports originated in non-member countries (Table 2-10). The amount of trade which could potentially be lost was thus $4.5 billion, of which over $1 billion came from the United States alone.

TABLE 2-10

Imports of Manufactured Products by EEC Countries, by Source, 1958[a]

(Dollar amounts in millions)

Importing Country	Total	EEC	Nonmembers						
			Total	United States	EFTA			All Other
					Total	United Kingdom	Other	
Total EEC	$8,910	$4,456	$4,454	$1,130	$2,110	$948	$1,162	$1,214
Belgium-Luxembourg	1,636	941	695	150	333	197	136	212
France	1,687	773	914	328	356	161	195	230
Germany	2,702	1,062	1,640	336	770	254	516	534
Italy	1,019	452	567	169	285	125	160	113
Netherlands	1,866	1,228	638	147	366	211	155	125
			Percentage Distribution					
Total EEC	100.0	50.0	50.0	12.7	23.7	10.6	13.0	13.6
Belgium-Luxembourg	100.0	57.5	42.5	9.2	20.4	12.0	8.3	13.0
France	100.0	45.8	54.2	19.4	21.1	9.5	11.6	13.6
Germany	100.0	39.3	60.7	12.4	28.5	9.4	19.1	19.8
Italy	100.0	44.4	55.6	16.6	28.0	12.3	15.7	11.1
Netherlands	100.0	65.8	34.2	7.9	19.6	11.3	8.3	6.7

Source: U.N., *Commodity Trade Statistics*, Vol. VIII.
[a] Manufactured products include SITC groups 5, 6, 7, and 8 as defined in App. Table C-1. Detail may not add to totals because of rounding.

In addition to the amount of trade involved, the height of pre-integration external tariffs is important in determining the amount of expected trade loss. As noted previously, the old national tariffs of Italy and France were quite high on most manufactured products, while those of Germany and the Benelux countries were much more modest. The new common external tariff is midway between these two groups, since it was formed, in general, by taking an arithmetic average of the four tariff areas.[15] Most tariffs on manufactured products in the CXT range from 3

[15] Because the tariff average was unweighted, this method may have led to a somewhat higher CXT than a weighted average would yield. Also, the national

to 29 percent, with an approximate mean value of 15 percent. Considering the level of tariff rates and the amount of trade involved, a significant trade loss for nonmember countries was possible. If there were supply limitations in the member countries, not all of this potential trade loss would be realized. This was unlikely to be a problem for the EEC, given the length of the transition period, the gradualness of the internal tariff reduction, and the large size of the countries (counting Benelux as a single unit).

The estimates indicate that nonmember countries might have been expected to lose approximately $975 million in sales to the EEC (in 1958 prices) as a result of the trade-pattern effects of integration (Table 2-11).[16] These expected losses are relatively greater in the German and Dutch markets because the tariffs facing nonmember exporters in these areas had to be increased to reach the CXT level, while in Italy and France the tariff declined. If member countries had increased their trade at the expense of nonmembers by this amount, intra-Community trade would have risen to 62.1 percent of total trade from the 1958 share of 50 percent.

For the United States, the expected loss of sales to the EEC of manufactured products is estimated at about $275 million: 24 percent of the 1958 level of Community imports from the United States.[17] This expected loss for U. S. sales is slightly greater than for most other nonmember exporters because the products in which the United States appears to have a comparative advantage tend to face a higher-than-average EEC tariff.

The United Kingdom is estimated to be the second largest loser from the trade-pattern consequences of tariff discrimination by the EEC. The indicated loss of over $200 million represents 23 percent of the 1958

---

tariffs used in the calculations of the average were the statutory rates, rather than the rates actually in use on January 1, 1958. The German tariff used for the calculation excluded the 25 percent tariff reduction of August 1957. The Italian rates excluded the reductions of 1951. A hypothetical Benelux tariff of 12 percent on most chemicals was also averaged in, to provide a more rational structure. Rome Treaty, Articles 19(2), 19(3)(d), and List E.

[16] See App. C for a description of the method used in this calculation.

[17] Using an approximate method, an estimated loss of $200 million was calculated by the author and presented in *The United States Balance of Payments in 1968*, by Walter S. Salant and others (Brookings Institution, 1963). In reviewing that book, Harry Johnson indicated that the estimate was biased on the low side, which seems to be confirmed by these calculations. See Johnson in *Review of Economics and Statistics*.

level of imports of British manufactured products by the EEC. The United Kingdom and the United States together account for over 50 percent of the total loss of nonmember trade. The United Kingdom is a particularly heavy loser in the Netherlands market, absorbing over one-third of the total $160 million loss in that market.

TABLE 2-11

Expected Loss of Sales to EEC of Manufactured Products by Nonmembers During Transition Period[a]

(Dollar amounts in millions, 1958 prices)

Importing Country			Nonmembers Losing Sales			
	Total	United States	EFTA			All Other
			Total	United Kingdom	Other	
Total EEC	$975	$273	$485	$220	$265	$217
Belgium-Luxembourg	140	45	91	41	50	4
France	174	66	73	33	40	35
Germany	394	86	141	64	77	167
Italy	109	35	60	27	33	14
Netherlands	159	40	120	54	66	0
Loss as Percentage of 1958 Imports						
Total EEC	*21.9*	*24.2*	*23.0*	*23.2*	*22.8*	*17.9*
Belgium-Luxembourg	*20.1*	*30.0*	*27.4*	*20.9*	*36.8*	*1.9*
France	*19.0*	*20.2*	*20.6*	*20.7*	*20.5*	*15.2*
Germany	*24.0*	*25.6*	*18.3*	*25.1*	*14.9*	*31.3*
Italy	*19.2*	*21.0*	*21.1*	*21.7*	*20.6*	*12.4*
Netherlands	*24.9*	*27.5*	*32.9*	*25.8*	*42.6*	*—*

Source: See App. C for description of method used in this calculation.
[a] Detail may not add to totals because of rounding.

The estimates indicate that the other members of EFTA are also substantial losers from the trade-pattern effects of EEC integration. In the aggregate, their losses amount to over $250 million, or 23 percent of their total sales of manufactured products to the EEC in 1958. Approximately half of the total loss is borne by all EFTA countries combined. Since the EFTA countries are themselves diverting trade away from the EEC, it is possible that a substantial offsetting of losses occurred.

First Direct Approach to EFTA Estimates

In the European Free Trade Association, a situation parallel to that of the EEC exists with respect to discriminatory internal tariff reductions. As

TABLE 2-12

Imports of Manufactured Products by EFTA Countries, by Source, 1958[a]

(Dollar amounts in millions)

Importing Country	Total	EFTA	Nonmembers			
			Total	United States	EEC	Other
Total EFTA	$7,613	$1,781	$5,832	$786	$3,591	$1,455
Austria	605	94	511	26	447	38
Denmark	764	308	456	35	354	67
Norway	951	409	542	48	392	102
Portugal	286	90	196	20	169	7
Sweden	1,482	431	1,051	160	771	120
Switzerland	981	138	843	105	661	77
United Kingdom	2,544	311	2,233	392	797	1,044
	Percentage Distribution					
Total EFTA	*100.0*	*23.4*	*76.6*	*10.3*	*47.2*	*19.1*
Austria	*100.0*	*15.5*	*84.5*	*4.3*	*73.9*	*6.3*
Denmark	*100.0*	*40.3*	*59.7*	*4.6*	*46.4*	*8.8*
Norway	*100.0*	*43.0*	*57.0*	*5.1*	*41.2*	*10.7*
Portugal	*100.0*	*31.5*	*68.5*	*7.0*	*59.2*	*2.4*
Sweden	*100.0*	*29.1*	*70.9*	*10.8*	*52.0*	*8.1*
Switzerland	*100.0*	*14.1*	*85.9*	*10.7*	*67.4*	*7.8*
United Kingdom	*100.0*	*12.2*	*87.8*	*15.4*	*31.3*	*41.0*

Source: U.N., *Commodity Trade Statistics*, Vol. VIII.
[a] Manufactured products include SITC groups 5, 6, 7, and 8, as defined in App. Table C-1. Detail may not add to totals because of rounding.

seen in Table 2-12, the value of EFTA imports of manufactured products in 1958 was $7.6 billion—over $1 billion less than the value of EEC imports in that year—but more than 75 percent of the total, $5.8 billion, came from nonmember countries. Thus, the amount of imports subject to trade loss by nonmembers was considerably more than in the case of the EEC.

The height of external tariffs (different for each member of EFTA) is also important in determining the amount of nonmember trade loss to be expected. The tariff levels of the EFTA countries for manufactured products, as noted previously, are rather hard to characterize. Portuguese tariffs are very high (probably because it was a late joiner of GATT). Portugal, however, is a small country and therefore should not be weighted very heavily in the overall EFTA picture. The tariffs of the United Kingdom, by far the largest EFTA country, also fall in the high range. Those of Austria and Norway are somewhat lower than the United Kingdom. On the other hand, Sweden, Switzerland, and especially Denmark can be classified as very low-tariff countries.

As in the case of the EEC, empirical estimates of the equation were made to measure trade loss for nonmembers, but with one important difference: It was assumed that half of the potential trade diversion to EFTA countries other than the United Kingdom would be absorbed by higher producer prices. Because of the short transition period, the large discrete reductions of internal tariffs, and most important, because of the relatively small size of the EFTA countries (with the exception of the United Kingdom), it could not be assumed that producers in these countries could supply (at constant prices) the increases in demand coming from tariff discrimination.

The results are shown in Table 2-13. The total expected nonmember country trade loss is over $800 million (in 1958 prices), somewhat less than the corresponding figure for the EEC. If this amount of trade were diverted to member countries, intra-EFTA trade would rise to 34.3 percent of total trade from the 1958 level of 23.4 percent, or a rise of 10.9 percentage points. The amount of nonmember trade loss expected from the formation of EFTA, surprisingly large in view of the low level of external tariffs in most member countries, is due to the small percentage of intra-EFTA trade existing prior to the creation of the free trade area, and to the fact that the major EFTA country, the United Kingdom, has high external tariffs. In fact, the losses in the United Kingdom market account for 37 percent of the total trade loss expected by nonmember countries.

The expected loss of the United States due to EFTA tariff discrimination is only about $100 million, compared with a $275 million expected loss due to the formation of the EEC. The discrepancy comes from the fact that the United States provided less than $800 million of the base-year imports of EFTA, but over $1.1 billion of the imports of the EEC in that year. Furthermore, the tariff structure of the EFTA countries is more favorable to the kinds of products exported by the United States.

The European Economic Community absorbs the brunt of the nonmember trade loss expected from EFTA. The loss amounts to over $500 million, at 1958 prices and levels of trade—63 percent of the total loss of all nonmember countries. The fact that most of the trade-pattern effects from EFTA should fall on the EEC is to be expected, in view of the

TABLE 2-13

Expected Loss of Sales to EFTA of Manufactured Products by Nonmembers During Transition Period[a]

(Dollar amounts in millions, 1958 prices)

Importing Country	Nonmembers Losing Sales			
	Total	United States	EEC	Other
Total EFTA	$828	$108	$523	$197
Austria	119	6	104	9
Denmark	37	3	29	5
Norway	68	6	49	13
Portugal	72	7	62	3
Sweden	129	20	95	14
Switzerland	94	12	74	8
United Kingdom	309	54	110	145
	Loss as Percentage of 1958 Imports			
Total EFTA	*14.2*	*13.7*	*14.6*	*13.5*
Austria	*23.3*	*23.1*	*23.3*	*23.7*
Denmark	*8.1*	*8.6*	*8.2*	*7.5*
Norway	*12.5*	*12.5*	*12.5*	*12.7*
Portugal	*36.7*	*35.0*	*36.7*	*42.9*
Sweden	*12.3*	*12.5*	*12.3*	*11.7*
Switzerland	*11.2*	*11.4*	*11.2*	*10.4*
United Kingdom	*13.8*	*13.8*	*13.8*	*13.9*

Source: See App. C for description of method used in this calculation.
[a] Detail may not add to totals because of rounding.

EEC's position as the dominant supplier to some of the EFTA countries.[18]

The Second Direct Approach

The measurement of expected trade loss detailed above depends primarily upon two variables: the pre-integration distribution of trade between member and nonmember countries, and the height of the external

[18] If Austria should join, the EEC would avoid about 20 percent of the total expected loss.

tariff for each product. Estimating empirical values of the equation in footnote 13 on page 50, when using these factors as independent variables, yields an estimate of expected shifts of trade from nonmember to member countries, product by product.[19] Because several years have elapsed since the formation of the EEC and EFTA, the expected shifts might already be apparent in changes in the structure of trade of member countries. Some confirmation of the measurement of expected trade losses can be obtained (by cross-section analysis) if the observed shifts in trade, product by product, reflect the expected shifts, as determined by the foregoing analysis.

Before proceeding, it is worth examining the question of the length of time it might take for the expected shifts in trade shares to materialize. The expected shares of trade of member countries refer to a new state of equilibrium. The time period required to reach the new equilibrium level will depend on the speed of internal tariff reductions, the time needed by businessmen to react to changes in tariffs, and, for the EEC, the speed of the erection of the external tariff wall. The reaction lag may not be too great, since businessmen could anticipate further tariff reductions once the process was begun. But some lag would still occur, unless they were able to predict perfectly the accelerated schedule of tariff reductions.

The time-path of tariff reductions in the EEC and EFTA can be seen in Table 2-14. For the EEC, the reduction of internal tariffs was well advanced by the end of 1965, and the second step toward aligning external tariffs was taken in the middle of 1963.[20] For EFTA, tariff reductions

[19] Literally, $yi = \dfrac{\Sigma_j (\dot{x}_{ij} X_{ij})}{\Sigma_j M_{ij}}$,

where

y_i = expected shift in shares from nonmember to member,

X_{ij} and $\dot{x}_{ij}$ are the same as before, and

M_{ij} = total imports of product i by member country j.

[20] It can be argued that the more recent tariff changes have had a much greater effect upon trading patterns than the earlier ones. In the first place, the first two rounds of internal reductions were made applicable to nonmembers as long as the country tariff did not fall below the CXT. Also, Germany was not required to make internal reductions immediately, since she had previously reduced her tariffs unilaterally. In addition, the external tariff wall was erected in large discrete steps and these were not begun until the process of internal reductions was well along. Finally, the margin of preference in the early stages was relatively slight, which might have encouraged nonmember suppliers to cut profit margins in order to maintain sales. This business behavior on the part of European exporters to the EEC might have been encouraged by the hope of a preferred entrance for some European nonmember suppliers into the market.

TABLE 2-14

Time-Path of Internal Tariff Reductions in the EEC and EFTA

	EEC		EFTA[a]	
Date	Percentage of EEC Tariff Remaining on Intra-Trade	Movement Toward CXT[b]	Date	Percentage of EFTA Tariff Remaining on Intra-Trade
January 1958	100	0		
January 1959	90	0	January 1959	100
July 1960	80	0	July 1960	80
January 1961	70	30	July 1961	70
January 1962	60	30	March 1962	60
July 1962	50	30	November 1962	50
July 1963	40	60	January 1964	40
January 1965	30	60	January 1965	30
January 1966	20	60	January 1966	20
July 1967	15	60	January 1967	—
July 1968[c]	—	100		

[a] Special timetables apply to several of the EFTA countries:
Norway: to meet special problems with respect to a small range of industries, the following timetable applies to a few consumer goods:

Date	Percent of Base-Date Tariff
January 1966	40
January 1967	30
January 1968	20
January 1969	10
January 1970	—

Portugal: an extended timetable for tariff reductions operates for a wide range of goods, as provided in Annex G of the EFTA Convention. The EFTA Convention states that before January 1970, the Council shall decide the subsequent timetable, provided that all Annex G duties are eliminated before January 1980.

Date	Percent of Base-Date Tariff
July 1960	80
January 1963	70
January 1967	60
January 1970	50

Finland: entered into association with EFTA in June 1961. Her normal timetable for tariff reductions is now as follows:

Date	Percent of Base-Date Tariff
July 1961	70
August 1962	60
May 1963	50
May 1964	40
March 1965	30
January 1966	20
January 1967	10
January 1968	—

For a few items listed in Annex I to the FINEFTA Agreement, there is a timetable extending to January 1969.
[b] Figures refer to the percentage of adjustment between the old national level of tariffs and the CXT completed on the date indicated.
[c] Anticipated.

58

were started considerably later than in the EEC, and even though the schedule was accelerated to match and then precede that of the EEC, the later starting date, plus the general insecurity of the whole organization, may have dampened the speed of business reaction.

The product-by-product shifts in the trade shares of member countries (for the 61 products) between 1958 and 1963, 1964, and 1965 were calculated for both the EEC and EFTA. The actual shifts were then compared to the expected shifts predicted from the tariff adjustments by regression analysis.[21] The results for both the EEC and EFTA are shown in Table 2-15.

Two measurements coming from the regression analysis are of special importance: the test of significance of the equation as a whole, and the estimated size of the reaction coefficient. The test of significance gives an indication of whether the entire analysis is meaningful. Unless the predicted changes in shares of trade provide a statistically significant explanation of actual changes, little confidence can be attached to the estimates of the trade loss of nonmember countries. If the equation does prove to be significant, then the estimated size of the reaction coefficient will give a broad indication of what percentage of the expected adjustment has already been completed.[22]

The results of the regression analysis for the European Economic Community are encouraging. The calculations for all three years are significant at the .001 level (as measured by the F ratio). The estimates of the reaction coefficient indicate that, by 1963, almost 40 percent of the adjustment to the new equilibrium level of trade shares had been accomplished, and that it had increased to almost 50 percent by 1965. While these figures are somewhat lower than might have been expected, given the progress in internal tariff reductions, they are certainly reasonable.

---

[21] A simple equation of the type $x = ay$ was fitted by the least squares technique. where x is the actual shift in member trade shares between 1958 and 1963, 1964, and 1965, y is the expected shift in member country trade shares, and a is a reaction parameter.

[22] The reaction coefficient can be interpreted directly for the EEC, since its expected value at equilibrium is 1.000. For the EFTA, however, the expected value is 0.633, because of the adjustment made for supply elasticities of the smaller EFTA countries.

TABLE 2-15

Regression Analysis of Actual Shifts in Intra-Community Trade Explained by Expected Shifts, EEC and EFTA[a]

Area	Year	Reaction Coefficient[b]	Coefficient of Determination[c] (R^2)	Level of Reliability[d] (F ratio test)
EEC				
	1963	.3895 (.0433)	.24	.001
	1964	.4634 (.0488)	.31	.001
	1965	.4873 (.0564)	.24	.001
EFTA				
	1963	.0652 (.0352)	.03	Not significant
	1964	.0639 (.0246)	.06	.050
	1965	.0971 (.0290)	.09	.025

[a] Data weighted by value of trade in 1958.
[b] Figures in parentheses are standard errors of parameters.
[c] R^2 corrected for degrees of freedom.
[d] A test at the .001 level implies that there is less than one case out of one thousand where the observed result could have occurred by chance when the true value is zero.

Unfortunately, the results of the calculations for the European Free Trade Association are not as encouraging. The calculations as a whole are much less significant, and this can be only partially explained by the later start of EFTA. The reaction coefficient has the expected sign and indicates that 15 percent of the adjustment had been completed by 1965 (.0971 divided by 0.633). The EFTA trade effect may well have been dominated by the deterioration of the United Kingdom's competitive position between 1958 and 1963-65.[23]

While the evidence is far from conclusive, it does appear that the

[23] An attempt was made to test for this possibility through use of a dummy variable. On the theory that the products most likely to be affected by a deterioration in the United Kingdom's competitive position would be the ones in which it was the dominant supplier in member trade in 1958, the digit "one" was assigned to these products and "zero" was given to products in which any other EFTA country was dominant. The results of calculating this equation were statistically significant, but the estimates of the coefficient are difficult to evaluate.

measure of expected trade loss has been partially confirmed for the European Economic Community. For the European Free Trade Association, the regression analysis was able to pick up some indications of significance, but little more. If the member countries—primarily the United Kingdom—did lose some of their competitive position during this time period, then the potential for diverting trade may not have been realized.

Indirect Approach to EEC Estimates

An alternative and indirect approach to measuring the trade loss of nonmember countries is possible. The major factor normally determining the change in a country's share of a foreign market is its relative competitive position. By examining changes in competitive position over time (before and after the start of economic integration), it is possible to stipulate what the market share should be, in the absence of changes in barriers to imports into that market. The difference between actual trade developments and the "normal" pattern can be attributed to changes in those barriers, if it is assumed that economic integration itself does not affect the competitive positions of the countries involved.[24] The indirect method can at best give only a rough approximation of the consequences of economic integration, since it is derived as a residual, and other factors not explicitly recognized might also be influencing trade. While economic integration may well be the most important factor in determining market shares, other than competitive conditions, it is certainly not the only factor, and the interpretation of the results should recognize this.

The actual shares of the EEC import market for manufactured products are shown in Chart 2. Annual shares from 1953 through 1965 are included to give a somewhat greater historical perspective, but the analysis will be confined to a comparison between 1958 and 1963.[25] In the early 1950's, member shares rose because of OEEC-sponsored intra-European trade liberalization. This factor was dissipated by the mid-1950's, and the shares became relatively stable. Just before integration, member countries provided about 50 percent of total EEC imports of manufactured products. After five years of changes in tariffs in the process of forming a customs union, manufactured imports provided by member

[24] The measurement of competitive conditions is independent of tariffs or tariff changes.
[25] These dates were determined by the availability of data.

CHART 2

Member Country Share of Imports of Manufactured Products of EEC Countries, 1953–65

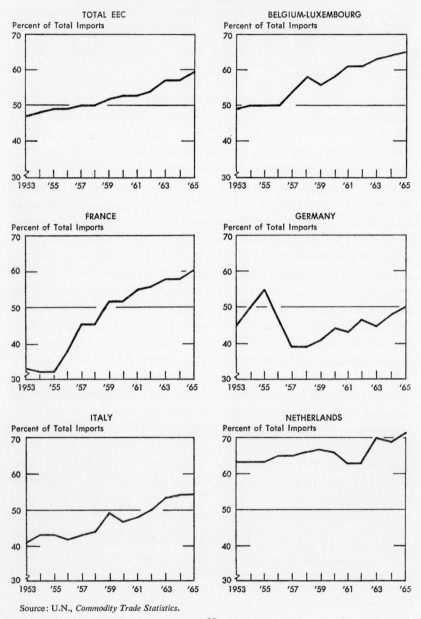

Source: U.N., *Commodity Trade Statistics.*

countries had risen to 57 percent. As noted previously, this change reflects tariff changes, shifts in competitive position, and possibly other factors.

In order to determine whether any of the increase in intra-Community trade should be attributed to shifts in competitive position, the export prices of member countries must be compared to the prices of other industrial countries. Between 1958 and 1963, the export prices of manufactured products of Italy, Belgium, and France declined by 6 percent, 4 percent and 3 percent, respectively, while those of the Netherlands and Germany rose by 3 percent and 6 percent.[26] These figures, however, refer to the industrial exports of these countries to all areas. What is required is a measure of the relative prices of the EEC exporting countries in the specific markets of other EEC countries. A separate measure is needed for each importing market, reflecting the relative country shares of that market.[27] The relative export prices of the EEC countries in the markets of member countries for 1963 are shown in Table 2-16. The entry for the Netherlands in the German market, for example, indicates that, compared with 1958, Dutch industrial products lost in price competitiveness by 5 percent relative to other industrial countries exporting to the German market.[28] Table 2-16 shows that Italy, France, and Belgium gained in competitiveness in member country markets, while the Netherlands and Germany generally lost some of their competitive position, reflecting the upward revaluation of the German mark and the Dutch guilder in 1961.

By making use of the indexes of price competitiveness in Table 2-16, and taking a constant value of the elasticity of substitution for each supplier to each member country market, based on recent European experience, it is possible to get an estimate of the share that intra-Community imports would have been in total member country imports of industrial products in 1963, in the absence of tariff changes.[29] Despite the fact that

[26] Export prices are measured as unit value indexes of dollar prices and thus reflect changes in exchange rates. Sources: Helen B. Junz and Rudolph R. Rhomberg, "Prices and Export Performance of Industrial Countries, 1953-63," International Monetary Fund, *Staff Papers* (Washington, D.C., 1965); United Nations, *Monthly Bulletin of Statistics* (New York, June 1965).

[27] The Junz-Rhomberg article, in IMF *Staff Papers,* discusses price competitiveness in separate markets at some length, and also provides the source of the price data cited.

[28] The exporting countries are Austria, Belgium, Canada, France, West Germany, Italy, Japan, Netherlands, Sweden, United Kingdom, and the United States.

[29] A constant elasticity of substitution of —2.0 was used for each market. This value is the median value found in the Junz-Rhomberg study. Because of the off-

the competitive position of three member countries improved in the EEC market and only two deteriorated, the losses slightly outweighed the gains because of the losses of Germany, the largest exporter of the EEC. The results of the calculations are shown in Table 2-17, and indicate that, based solely on competitive conditions, intra-Community trade would

TABLE 2-16

*Export-Price Competitive Indexes of EEC Countries
in the Markets of Member Countries, 1963*[a]

(1958 = 1.000)

Exporting Country	Market				
	Belgium-Luxembourg	Nether-lands	Germany	France	Italy
Belgium-Luxembourg	—	.924	.971	.942	.922
Netherlands	1.011	—	1.053	1.020	.994
Germany	1.070	1.082	—	1.093	1.053
France	.949	.962	.994	—	.934
Italy	.911	.917	.932	.907	—

Source: Helen B. Junz and Rudolph R. Rhomberg, "Prices and Export Performance of Industrial Countries, 1953–63," International Monetary Fund, *Staff Papers* (Washington, D.C., 1965).
[a] Value greater than 1.0 indicates loss of price competitiveness.

have declined to 49.5 percent of total imports of industrial products in 1963 from the 50.0 percent figure in 1958.

Comparing Results of Direct and Indirect Approaches for the EEC

The actual percentage of EEC intra-Community trade of industrial products was 56.6 percent in 1963 (Table 2-17). Since competitive conditions would have resulted in a 49.5 percent figure, the difference of 7.1 percentage points can be attributed to the effects of economic integration. According to our previous analysis of the impact of tariff adjustments, the intra-Community trade share should rise to 62.1 percent of total member

---

setting nature of the competitive changes of member countries, the resulting estimated intra-Community share is not sensitive to the particular number used for the elasticity of substitution. (See App. C for further discussion of this point.) It is sensitive, however, to the assumption of constancy of the elasticity of substitution for all countries in all markets. Constancy was assumed because of the lack of statistical reliability of the *differences* between the calculated parameters.

imports when the new equilibrium is reached (see page 52), or an increase of 12.1 percentage points. Thus, by this measure, 59 percent of the adjustment was completed by the end of 1963; this contrasts with the 40 percent figure measured by the reaction coefficient in the regression analysis (second direct approach, Table 2-15). The difference between the two measures of adjustment completed by 1963, while substantial, is not very significant, given the crudeness of both measures. Another compari-

TABLE 2-17

Actual and Estimated Shares of EEC Market Held by Members,
1958 and 1963, and Difference Due to Integration

(In percentages)

| Country | 1958 | 1963 | | |
| | Actual Share | Actual Share | Estimated Share | Difference Due to Integration[a] |
	(1)	(2)	(3)	(4)
Total EEC	50.0	56.6	49.5	7.1
Belgium-Luxembourg	11.6	11.3	12.9	−1.6
Netherlands	6.9	6.4	6.6	−0.2
Germany	18.8	21.9	16.0	5.9
France	8.3	10.6	8.9	1.7
Italy	4.4	6.4	5.1	1.3

[a] Col. 2 minus col. 3.

son can be made of the results of the direct and indirect approaches. According to the direct approach (first and second combined), economic integration was estimated to have increased member shares of the market by about 5 percentage points by 1963 compared to the 7 percentage points indicated by the indirect approach.

The previous analysis does not give any indication of which of the Common Market countries would benefit the most from static trade diversion. Such an analysis, which would require an examination of product and market specialization and supply elasticities of the member countries, is beyond the scope of this study. However, Table 2-17 does give an estimated measure of the distribution of export benefits among member countries, and the contrasts are so great as to be worth noting. The country which apparently obtained most of the export benefits is Germany, followed by France and Italy, while the Benelux countries appear to have

CHART 3

Member Country Share of Imports of Manufactured Products of EFTA Countries, 1953–65

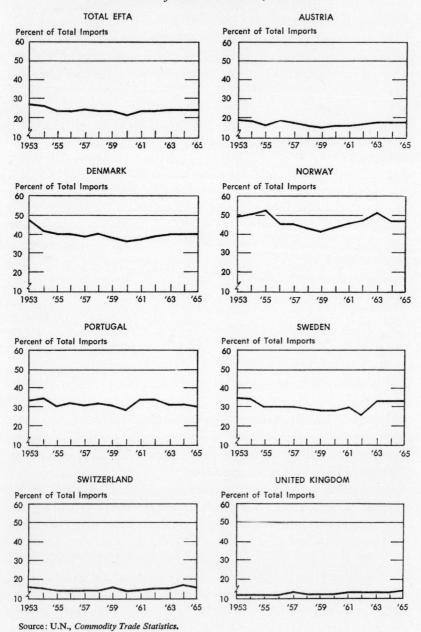

Source: U.N., *Commodity Trade Statistics.*

66

lost exports. The actual shares of both the Netherlands and Belgium-Luxembourg in the EEC market fell from 1958 to 1963. One fact that might explain this behavior is that in 1958 the Netherlands and Belgium-Luxembourg already had protected markets in the Benelux arrangement. After the formation of the EEC they were forced to share this preference with Germany, France, and Italy. It may be that this loss was of great importance, particularly in the early years of the Common Market, since intra-Benelux trade was quite large for both the Netherlands and Belgium-Luxembourg.

A preliminary test of this hypothesis was made by calculating the shares of Belgium-Luxembourg and the Netherlands in Common Market imports, exclusive of Benelux imports. The results seem to confirm the hypothesis. Belgium's share of this trade increased between 1958 and 1963, indicating that Belgium's decline in the market as a whole was due to a sharp decline in the Dutch market. To a lesser extent, the behavior of Dutch exports also seems to confirm the hypothesis. The Netherlands' share in the EEC market minus Benelux fell, although by less than its share in the market as a whole. Germany may have been the major beneficiary of the termination of Benelux preferences because of its geographical proximity to the major part of the market.

Indirect Approach to EFTA Estimates

The indirect method was also employed for estimating the trade-pattern effect of the European Free Trade Association. Chart 3 illustrates the change in member shares in EFTA between 1953 and 1963. Unfortunately, the price data required for the calculation of expected member country shares of EFTA trade, based solely on competitive conditions, were not available for all countries in all markets. This necessitated assigning relative export prices based on related, but not fully comparable, export-price data (Table 2-18).[30] This lack of data is not as serious as it appears, since data are available for the major exporting countries (except Switzerland), covering about two-thirds of intra-EFTA trade of in-

---

[30] Export unit values are available from Junz-Rhomberg, in IMF *Staff Papers*, for three exporting countries (the United Kingdom, Sweden, and Austria), in four markets (all of the above plus Switzerland). All other export price relatives were estimated from data on general export prices in International Monetary Fund, *International Financial Statistics* (Washington, D.C., 1965).

dustrial products. As seen in Table 2-18, there are very few instances in which the EFTA countries actually improved their competitive positions in the markets of other EFTA countries between 1958 and 1963. In particular, the export prices of industrial products of Switzerland and the United Kingdom rose substantially in relation to other industrial countries exporting to EFTA markets.

TABLE 2-18

Export-Price Competitive Indexes of EFTA Countries in the Markets of Member Countries, 1963[a]

(1958 = 1.000)

Exporting Country	Market						
	Austria	Denmark	Norway	Portugal	Sweden	Switzerland	United Kingdom
Austria	—	1.030[b]	1.020[b]	1.040[b]	1.026	1.045	1.063
Denmark	1.010[b]	—	1.000[b]	1.030[b]	1.020[b]	1.050[b]	1.070[b]
Norway	.970[b]	.980[b]	—	1.000[b]	.980[b]	1.020[b]	1.040[b]
Portugal	1.020[b]	1.040[b]	1.030[b]	—	1.040[b]	1.070[b]	1.080[b]
Sweden	1.007	1.010[b]	.990[b]	1.020[b]	—	1.031	1.052
Switzerland	1.040	1.050[b]	1.040[b]	1.060[b]	1.050[b]	—	1.090[b]
United Kingdom	1.027	1.040[b]	1.030[b]	1.050[b]	1.041	1.076	—

Sources: Helen B. Junz and Rudolph R. Rhomberg, in IMF *Staff Papers;* International Monetary Fund, *International Financial Statistics* (Washington, D.C., 1965).
[a] Value greater than 1.0 indicates loss of price competitiveness.
[b] Estimated.

Comparing Results of Direct and Indirect Approaches for EFTA

Following a procedure identical to that employed for the EEC, the price indexes in Table 2-18 were used to estimate the 1963 shares of EFTA trade that should have been supplied by other EFTA countries on the basis of competitive conditions alone. The results are shown in Table 2-19.[31] Because of the general deterioration in the competitive position of the EFTA countries, the intra-EFTA share of trade in industrial products

[31] The same price elasticity of substitution, -2.0, was used as for the EEC calculations. However, the EFTA results are more sensitive to the value of the parameter than are those for the EEC. See App. C.

in 1963 should have declined to 21.7 percent of total imports compared to 23.6 percent in 1958. The actual intra-EFTA share of total imports in 1963 was 24.4 percent, 2.7 percentage points larger than expected from competitive conditions. This residual can be attributed to the effects of the freeing of intra-EFTA trade. The estimated difference of 2.7 percentage points is not very large in view of the equilibrium amount of trade estimated to be diverted to member countries—10.9 percentage points—by the direct approach (p. 55).

TABLE 2-19

Actual and Estimated Shares of EFTA Market Held by Members, 1958 and 1963, and Difference Due to Integration

(In percentages)

Country	1958	1963		
	Actual Share (1)	Actual Share (2)	Estimated Share (3)	Difference Due to Integration[a] (4)
Total EFTA	23.6	24.4	21.7	2.7
Austria	1.1	1.4	0.9	0.5
Denmark	1.7	2.2	1.7	0.5
Norway	2.2	2.2	2.1	0.1
Portugal	0.3	0.4	0.2	0.2
Sweden	5.8	6.1	5.6	0.5
Switzerland	3.1	3.1	2.7	0.4
United Kingdom	9.4	8.9	8.3	0.6

[a] Col. 2 minus col. 3.

If the estimate of the trade-pattern effect obtained from analyzing tariff changes in the direct approach is correct, then only 25 percent of the EFTA adjustment had been completed by 1963. This figure is at best only roughly comparable to the reaction coefficient obtained from the regression analysis (10 percent), but neither estimate is statistically very satisfying nor plausible, in view of the progress made in internal tariff reductions in EFTA. One could argue that economic integration has been more important than it appears because the consequences of the loss of competitiveness by member countries of EFTA have been underestimated. If the numerical value for the elasticity of substitution is greater than the -2.0 figure used in this analysis, then support could be given to this proposition.[32] On the other hand, it may simply be that the estimate of the trade-pattern effect by the direct approach is too great.

Some indications of the distribution of gains from the trade-pattern effect among the member countries of EFTA are shown in Table 2-19. Unlike the EEC, all of the member countries of EFTA seem to have benefited, and by roughly equal amounts. As might have been expected, the larger countries appear to have benefited somewhat more than the smaller ones. It must be remembered, however, that all the analyses of the consequences of EFTA are tentative, in view of the inability to isolate very pronounced trade effects reasonably attributable to economic integration.

Net Results of Income and Trade-Pattern Effects

Income and trade-pattern effects can now be combined to arrive at the net effect of economic integration upon imports of manufactured products from nonmember countries.

The direct and the indirect approaches to estimating the trade-pattern effect of integration all yielded somewhat different results. It was decided to use only the estimates from the direct method (Tables 2-11 and 2-13) for subsequent analysis, in the belief that these estimates are more firmly based. As seen in Table 2-20, the two effects taken together indicate that there are net losses for nonmembers. These losses represent the difference between the actual sales of manufactured products to the EEC and EFTA by nonmember countries during the respective transition periods and the sales that would have been expected in the absence of economic integration (measured in 1958 prices). The losses due to the formation of EFTA are somewhat greater than those due to the EEC. This results from the fact that the income effects of the EEC are substantially greater. For the United States, however, the net loss due to the formation of EEC is twice as great as that due to EFTA, $161 million compared to $77 million. The major losers in the EFTA market are the EEC countries, as are the EFTA countries in the EEC market.

The question arises, in evaluating these figures, whether the bilateral losses inflicted by EFTA on the EEC are offset by the losses expected in

[32] An elasticity of substitution of −3.0 yields an estimated EFTA effect of 3.5 percentage points (24.4 percent, actual share, minus 20.9 percent, normal share), compared to the 2.7 percentage points noted above. See App. C.

TABLE 2-20

Expected Net Losses for Nonmember Countries in Trade of Manufactured Products Due to Income and Trade-Pattern Effects, EEC and EFTA During Transition Periods

(Millions of dollars, 1958 prices)

Importing Country	Area with Net Loss				
	All Non-members	United States	EFTA	EEC	Other
Total EEC	548	161	279	—	108
Belgium-Luxembourg	68	30	56	—	18ᵃ
France	89	33	39	—	17
Germany	245	56	71	—	118
Italy	48	16	29	—	3
Netherlands	98	26	84	—	12ᵃ
Total EFTA	597	77	—	378	142
Austria	90	4	—	79	7
Denmark	9	1	—	7	1
Norway	64	6	—	46	12
Portugal	65	6	—	56	3
Sweden	93	14	—	68	11
Switzerland	55	7	—	43	5
United Kingdom	221	39	—	79	103
Total EEC and EFTA	1,145	238	279	378	250

Sources: Tables 2-9, 2-11, and 2-13. ᵃ Gain.

the reverse direction, allowing the consideration of only an adjusted net figure.[33] The extent to which these trade losses can be regarded as offsetting depends in large measure on the similarity of the products structure of the respective diversions. A careful analysis of this question would require much finer product detail than used in this study; however, a rough

[33] For instance, the United Kingdom might be prevented from selling a particular chemical in the Netherlands because of the CXT. Instead it could increase its sales of the chemical to Austria by an equivalent amount, at the expense of German exporters, because of the trade preference provided by the Austrian external tariff (with the Germans switching markets in the opposite direction). In such a situation, what are the real losses involved? Clearly, transportation costs might be increased by the shifting of markets, and the structure of prices in both the Netherlands and Austria might be distorted somewhat, but these effects are not likely to be great. This conclusion is underscored if one compares this situation to that of a third country such as the United States, which is losing markets in both the EEC and EFTA without a corresponding increase in preference elsewhere.

TABLE 2-21

Bilateral Trade Diversion, EEC and EFTA, by Product Class[a]

(Thousands of dollars, 1958 prices)

Type of Loss	SITC 5	SITC 6	SITC 7	SITC 8	Total
Loss of EEC from EFTA[b]	89	257	405	107	858
Loss of EFTA from EEC	60	165	206	55	485
Net loss:					
EEC minus EFTA	29	92	199	52	373

[a] These figures refer to the trade-pattern effect only, since the growth effect cannot be distributed by products. Product classes are from the Standard International Trade Classification.

[b] The EFTA figures represent the gross trade-pattern effect, before the correction for supply elasticities of the smaller EFTA countries.

order of magnitude can be obtained by looking at the broad product divisions shown in Table 2-21. The product structures are quite similar in their gross outline because, for each of the product classes, the loss inflicted on the EEC by EFTA is almost twice as great as the reverse loss. It appears, therefore, that a concept of a net loss which overlooks offsetting trade diversions between the EEC and EFTA might have some merit.

The evaluation of the total impact of the EEC and EFTA based on the two concepts (with and without offsetting trade diversion) can be seen in Table 2-22. The total amount of trade loss is reduced from $1,145 million

TABLE 2-22

Loss of Trade in Manufactured Products Before and After Offsetting Trade Diversion

(Dollar amounts in millions, 1958 prices)

Type of Loss	Area with Loss				
	Total	United States	EFTA	EEC	Other
Loss before offsetting trade diversion	$1,145	$238	$279	$378	$250
Loss after offsetting trade diversion	587	238	—	99	250
	Percentage Distribution				
Loss before offsetting trade diversion	100.0	20.8	24.4	33.0	21.8
Loss after offsetting trade diversion	100.0	40.5	—	16.9	42.6

Source: Table 2-20.

to $587 million, if a net concept is considered, and the major impact falls on the United States and other nonintegrated countries. The loss of $238 million of trade by the United States as a result of the EEC and EFTA is only the direct impact. A secondary effect upon the United States would be expected to arise from indirect repercussions of the $250 million of the expected trade loss of other nonintegrated countries. Canada and Japan are among those most significantly affected, and they are the major trading partners of the United States. While the potential indirect effects of the trade losses upon the United States cannot be measured, it is clear that important economic developments in Japan, Canada, Australia, and other countries do have a substantial and immediate feedback on the United States. Because of the multitude of responses possible in these countries, and because these feedbacks on the United States occur simultaneously with many other economic factors, further analysis of this effect does not appear to be fruitful.

Implications for the United States and Conclusions

The weight of the evidence examined in this chapter points to the conclusion that economic integration can be extremely important in shaping the whole environment of the sector producing manufactured products in member countries: Income can be stimulated and trade patterns can be affected. These consequences do, in fact, seem to have resulted from the European Economic Community. The income of member countries has been stimulated with beneficial results radiating beyond the Community's borders. Also, trade of member countries has been profoundly influenced by the existence of Community preferences. Much closer interdependence of markets has occurred than could have been expected in the absence of economic integration.

It is also apparent that economic integration has not affected all member countries of the EEC equally. All have increased their trade with other members, but only some have done so without sacrificing their trade with nonmembers. Most have been stimulated to a higher level of income, but apparently not equally. Certainly the pre-existing conditions in a country and the economic policies it follows will influence how the forces of economic integration are transmitted throughout the economy.

Through its impact on member countries, economic integration has also greatly affected the trade of the EEC with nonmember countries. The inherent discrimination that accompanies economic integration has resulted in a loss of markets for manufactured products by nonmember countries that appears to have been only partially offset by the expansionary effects of integration. The amounts involved are not overwhelming. The impact on nonmember countries has been softened, because the integration adjustments have proceeded against the background of rapid economic growth. While nonmember countries have suffered from being denied opportunities to expand their trade as much as they would have been able to if the EEC and EFTA had not been formed, they have not been faced with an actual decline in sales.

The trade of the United States has been greatly affected, with U. S. sales increasing but its share decreasing. No doubt the removal of quantitative barriers against dollar products—the vestige of earlier dollar shortages—during this period helped to ease the adjustment for American exporters. The fact that the adjustment came during a period of weakness in the United States balance of payments made it more painful than the amounts involved would signify. The improvement in the U. S. payments position during this period, therefore, is all the more remarkable. Possibly the two are not unrelated. The Common Market typified the change in world economic conditions from postwar recovery to the new prosperity, and the United States responded to the challenge with renewed competitive strength.

But the United States is not the only nonmember country affected by the EEC. The neighboring countries in Europe—mainly in the European Free Trade Association—have to bear the major share of the adjustment. The existence of EFTA does potentially provide a substantial offset for them, but the analysis indicates that not much of the potential has so far been realized. The major conclusion to be drawn from the experience of EFTA is that a trading arrangement can be beneficial, but only if domestic economic conditions permit change. While this conclusion suggests that the substantial potential benefits of EFTA are still available, some of the difficulties are permanent. The geographical dispersion of the group will always remain to limit even the potential benefits of union. EFTA could become an important stimulus for most of its members, but whether or not it will remains questionable.

CHAPTER THREE

Agriculture

THE AGRICULTURAL ASPECTS of European economic integration have received a substantial amount of attention in both Europe and the United States. The European interest stems from the great difficulty of encompassing agriculture in the schemes for integration, while the U.S. interest arises from the manner in which that difficulty has been met.[1]

Attempts to include agriculture in the Benelux Customs Union, for instance, were never completed, despite the success of Benelux in reducing barriers to nonagricultural products. The more ambitious Green Pool idea for European agriculture, similar to the European Coal and Steel Community, failed to reach even a point of serious negotiation. This difficulty is apparent in the Rome Treaty, where the vagueness with which agriculture is treated is in marked contrast to the precision of the articles for manufactured products. Conflict over agriculture was a major cause of the failure to negotiate a continent-wide free trade area in 1958, and was one of the reasons for the breakdown of negotiations for the United Kingdom's entry into the Common Market in 1963. It has caused numerous crises within the EEC itself, and was partially responsible for the major crisis of July 1965-January 1966. Furthermore, the argument over poultry between the United States and the Common Market became so heated that it was named "the chicken war."

It is not hard to understand why agriculture has been an obstacle to the harmonious relationship of advanced industrial nations. The problems of farmers have been thought of as purely national problems and agricul-

---

[1] Most of this chapter concerns the EEC. While EFTA has made some provision for agricultural trade, the Community has given it more attention.

tural policies have been formulated without consideration of international implications. The agricultural dilemma is viewed as a welfare problem, requiring the state to intervene in the market place to protect a disadvantaged segment of the population. The fact that the form of intervention has often seriously disrupted international trade in agricultural products has not prevented this basically national outlook from persisting.

Some writers have traced governmental protection of agriculture on the Continent to the nineteenth century.[2] Lamartine Yates suggests that, unlike the situation in Great Britain, the rapid expansion of population on the Continent preceded the increase in demand for industrial workers caused by the Industrial Revolution. This led to overcrowding in the countryside and to reduced per capita returns in agriculture. Diminishing returns to farmers forced governments to come to their aid. Agricultural policies were formulated which treated land and capital as the scarce factors of production and labor as the abundant, if not redundant, factor. Whatever the cause, agricultural protectionism has a long tradition on the Continent, and should be viewed in this historical context.[3]

In order to appraise the consequences of integration for agricultural exports of nonmember countries, the total impact of the EEC and EFTA on the agricultural sectors of member countries must be examined. When a government decides to influence the production and consumption of agricultural products (as all member governments have, to some degree) it must formulate a commercial policy in support of those aims, or face insupportable financial burdens. In statisticians' language, it has already used up its degrees of freedom. Thus agriculture in general will be examined in this chapter, not just the trade in agricultural products.

The analysis will proceed as follows: European agriculture before integration will be reviewed to arrive at a judgment of how it might have developed without the EEC; the policies of the EEC will be examined to determine their probable consequences for the agricultural sector; and estimates will be attempted of the consequences of integration in general and the effects on nonmember trade in particular. This requires an examination of both production and consumption effects, since net imports (or exports) result only from the difference between them. In a briefer form, the same will be done for EFTA.

[2] P. Lamartine Yates, *Food, Land and Manpower in Western Europe* (London: Macmillan, 1960).

[3] Some countries, such as Denmark and the Netherlands, resisted this historical trend, much to their own benefit.

European Agriculture Before Integration

Most European countries had restrictive agricultural policies following World War II, and there is no reason to believe that they would have changed the direction of these policies.[4] These governments not only had a long history of agricultural protectionism, but also faced a number of factors in the postwar period that appeared to require further restrictions. First, the rapid increases in income and personal welfare in many European countries either were not shared by the agricultural sector, or were much less than in other occupations. Since per capita income in agriculture was already below that in the nonagricultural sector, this divergence of trends increased the absolute gap between the economic welfare of the two groups. An equity argument could thus be made for "doing something" for agriculture.

Second, most European countries suffered from balance-of-payments problems in the immediate postwar period and, therefore, import replacement had a rationale of its own. While a balance-of-payments argument was frequently used in support of restrictive agricultural policies, it was clearly not of overriding importance, since these policies have survived even in those countries having balance-of-payments surpluses.[5] What is more likely is that the balance of payments provided an excuse for following agricultural policies desired for other reasons. Such an excuse was very convenient and necessary to placate domestic nonagricultural interests and to resist pressures from agricultural exporting countries for a more liberal commercial policy.

Third, it was argued that a reasonable degree of self-sufficiency in agriculture was needed for reasons of national defense. European countries

---

[4] The term "restrictive agricultural policies" refers to policies restricting the operation of the market mechanism in both domestic and foreign commerce.

[5] The United Kingdom may be unique in that the balance of payments may have been a greater factor in determining agricultural policy than for other countries. This may be due to the greater dependence of the United Kingdom on imported food, and also to the persistence of the U.K. balance-of-payments deficit. Even the British Plan for 1964-1970 indicates that the contribution of agriculture to the plan will be to increase production to meet the growth in demand and thus will "ease the pressure on our (U.K.) bill for imports of temperate agricultural produce." Great Britain, Department of Economic Affairs, *The National Plan* (London, 1965), p. 135.

had recently experienced the suffering that can occur to a population greatly dependent on imported foodstuffs when a war or some other calamitous political event interrupts normal international trade. Thus, this argument had much popular appeal. The concept of self-sufficiency in food is undermined when agricultural output is crucially dependent upon imported animal feed, imported seed, imported fertilizer, imported petroleum, imported spare parts and machinery, and in some cases even imported workers. Yet the argument survives, and seems to be an important determinant of agricultural policy for the politically neutral countries of Europe—Sweden, Switzerland, and Austria.

These arguments influenced the governments of most European countries to interfere in the markets for agricultural products. Also of great importance was the strong political position of the agricultural population of most European countries in this period. Given the delicate balance between political groups in Europe, it is easy to understand how agricultural policies favored by the farmers receive attention.[6] Furthermore, the costs of "doing something" for agriculture are not overly burdensome. All of these countries are relatively rich by world standards, and the cost of protecting inefficient agriculture is not great for the population as a whole. Also, the real costs of protecting agriculture are usually well-hidden. The true economic costs involved are the losses of real income that could have been earned if the resources of the country were not artificially maintained in agriculture. There is obviously no way of observing these costs. Even in the case of the Netherlands, where the major protection of agriculture comes in the form of excessive government aids to farming, the opportunity costs of not putting these funds to alternative uses are not clearly discernible. The problems caused by restrictive agricultural policies are usually visible only when questions concerning international trade arise. However, when the agricultural problem is looked at from this point of view, the conflict appears, however incorrectly, to be one between domestic and foreign agricultural interests (rather than primarily as domestic agriculture versus the rest of the domestic economy). When issues are presented in this form, domestic agricultural interests will usually prevail.

[6] Even the French government during the Fifth Republic has been very sensitive to farmer opinion. Despite the strong political position of General de Gaulle, the French president has been more sympathetic to the demands of agricultural organizations than to similar pleas of other groups, such as miners or civil servants.

The Common Market Countries

The form of governmental interference in the market has differed from country to country, depending in part on the degree of agricultural self-sufficiency prevalent, and in part on the particular policy goals. For countries importing a substantial portion of their agricultural needs, trade restrictions, combined with price supports, were generally sufficient to provide an income supplement to farmers. German and Belgian agricultural policies were of this type. Possibly because of a smaller percentage of population in agriculture, however, price supports in Belgium did not exceed world market prices to the extent that they did in Germany. In contrast, France, having a higher degree of self-sufficiency in agriculture, with actual surpluses in some crops, could not depend on import restrictions alone to maintain prices at their desired level. For grains in particular, the French government was forced both to make direct expenditures to underwrite the cost of diverting bread grains from human to animal uses, and to subsidize exports. The Italian situation was similar to the French, but surpluses were only a problem in soft wheat, and these were handled through export subsidies. Of the EEC countries, only the Netherlands had anything resembling a liberal agricultural policy. The Netherlands imported a substantial amount of intermediate agricultural products, such as feed grains, and exported "final goods," such as meat and cheese, at world market prices. Dutch farmers, being efficient, were able to reach an income parity with nonagricultural workers without government restrictions, but with substantial government help. The Dutch government subsidized agriculture through a host of means—all aimed at increasing agricultural efficiency.

Most EEC countries considered foreign agricultural trade as a cushion to absorb the shocks of domestic policy. Thus, the international consequences of their policies can be judged only after an evaluation is made of the total effect of all agricultural measures on production and consumption within these countries in the pre-Rome Treaty period.

PRODUCTION. In trying to achieve the major goal of agricultural policy—increasing agricultural income—all of these governments found it necessary to increase producer prices (with the exception of the Netherlands, where producer prices followed market forces). As seen in Table 3-1, producer prices during the decade 1948-58 followed a rather unsteady but upward course in the major producers, France and Germany. Prices in the Benelux countries and Italy increased until the end of the Korean War, declined somewhat, and then held steady until the start of the EEC.[7]

TABLE 3-1

Indexes of Current Agricultural Producer Prices, Deflated Prices,[a] *and Ratios of Prices Received to Prices Paid by Farmers, EEC Countries, Selected Years, 1948–66*

(1957–59 = 100)

Type of Index and Country	1948	1952	1956	1958	1960	1962	1964	1966
Current Prices								
Belgium-Luxembourg	86	109	100	97	101	104	115	121
France	63	84	84	108	107	116	125	127
Germany	84	92	97	99	97	108	116	124
Italy	85[a]	97	101	96	98	115	122	129
Netherlands	85	104	104	99	97	96	113	122
Deflated Prices[b]								
Belgium-Luxembourg	n.a.	n.a.	103	98	98	99	103	104
France	n.a.	n.a.	97	106	95	95	95	94
Germany	n.a.	n.a.	101	99	95	100	97	103
Italy	n.a.	n.a.	104	95	95	104	97	99
Netherlands	n.a.	n.a.	114	98	94	89	95	97
Ratio of Prices Received to Prices Paid								
Belgium-Luxembourg	n.a.	124	104	97	95	92	94	90
France	n.a.	n.a.	94	109	97	101	103	105
Germany	n.a.	n.a.	101	98	93	94	95	98
Italy	n.a.	89	97	96	98	109	107	108
Netherlands	n.a.	125	113	99	90	82	83	87

Sources: Food and Agricultural Organization, *The State of Food and Agriculture, 1966* (Rome, 1966) and earlier annual volumes.

n.a. Not available.

[a] Estimated.

[b] Current producer prices deflated by cost of living.

These prices gave an incentive for increased output in all of these countries, as seen in Tables 3-2 and 3-3. During the decade 1948-58, agricultural output increased by 85 percent in Germany, 70 percent in the Netherlands, about 60 percent in Belgium and Italy, and 35 percent in France.

[7] It is an open question whether farmers respond to producer prices, to deflated producer prices, or to the ratio of prices received to prices paid. All are shown in Table 3-1. In recent years, there has been an upward movement in all measures, but in different degrees.

For the EEC countries as a whole, agricultural output increased by about 65 percent. Higher producer prices, of course, were not the only factor stimulating greater output. Other factors, such as the improvement in agricultural techniques through mechanization, seed selection, pest and weed control, and increased fertilization, were all of great importance,

TABLE 3-2

Indexes of Aggregate Agricultural Production, EEC and EFTA Countries, 2-Year Averages, Crop Years, 1948–65

(1957–59 = 100)

Country	1948–1950	1950–1952	1952–1954	1954–1956	1956–1958	1958–1960	1960–1962	1962–1964	1964–1965[a]
EEC									
Belgium-Luxembourg	67	78	85	93	95	98	108	116	125
France	77	84	91	100	98	102	117	122	125
Germany	62	81	90	92	96	102	108	118	119
Italy	72	80	90	92	94	108	106	104	109
Netherlands	67	77	83	90	94	106	113	113	126
EFTA									
Austria	60	76	85	90	98	98	106	116	122
Denmark	68	80	86	88	94	103	103	101	104
Norway	90	96	97	101	102	104	105	102	100
Portugal	82	95	96	102	102	98	110	126	122
Sweden	100	102	102	98	102	100	98	95	102
Switzerland	84	90	96	96	96	104	110	118	121
United Kingdom	76	82	89	94	100	101	107	109	113

Sources: FAO, *The State of Food and Agriculture, 1966;* Organization for Economic Cooperation and Development, *Agricultural and Food Statistics, 1959* (Paris, 1959) and *Agricultural and Food Statistics, 1962;* U.S. Department of Agriculture, *The 1965 Western Europe Agricultural Situation* (Washington, D. C., 1966).
 [a] Preliminary.

along with certain structural changes such as improved cropping patterns and farm consolidation. In addition, prices were not so high as to prevent a modest reduction in land under cultivation and a substantial migration from the farms to industrial employment. Nevertheless, prices were high enough to provide a growing stream of money receipts to farmers and to allow them to purchase the nonfarm ingredients of modern agriculture which contributed to the large increase in output.[8]

[8] John O. Coppock has estimated that increments to agricultural output have required nonfarm inputs equal in value to as much as 50 percent of output prices in Europe and more than 80 percent of those in the United States. This led him to conclude that high price supports lead to high-yield, high-cost agriculture. *Atlantic Agricultural Unity: Is It Possible?* (McGraw-Hill, 1966).

TABLE 3-3

*Growth of Agricultural Production in EEC and EFTA
Countries, by 5-Year Periods, 1948–64*

(In percentages)

Country	Compound Annual Rate of Increase		
	1948–49 to 1953–54	1953–54 to 1958–59	1958–59 to 1963–64
EEC			
Belgium-Luxembourg	6.4	3.3	2.2
France	4.8	1.0	4.4
Germany	10.8	2.3	3.3
Italy	6.6	2.4	−1.0
Netherlands	7.0	4.2	1.5
EFTA			
Austria	9.9	2.8	3.0
Denmark	7.6	2.8	−0.4
Norway	3.2	0.8	0.8
Portugal	5.6	−2.6	5.4
Sweden	1.2	−0.6	−0.6
Switzerland	2.5	1.8	2.2
United Kingdom	4.2	1.7	1.8

Sources: FAO, *The State of Food and Agriculture, 1966;* OECD, *Agricultural and Food Statistics;* U. S. Department of Agriculture, *The 1965 Western Europe Agricultural Situation.*

CONSUMPTION. Agricultural policies in Europe seem to have had a smaller impact on consumption than on production. In the aggregate, food consumption appears to be little affected by changes in the relative price levels of agricultural and nonagricultural products, although demand is quite responsive to a change in the price of a single agricultural product in relation to other agricultural products.[9] We can, therefore, disregard price changes in explaining past changes in consumption, and attribute the trends in aggregate consumption of agricultural products in Europe to changes in population and in per capita income. Table 3-4 gives popula-

[9] This statement refers to the "pure" price effects and not to the real income effects of price changes. Also, it is strictly true only for the range of relative price changes actually experienced. Drastic changes in relative prices might possibly have a more profound impact. Furthermore, it does not apply to nonfood agricultural products, since products such as cotton do face competition from manufactured substitutes and are responsive to price changes. However, only a very small portion of European agriculture is devoted to industrial raw materials.

tion figures for the Common Market countries from 1948 to 1965. During the decade 1948-58, the population of these countries increased by 11.5 percent, providing an important element in the upward trend of agricultural consumption. Also, per capita consumption increased substantially, reflecting the rising levels of per capita income. An aggregate index of the

TABLE 3-4

Population of EEC and EFTA Countries, Selected Years, 1948-65[a]

(In millions)

Country	1948	1953	1958	1963	1965
Total EEC	151.9	159.1	166.4	177.5	181.6
Belgium	8.6	8.8	9.1	9.3	9.5
Luxembourg	0.3	0.3	0.3	0.3	0.3
France	41.2	42.8	44.8	47.9	48.9
Germany	46.3	49.2	52.1	57.6	59.0
Italy	45.7	47.6	49.0	50.5	51.6
Netherlands	9.8	10.5	11.2	12.0	12.3
Total EFTA	84.1	86.2	88.3	91.8	93.2
Austria	6.9	7.0	7.0	7.2	7.3
Denmark	4.2	4.4	4.5	4.7	4.8
Norway	3.2	3.4	3.5	3.7	3.7
Portugal	8.3	8.5	8.8	9.0	9.2
Sweden	6.9	7.2	7.4	7.6	7.7
Switzerland	4.6	4.9	5.2	5.8	5.9
United Kingdom	50.1	50.9	51.9	53.8	54.6

Sources: OECD, *Main Economic Indicators* (Paris, January 1967); OECD, *General Statistics* (Paris, November 1963, November 1964); U.N., *Demographic Yearbook* (New York, 1951).
[a] Population figures are at midyear. Detail may not add to totals because of rounding.

volume of per capita food consumption is shown in Table 3-5.[10] It appears that per capita consumption in the EEC countries increased by roughly 30 percent during the period 1948-59, but only one-third of the increase, or 10 percent, occurred between 1953 and 1959. The rise reflected an increase in caloric intake, but more important was an im-

[10] The concept of aggregate food consumption is ambiguous since the human diet can be measured in more than one dimension. The indexes in Table 3-5 were taken from the work of John Coppock and extended to recent years according to the method he described. The method involves converting different food items into wheat equivalents. *North Atlantic Policy—The Agricultural Gap* (The Twentieth Century Fund, 1963), App. III.

provement in the "quality" of food consumed (more meat and fruit, less wheat and potatoes).

Summing the two factors—population growth and increased consumption per capita—total consumption of agricultural products in the EEC countries appears to have increased by about 40 percent during the decade preceding the Rome Treaty. Since production increased by about 65 percent, the EEC countries experienced greater agricultural self-sufficiency in 1958 than they did in 1948. This was not the case for every

TABLE 3-5

Indexes of Volume of Per Capita Food Consumption,
EEC Countries, Prewar to 1963

(1950–52 = 100)

Country	Pre-war	1947–1949	1950–1952	1953–1955	1956–1957	1959	1963
Total EEC	100	87	100	107	110	115	132
Belgium-Luxembourg	91	94	100	105	106	107	114
France	94	92	100	106	107	110	120
Germany	112	78	100	109	115	116	149
Italy	96	87	100	107	112	120	138
Netherlands	103	92	100	104	105	112	122

Sources: John O. Coppock, *North Atlantic Policy—The Agricultural Gap;* OECD, *Agricultural and Food Statistics;* FAO, *Production Yearbook, 1960* (Rome, 1961).

product, however, as seen in Table 3-6. Total cereal self-sufficiency, for instance, grew from 77 percent in 1948-49 to 84 percent in 1958-59, but only as a result of bread grains (mainly wheat) increasing from 76 percent to 94 percent, while coarse grains (animal feed) declined from 77 percent to 73 percent.

NET IMPORTS. The movement toward agricultural self-sufficiency had its inevitable effect upon net imports (imports minus exports) of agricultural products by EEC countries. As shown in Table 3-7, net imports increased after 1950, but by a smaller percentage than consumption. For France and the Netherlands, there was an absolute decline in net imports (or increase in net exports). There was relative stagnation in the imports of Belgium-Luxembourg, and some increase in Germany and Italy. These aggregate figures understate the impact of the movement toward self-sufficiency on nonmember competitive exports, since they include both temperate zone products which meet domestic competition, and tropical zone products which do not. Great increases in self-sufficiency in temperate products were needed to cause a decline in the import-consumption ratio, since imports of tropical products increased substantially.

As an important part of total EEC supplies, United States exports were greatly affected by the trend toward self-sufficiency. Between 1948 and

TABLE 3-6

*Percentage of Domestic Needs for Selected Food Products
Provided by Domestic Production, 1948–65*

Food Product	Crop Year				
	1948–1949	1953–1954	1958–1959	1962–1963	1964–1965
Total cereals	77	85	84	86	87
Bread grains	76	86	94	99	106
Coarse grains	77	82	73	73	75
Potatoes	101	102	102	102	n.a.
Butter	99	103	102	102	n.a.
Fats and oils	42	42	41	44	n.a.
All meat	95	99	95	94	n.a.
Sugar	81	99	96	103	109
Eggs	99	95	89	96	n.a.
Cheese	101	100	99	99	n.a.
Vegetables	102	100	n.a.	n.a.	n.a.

Sources: Statistical Office of The European Communities, *Agricultural Statistics*, Nos. 1 and 2 (Brussels, 1966); OECD, *Agricultural and Food Statistics*.
n.a. Not available.

1958, U. S. exports of agricultural products to the EEC actually declined. However, the unusually high level in the earlier period was not likely to be maintained. The United States did not fare as well as other exporters in this period because most U.S. exports were competitive temperate products. In particular, the United States was the principal supplier of wheat to Europe, and wheat imports, more than any other product, have absorbed the brunt of increases in local agricultural output.[11]

[11] U. S. cotton exports also declined noticeably, but not as a result of European agricultural policy. The decline resulted from the deterioration in the position of cotton among textile fibers, and also because of the noncompetitive pricing policy of the U. S. government.

TABLE 3-7

Foreign Trade in Food and Agricultural Products, EEC Countries, 1950–65[a]

(Millions of dollars)

Country and Type of Trade	1950	1953	Average 1953–56	1957	1958	1959	1960	1961	1962	1963	1964	1965
Total EEC[b]												
Imports	n.a.	n.a.	n.a.	n.a.	6,920	7,822	8,706	8,784	9,626	10,273	11,136	12,289
Exports	n.a.	n.a.	n.a.	n.a.	2,672	3,027	3,388	3,680	3,921	4,447	4,886	5,631
Net imports	n.a.	n.a.	n.a.	n.a.	4,248	4,795	5,318	5,104	5,705	5,826	6,250	6,658
Total EEC[c]												
Imports	3,684	4,315	5,023	6,182	6,020	6,263	6,824	7,014	7,929	8,510	9,333	10,515
Exports	1,632	1,966	2,348	2,853	2,730	2,927	3,314	3,592	3,823	4,263	4,720	5,459
Net imports	2,052	2,349	2,676	3,329	3,290	3,336	3,510	3,422	4,106	4,247	4,613	5,056
Belgium-Luxembourg												
Imports	478	498	527	565	545	584	603	594	650	696	819	939
Exports	128	136	143	158	185	186	198	229	286	358	371	484
Net imports	350	362	384	407	360	398	405	365	364	338	448	455
France												
Imports	1,041	1,309	1,441	1,667	1,724	1,481	1,605	1,557	1,799	1,898	2,153	2,151
Exports	509	502	668	817	726	720	960	1,125	1,101	1,327	1,522	1,689
Net imports	532	807	774	850	998	761	645	432	698	571	631	462
Germany												
Imports	1,317	1,487	1,888	2,507	2,348	2,673	2,809	3,025	3,545	3,305	3,636	4,360
Exports	52	129	177	229	234	268	290	296	316	362	433	538
Net imports	1,265	1,358	1,712	2,278	2,114	2,405	2,519	2,729	3,229	2,943	3,203	3,822
Italy												
Imports	342	503	536	684	677	717	974	988	1,060	1,610	1,557	1,841
Exports	317	380	441	638	547	575	612	675	767	740	771	918
Net imports	25	123	95	46	130	142	362	313	293	870	786	923
Netherlands												
Imports	506	518	631	760	726	808	833	850	875	1,001	1,168	1,226
Exports	626	818	919	1,011	1,038	1,179	1,254	1,267	1,353	1,476	1,623	1,831
Net imports	-120	-300	-288	-251	-312	-371	-421	-417	-478	-475	-455	-605

Sources: U.N., *Commodity Trade Statistics*; OECD, *Agriculture and Food Statistics, 1962.*   n.a. Not available.
[a] Two sets of EEC totals are shown. The first is for a more inclusive definition of agricultural products and is more appropriate for this discussion (see note b). The second, covering a more restrictive definition (note c), allows comparison over a longer period of time. Detail may not add to totals because of rounding.
[b] Includes SITC groups 0 (less 031, 032), 1 (less 112.4, 122), 211, 221, 231, 261, 262, 263, 264, 265, 291, 292, and 4.   [c] Includes SITC groups 0, 1, 22, 29, and 4.

Prospects for Agriculture Without Integration

Given the earlier trends in production and consumption in the EEC countries, it is questionable whether the market would have been buoyant for imported agricultural products even without the Common Market. In fact, it is possible to argue that the EEC has had little effect upon agricultural trade, and will not have an effect until the price harmonization provisions come into existence in mid-1968 (for grain this took place on July 1, 1967). This hypothesis, however, seems too extreme. Without the prospect of a unified market for agricultural products, the rather powerful constraints operating on the individual countries would have forced them to take a more rational approach to agriculture.

In the first place, food is still a sufficiently large item in the budget of European workers so that agricultural price increases can give an inflationary push to the entire economy by stimulating demands for higher wages in industry. Since there were inflationary pressures in these countries from 1959 on, overall economic policy demanded a careful scrutiny of agricultural policy for its implications for price stability.

Second, conditions in the labor market in most of these countries demanded that the movement of workers from farms to factories be unhindered by agricultural policy. Member countries had reached a condition of full employment, and moving labor from low to high productivity occupations was required to maintain a rapid rate of economic growth. Italy was the only country that continued to have surplus labor in the early 1960's, but even in Italy the supply of skilled workers and those easily trained was drying up. Under these conditions, agricultural policy might well have shifted from subsidizing farm products to helping farmers themselves, which in many cases might have meant moving them out of agriculture.

Third, fiscal constraints were operating on individual governments to keep agricultural policy within reasonable bounds. A program of agricultural price supports can be very expensive. Once self-sufficiency is achieved in any product, domestic prices can be supported above world prices only by the government's willingness to buy all surplus supplies while restricting imports, and these surplus supplies can be disposed of only at a substantial loss. Surplus disposals are not only expensive; they are very visible (unlike trade restrictions). Political resistance can build up against such programs and substantially limit their scope.

These pre-EEC constraints on irrational national policies were obviously at work in the member countries during the mid-1950's. Between 1953 and 1958, agricultural producer prices increased very little (except in France, as part of the general rise in price level) (Table 3-1). Agricultural output expanded more or less in line with the growth of consumption. Referring again to Table 3-6, there was little or no increase in overall agricultural self-sufficiency in this period. Even agricultural imports, including some from the United States, revived and increased.

With these constraints, it is difficult to imagine the nature of the agricultural policies that would have existed in these countries in the absence of integration. While it is clear that a drastic shift toward "free enterprise" agriculture would not have taken place, a movement toward less drastic government interference in the market might have occurred, and an overall move toward a more rational policy aimed at the reallocation of the agricultural population would have been likely. Because real costs are converted to visible money costs when self-sufficiency in a product is reached, changes in world market prices were bound to have had a growing influence on policy even in the most restrictive countries. Thus, it is possible to assume that incentive pricing leading to excessive production would, in general, have been discontinued. Prices might have been set to limit increases in output to the growth in consumption, for most temperate agricultural products. This would have left room for a rate of growth of agricultural imports greater than that for consumption of agricultural products.

The Rome Treaty
and the Common Agricultural Policy

The development of national agricultural policies was upset by the signing of the Rome Treaty. While the treaty did not provide a detailed plan for unifying the separate agricultural markets of the Community, it did place emphasis on agriculture, leaving little doubt that detailed plans would be forthcoming. It was made clear during the process of negotiation that France considered agriculture to be an extremely important part of the Community and would not consider a Common Market without it. Thus, beginning in 1957, individual governments had to take cognizance of the implications of the Rome Treaty for national policies even though the Common Agricultural Policy (CAP) itself was not approved by the Council of Ministers until January 14, 1962.[12]

Following the mandate in the treaty, the EEC Commission set to work to formulate a detailed agricultural proposal. The task was most difficult. The existing differences between national agricultural policies had to be reconciled; however, the objectives of the new policy as set out in the treaty were clearly contradictory. The desired increase in agricultural earnings could come either from increased productivity, which would in practice require a drastic disregard of structural problems in the member countries, or from higher producer prices, which would disregard the consumer interest. After much consultation, the Commission brought forth a proposal known as the Mansholt Plan.[13] When finally adopted, the CAP reflected this plan, but with some substantial modifications.

The original Mansholt Plan attempted to compromise conflicts of interest by having two separate programs. One was a long-term program, aimed at improving the structure of agriculture in the Community. The

[12] Title II of the Rome Treaty is devoted to agriculture, and includes ten separate articles. The treaty sets down the objectives of agricultural policy as follows:

(a) To increase agricultural productivity by developing technical progress and by insuring the rational development of agricultural production and the optimum utilization of the factors of production, particularly labor;

(b) To insure thereby a fair standard of living for the agricultural population, particularly by the increasing of the individual earnings of persons engaged in agriculture;

(c) To stabilize markets; and

(d) To insure reasonable prices in supplies to consumers (Article 39, No. 1).

The treaty further states that, in putting into practice the goals as directed, due account must be taken of:

(a) the particular character of agricultural activities, arising from the social structure of agriculture and from structural and natural disparities between the various agricultural regions;

(b) the need to make the appropriate adjustments gradually; and

(c) the fact that in member states agriculture constitutes a sector which is closely linked with the economy as a whole (Article 39, No. 2).

The treaty also provides direction as to the procedure for formulating and approving a detailed common agricultural policy, and sets out alternative organizational forms and methods for reaching the objectives of the treaty.

[13] The plan takes its name from Sicco Mansholt, EEC Commissioner specializing in agriculture. The appellation is unfortunate in that subsequent agricultural proposals were also called Mansholt Plans, causing some confusion. The Commission's proposals for treating agriculture in the Kennedy Round of GATT negotiations were distinguished from each other by being called Mansholt One and Mansholt Two, but some improvement in nomenclature would clearly be desirable.

other program was aimed at immediate needs, and dealt with marketing questions. Even in conception, however, the conflict of interest could not be completely resolved, for the desired improvement in structure could easily be frustrated in the long run by pricing policies which were not geared to stimulate resource mobility. The conflict was settled when the Council of Ministers approved only the marketing policy. There was no clear rejection of structural policy, but only a relegation of its aims to a secondary position. The CAP was approved after a series of marathon negotiating sessions in which the future of the EEC itself was at stake. The French refused to allow the passing of the Community into its second transitional stage without an agricultural policy. Clocks were stopped until agreement was reached. But reaching agreement was so difficult that only the most pressing issues, as determined by the Ministers, were settled and it was decided that structural policy could be postponed.[14]

The major outline of the procedure for the marketing of agricultural products within the EEC was laid out in the January 1962 decisions. The goal of policy was the establishment of a single unified market for the entire Community. In such a market, prices for identical goods would differ only by transportation costs. To accomplish this, all national policies affecting prices, such as trading restrictions, local usage regulations, and subsidies would have to be replaced by regulations for the Community as a whole. Different types of marketing arrangements were contemplated, depending on the nature of the product involved. Products not directly competitive with local production could be marketed with little or no interference. The major products of this type which are of interest to the United States are cotton and soybeans, which enter the market free of duty.[15] Other products, such as sugar and tobacco, which are partially competitive with local production, have been supported only by import

[14] The political and economic importance of the January 14, 1962, decisions cannot be overemphasized. Despite the deletion of the structural section, the agreement can rightly be described as ". . . the first detailed legislated code on agriculture ever to have been adopted at the European level; even at the national level there is no precedent for such a complex of measures adopted concurrently and as an organic whole." EEC, "An Agricultural Policy for Europe," *Information Memo 300/62-E* (Brussels, January 23, 1962).

[15] It has been argued that U. S. strategy in agricultural tariff negotiations should be aimed primarily at maintaining the duty-free status of soybeans and soybean meal because of the bright prospects for future U. S. exports. Reynold P. Dahl, "Demand for U. S. Soybeans in the European Common Market: A Case for Optimism," *Journal of Farm Economics*, Vol. 47 (November 1965), pp. 979-92.

tariffs. These tariffs are theoretically subject to reduction through tariff negotiations.

The marketing conditions for most of the remaining products—the bulk of temperate agriculture—are fully controlled through market intervention. Target prices for individual products are set for the market as a whole, with some slight deviations. To ensure that these prices cannot be undermined by world market conditions, a system of variable import levies is provided. These levies are calculated to offset completely any price advantage that imported products may have over domestic products. Since these levies are easily adjusted, the EEC market is completely insulated from world price developments. Aside from the variable levy, an additional fee is attached to imports to give domestic products a clear competitive edge. This system is adequate for products in which the EEC is not completely self-sufficient, but for products in surplus further measures are needed. In order to ensure that surpluses (domestic production above domestic consumption at target prices) will not undermine target prices, the CAP provides for disposal of the excess, through either subsidized exports or subsidized consumption in less than optimum usage, for example, wheat for animal feed.

Before unified prices are reached, a transitional period is provided in which the variable levy schema would operate. Since member country prices differ during this period, the variable levies apply to intra-Community trade to maintain protection of members from each other. These levies are calculated so that member country supplies are given a competitive advantage over nonmember country products. The regulations on intra-Community trade will become unnecessary and disappear once the unified market price is reached. During the transition period, a three-tiered preferential system is in operation, so that demand for agricultural products in any member country will be met first by domestic sources of supply. If these are insufficient, imports from other member countries will be allowed. Finally, if no member country can supply the market, nonmember country supplies will be bought. When the single market is achieved, the first two preferences will be combined, leaving only imports from outside the Community in the residual position.

Many of the essential ingredients of the marketing provisions of the CAP were not decided in January 1962. Some products were not covered in the original regulations and were provided for in subsequent agreements. The details of the dairy, beef, and rice regulations were not de-

TABLE 3-8

EEC Basic Target Prices and Import Prices for Grains, 1964 and 1967

Grain	Basic Target Prices Effective July 1964						Mansholt Proposal Target Prices	Target Prices Effective July 1, 1967	Most Favorable Import Prices c.i.f. Rotterdam 1964[a]	1967 Target Prices as Percentage of 1964 c.i.f. Prices
	Germany	France	Italy	Netherlands	Belgium	Luxembourg				
	Dollars per Metric Ton, EEC Standard Quality									
Soft wheat	118.87	100.22	113.60	104.83	104.60	117.00	106.25	106.25	60.86	174.6
Durum wheat	—	117.26	143.20	—	—	—	125.00	125.00	75.15	166.3
Rye	108.13	81.79	—	74.59	83.60	108.00	93.75	93.75	60.78	154.2
Barley	103.00	83.00	72.22	82.32	89.00	89.00	92.50	91.25	58.21	156.8
Maize	—	98.32	68.42	—	—	—	93.75	90.63	60.01	151.0
	Relative Prices of Individual Grains (Soft Wheat Price=100)									
Soft wheat	100.0	100.0	100.0	100.0	100.0	100.0	100.0	100.0	100.0	
Durum wheat	—	117.0	126.1	—	—	—	—	117.6	123.5	
Rye	91.0	81.6	—	71.2	79.9	92.3	88.2	88.2	99.9	
Barley	86.6	82.8	63.6	78.5	85.1	76.1	87.1	85.9	95.6	
Maize	—	98.1	60.2	—	—	—	88.2	85.3	98.6	
	Percentage Change Resulting from Price Adjustments to New Levels[b]									
Soft wheat	-10.6	+ 6.0	- 6.5	+ 1.4	+ 1.6	- 9.2	—	—	—	
Durum wheat	—	+ 6.6	-12.7	—	—	—	—	—	—	
Rye	-13.3	+14.6	—	+25.7	+12.1	-13.2	—	—	—	
Barley	-11.4	+ 9.9	+26.4	+10.8	+ 2.5	+ 2.5	—	—	—	
Maize	—	- 7.8	+32.5	—	—	—	—	—	—	

Source: FAO, *Monthly Bulletin of Agricultural Economics and Statistics*, Vol. 14 (March 1965).
[a] As determined by the EEC Commission.
[b] These figures are approximate since the common basic target prices for 1967 apply to only one deficit area for the Community (Duisburg), while the target prices for 1964 apply to the main deficit areas in individual countries.

92

cided upon until December 1963 and others were delayed until July 1966. Furthermore, the provision of resources for the Guidance and Guarantee Fund, which is used in support of the CAP, was only temporarily settled. Indeed, the financing of the CAP became a point of dispute during the negotiation for British entry into the Common Market during the summer of 1962, and continues to be a difficult problem in reconciling British agriculture with the EEC. The renewal of the financial arrangement was one of the issues which led to the July 1965 crisis in the Community.

The most significant area in dispute, however, was the issue of prices. It was indicated that member governments would be asked to align their support prices slowly until they converged on the CAP target price. Since the price decision is at the very heart of the program, much uncertainty was created. Since, in general, the Germans had the highest prices and the French the lowest, it was assumed that the target price level would fall somewhere in between. The difficulty in reaching the pricing decision stemmed primarily from the reluctance of the Germans to lower their grain prices because of the adverse income effect on German farmers. It became abundantly clear that if a slow process of convergence were relied upon, target prices would be unified only near the highest prices ruling in the Community.[16] In order to break the negotiating deadlock and also to reach a more rational level of agricultural pricing within the EEC, it was decided in December 1964 that all member countries would align their support prices in one step in July 1967 (subsequently delayed to July 1968 for most products). The advantage of this arrangement is that the readjustment required of farmers whose prices were being drastically lowered would be so great that it would justify a compensation payment from the Community as a whole. The compensation payments are scheduled to decline over time and could be tied to measures to improve the structure of agriculture. The Community's experience in this matter illustrates that sometimes a more extreme and imaginative solution to a problem is negotiable, while a reasonable but less imaginative one is not.

The actual target prices for different grains, the most sensitive pricing problem, and the percentage change from the individual country prices of July 1964, are shown in Table 3-8. While the Community target prices involve substantial increases in many countries, in Germany there is a noticeable decline.

[16] Lawrence B. Krause, "The European Economic Community and American Agriculture," in *Factors Affecting the United States Balance of Payments,* Joint Economic Committee, 87 Cong. 2 Sess. (1962).

Impact of the Common Agricultural Policy

The impact of the CAP on production and consumption, and therefore on the international trade of member countries, is not easily measured. Even if we accept the usual assumption that price changes have no effect upon aggregate consumption of agricultural products, it is still necessary to calculate the effect of EEC-induced increases in income upon agricultural demand, and the effect on agricultural production of the price changes caused by the CAP. The estimating problem can be considered in two parts: the effects of the Common Market before the grain price decision of December 1964; and subsequent effects.

Effects on Members up to 1965

Even though the agreement for the CAP followed the signing of the Rome Treaty by four and one-half years, it was clear from the start that some sort of unified agricultural policy would have to be instituted if the Community were to succeed. This probably had a pronounced effect upon the national policies pursued in the interim. Since the Community as a whole was a net importer of temperate agricultural products, the expectation of a unified policy had the effect of relieving some of the previously existing constraints on national policies. In particular, governmental fears of stimulating production beyond the point of self-sufficiency were reduced by the knowledge that a unified agricultural policy would always give products of member countries preference over those of nonmembers.

The probable effect of the first years of the EEC on national policy was the encouragement of higher producer prices. This was especially true in those countries where prices were lowest. In the Netherlands, a policy was instituted of raising prices to levels more in line with those in other member countries. A trend in this direction was thought by policymakers to be inevitable, and it was decided to allow the economy to adjust to the inflationary consequences more slowly by beginning the process early. In France, resistance to a trend toward higher prices was undermined by the expected expansion of a protected market, and by the fact that French prices were substantially below those of Germany, the major deficit area. This trend toward higher prices was shown in Table 3-1. Producer prices were rather stable for a short period (fluctuating up and down around a stable mean), but then rose.

The quantitative impact of the EEC on producer prices in 1963-64 was estimated, using the assumption that the previous level of producer prices would have been maintained (with a moderate upward adjustment in France). The results show a 10 percent increase of prices in Belgium-Luxembourg, 14 percent in France, 11 percent in Germany, 12 percent in Italy, and 8 percent in the Netherlands. By multiplying these estimated price increases by price elasticities of supply for each member country, an estimate was obtained for the stimulation of agricultural output in

TABLE 3-9

Estimated Increase in Agricultural Production in 1963–64 in EEC Countries Due to the Common Agricultural Policy[a]

Country	Estimated Price Increase (Percent) (1)	Short-Run Price Elasticity of Supply (2)	Estimated Increase in Output[b] (Percent) (3)
Belgium-Luxembourg	10	0.1	1.0
France	14	0.2	2.8
Germany	11	0.2	2.2
Italy	12	0.2	2.4
Netherlands	8	0.1	0.8

[a] These calculations were made using both current producer prices and prices deflated by prices paid by farmers and a general cost-of-living index. This table reflects only the current price calculations, but the others did not differ appreciably with respect to estimated increases in output.
[b] Col. 1 multiplied by col. 2.

1963-64 arising from the CAP, as shown in Table 3-9.[17] For the EEC as a whole, agricultural output in 1963-64 was estimated to be about 2.5 percent greater than it would have been in the absence of the Common Market arrangement.

[17] The price elasticities of supply were obtained for each country through multiple regression analysis. A simple equation was fitted as follows:

$\text{Log } O_t = a + b(T) + c(P_{t-1}) + u$, where

O_t is the index of agricultural output in period t;

T is a linear measurement of time, taken as a proxy variable for technological change;

P_{t-1} is the index of producer prices in the previous year; and

u is an error term.

a, b, and c are the estimated parameters, with c being the lagged price elasticity of supply. There are many difficulties in such measurements and they should be considered as giving only an indication of the relative order of magnitude.

As discussed in Chapter 2, in the section on income effects, the EEC also stimulated the rate of growth of the entire economy in the member countries. By 1963-64, national income was at a higher level in all of the member countries because of economic integration (see Table 2-8). With a higher level of income, more agricultural products are purchased and consumed. The amount of the increase in demand is determined by the income elasticity of demand, which in turn depends upon per capita income levels and the nature of the products under consideration. In Table 3-10, the income effect on aggregate agricultural consumption is indicated for the EEC countries.

TABLE 3-10

Estimated Increase in Consumption of Agricultural Products in 1963–64 in EEC Countries Due to Common Market

Country	Change in Income[a] (Percent) (1)	Income Elasticity[b] (2)	Increase in Consumption[c] (Percent) (3)
Belgium-Luxembourg	*1.1*	0.16	*.18*
France	*0.8*	0.25	*.20*
Germany	*0.8*	0.20	*.16*
Italy	*1.2*	0.42	*.50*
Netherlands	*1.0*	0.26	*.26*

[a] Calculated from the values presented in Table 2-8.
[b] *Le Marché Commun des Produits Agricoles: Perspectives 1970*, Etudes #10 (Brussels, 1963).
[c] Col. 1 multiplied by col. 2.

A comparison of Table 3-9 with Table 3-10 shows that the estimated stimulus to production is greater than the estimated increase in consumption of agricultural products for each member country, and thus for the Common Market as a whole. It therefore appears that the formation of the Common Market did provide a stimulus toward self-sufficiency in agriculture during the period 1958-59 to 1963-64. An estimate of the value of import replacement of agricultural products stimulated by the Common Market in 1963-64 was obtained by multiplying the net stimulation percentage (production minus consumption, Tables 3-9 and 3-10) by the value of gross agricultural output in each member country.[18] This cal-

[18] Statistical Office of the European Communities, *General Statistical Bulletin*, No. 11 (Brussels, 1965), pp. 50-51. Data are in current prices expressed in local currencies. Conversion to dollars was made at average exchange rates, given on p. 198 of the *Bulletin*.

culation yielded an estimate of $550 million of agricultural production, valued at current prices within the Community. Since Community prices are substantially above world market prices, the estimate was corrected for overvaluation and reduced to $340 million.[19] Thus by 1963-64, the annual loss of agricultural exports of nonmember countries to the EEC exceeded $300 million.

While the figures are not large—certainly not large enough to imply absolute reductions of imports from nonmember countries—the impact on particular products could conceivably have been very great and could have substantially affected the trade of the countries exporting those products. As an illustration of possible adverse developments, one might examine the case of wheat. Producer prices for wheat were increased, leading to greater output. At the same time, greater per capita income reduced the demand for wheat for human consumption since, at high levels of income, wheat is an inferior good.[20] The result of the rise in output and the fall in consumption was the reaching of 100 percent (net) self-sufficiency in wheat in the Community in 1963, and a surplus in 1964-65, compared with less than 90 percent self-sufficiency when the Community began (Table 3-11).

This does not imply that all of the movement toward self-sufficiency can be attributed to the EEC; as mentioned previously, the trend of European agricultural policies was already in this direction. However, it appears to have accelerated because of the Common Market.

Another appraisal of the consequences of the Common Market for agriculture in the member countries can be obtained by examining the trade of the Community in farm products, as seen in Table 3-12. A number of factors were operating in the period 1958-65. Intra-Community trade as a percent of total trade increased for all farm products. From the beginning of the CAP in 1962, the increase of imports from member countries was particularly sharp for those products subject to Common Market regulations. Even for the products not regulated, but subject to the normal tariff preferences, the member country share of imports increased. The consequences of the Common Market can also be seen on

[19] The ratios of domestic prices to world prices were obtained by weighting the average variable levies applying to different crops during the year 1963-64. The variable levies as a percent of c.i.f. prices are found in the FAO publication, *Monthly Bulletin of Agricultural Economics and Statistics* (March 1965), p. 20.

[20] In the EEC study No. 10, *Perspectives 1970,* it was estimated that for the EEC as a whole, the income elasticity of demand for wheat is −0.24.

TABLE 3-11

*Production, Trade, and Available Supply of Selected Commodities
in EEC, Selected Years, 1952–63*[a]

(Millions of metric tons)

Commodity	1952–1953[b]	1956–1957[b]	1959–1960[b]	1960	1961	1962	1963
Wheat							
Domestic production	21.3	21.7	25.0	24.2	23.2	29.6	24.5
Imports	5.5	6.1	4.5	4.4	7.1	5.2	4.1
Exports	0.5	2.1	2.6	2.6	2.2	2.9	4.1
Available supply	26.3	25.7	26.9	26.0	28.1	32.0	24.5
Domestic production as percentage of available supply	*81.1*	*84.4*	*93.0*	*93.2*	*82.5*	*92.5*	*100.0*
Coarse Grains							
Domestic production	16.8	22.7	23.1	24.3	23.2	24.5	27.9
Imports	4.9	7.5	9.4	9.9	9.4	13.4	13.1
Exports	0.2	1.6	0.9	1.3	3.2	1.7	3.0
Available supply	21.6	28.1	31.6	32.9	29.4	36.3	38.0
Domestic production as percentage of available supply	*77.9*	*78.8*	*73.0*	*73.7*	*79.0*	*67.5*	*73.4*
Meat[c]							
Domestic production	6.5	7.7	9.4	9.6	10.2	10.9	11.2
Imports	0.2	0.4	0.6	0.6	0.6	0.7	1.0
Exports	0.2	0.3	0.4	0.5	0.4	0.5	0.5
Available supply	6.5	7.8	9.6	9.8	10.4	11.1	11.6
Domestic production as percentage of available supply	*99.8*	*97.8*	*98.0*	*98.3*	*98.3*	*98.2*	*96.2*

Sources: L. B. Krause, "The EEC and American Agriculture," Joint Economic Committee, U. S. Congress (1962); U. N., *Commodity Trade Statistics;* OECD, *Agricultural and Food Statistics, 1962;* U. S. Department of Agriculture, *The 1963 Western Europe Agricultural Situation;* Statistical Office of the European Communities, *Basic Statistics of the Community* (Brussels, 1963) and *Basic Statistics* (1964); OEEC, *Agriculture* (Paris, 1961).

[a] Detail may not add to totals because of rounding.
[b] Average.
[c] Crop year.

the export side. As Community agriculture became less competitive at world prices, a larger percentage of exports was directed to protected markets in other member countries. This was less true for regulated products, since in most cases the regulations provide for subsidies for exports outside the Community.

TABLE 3-12

EEC Trade in Farm Products, 1958–65[a]

(Dollar amounts in billions)

Type of Trade and Year	Total EEC Trade in Farm Products		Regulated Products		Nonregulated Products	
	Total	*EEC Share (Percent)*	Total	*EEC Share (Percent)*	Total	*EEC Share (Percent)*
Imports						
1958	$ 8.6	*14.5*	$2.7	*23.6*	$5.9	*10.3*
1959	8.9	*17.3*	2.8	*27.9*	6.1	*12.4*
1960	10.0	*17.8*	3.1	*30.2*	7.0	*12.3*
1961	10.2	*19.3*	3.2	*30.5*	7.0	*14.0*
1962	11.1	*20.0*	3.7	*30.0*	7.5	*15.1*
1963	11.9	*20.9*	3.8	*33.6*	8.1	*15.0*
1964	13.0	*21.8*	4.2	*35.1*	8.8	*15.4*
1965	13.9	*23.9*	5.0	*36.7*	8.9	*16.8*
Exports						
1958	3.1	*38.7*	1.4	*42.2*	1.7	*35.7*
1959	3.4	*44.5*	1.6	*48.5*	1.9	*41.2*
1960	3.9	*45.8*	1.8	*50.0*	2.0	*42.3*
1961	4.2	*46.9*	2.0	*49.4*	2.2	*44.7*
1962	4.5	*49.4*	2.1	*50.4*	2.3	*48.5*
1963	4.9	*50.3*	2.5	*50.9*	2.5	*49.7*
1964	5.4	*51.4*	2.8	*52.2*	2.6	*50.6*
1965	6.1	*54.4*	3.3	*55.1*	2.9	*53.5*

Sources: EEC, "The Community's Internal and External Trade in Farm Products," *Newsletter on the Common Agricultural Policy*, No. 41 (September 1965); Statistical Office of the European Communities, *Agricultural Statistics, 1966*, No. 5 (Brussels, 1966).
[a] More inclusive definition of agriculture than used elsewhere in this chapter. Detail may not add to totals because of rounding.

Effects on U. S. Exports Up to 1965

Despite the protective nature of the agricultural policies of the EEC, nonmember countries have been able to increase the value of their agricultural exports to the Community. While declining as a percent of consumption, net agricultural imports of the Community (imports from nonmembers minus exports to nonmembers) have increased from $4.2 billion in 1958 to $6.7 billion in 1965.

Some evidence of the consequences of the EEC for U. S. agricultural exports during the 1958-65 period can be seen by referring to Table 3-13. United States agricultural exports to the EEC grew from $800 million in

TABLE 3-13

Exports of U.S. Agricultural Products, Selected Years, 1948–65

(Dollar amounts in millions)

Year	Total Exports	Dollar Sales[a]	Exports to EEC	Exports to EFTA	Exports to EEC as Percentage of Total Exports	Exports to EEC as Percentage of Dollar Sales	Exports to EFTA as Percentage of Total Exports	Exports to EFTA as Percentage of Dollar Sales
1948	$3,472	n.a.	$1,476	$454	42.5	n.a.	13.1	n.a.
1953	2,847	n.a.	703	442	24.7	n.a.	15.5	n.a.
1955/56– 1957/58[b]	4,073	$2,535	941	614	23.1	37.1	15.1	24.2
1958	3,855	2,581	822	585	21.3	31.8	15.2	22.7
1959	3,955	2,723	926	620	23.4	34.0	15.7	22.8
1960	4,832	3,483	1,099	738	22.7	31.6	15.3	21.2
1961	5,024	3,586	1,157	662	23.0	32.3	13.2	18.5
1962	5,034	3,646	1,151	667	22.9	31.6	13.2	18.3
1963	5,584	4,191	1,171	648	21.0	27.9	11.6	15.5
1964	6,347	4,916	1,416	720	22.3	28.8	11.3	14.6
1965	6,229	5,062	1,477	655	23.7	29.2	10.5	12.9

Sources: U. S. Department of Agriculture, *Foreign Agricultural Trade*, January 1961; April 1963; July, August, and October 1964; May, July, and August 1965; and August and September 1966.

n.a. Not available.

[a] Dollar sales are commercial sales plus imputed dollar earnings from government programs. For 1958 and 1959, these are unadjusted commercial sales.

[b] Average.

1958 to $1.5 billion in 1965 (by 80 percent), after having been on a plateau of about $1.1 billion from 1960 through 1963. While individual years can, of course, show sharp changes because of weather conditions, the trend seems to be upward. The EEC has taken a rather constant share, about 23 percent, of total U. S. agricultural exports. Looking at this trade flow from the EEC side (Table 3-14), the United States supplied 12.6 percent of all EEC imports of agricultural goods in 1957-59 (including intra-Community trade). This increased to 14.0 percent in 1961, but after the start of the CAP, it declined to 13.1 percent in 1965. Excluding intra-Community trade, the U.S. share of nonmember trade increased from 1957-59 to 1965, indicating the competitive improvement of U.S. products in world markets. If the EEC had imported $150 million more of U.S. agricultural products in 1965, then the U.S. share of EEC imports would not have declined from the 1961 level, and the EEC's share of U.S. dollar exports would also have remained constant. If crop years rather than calendar years are used, the trends are all the same, but the increase in exports required to bring the two ratios in 1965-66 to their 1958-59 levels is $200 million. Thus an annual loss of export sales of

TABLE 3-14

Imports of Selected Agricultural Products by EEC, by Source, 1957–65

Product and Year	EEC Imports		Source of Imports (Percentage of total imports)				
	Millions of Dollars	Thousands of Metric Tons	Intra-EEC	Associates of EEC	United States	EFTA	Other
Total agricultural imports[a]							
1957–59 average	7,557	—	16.4	12.3	12.6	6.9	51.8
1960	8,706	—	17.7	11.4	13.0	5.9	52.0
1961	8,784	—	19.4	10.6	14.0	5.9	50.1
1962	9,626	—	20.0	10.3	12.8	5.8	51.1
1963	10,273	—	21.5	8.8	12.5	6.5	50.7
1964	11,136	—	22.5	8.6	13.8	6.0	49.1
1965	12,289	—	25.0	7.4	13.1	5.9	48.6
Wheat and wheat flour							
1958–60 average	—	4,455	18.1	2.0	18.5	1.9	59.5
1961	—	7,137	9.2	—	35.7	2.4	52.7
1962[b]	—	5,247	10.8	—	21.1	2.7	65.4
1963	—	4,053	9.1	—	26.3	5.2	59.4
1964	—	3,997	15.4	—	28.8	2.9	52.9
1965	—	4,651	24.2	0.7	20.7	1.8	52.6
Coarse grains							
1958–60 average	—	8,842	4.5	1.2	41.1	4.2	49.0
1961	—	10,387	17.8	—	39.9	3.1	39.2
1962	—	13,228	6.3	—	46.7	4.9	42.0
1963	—	13,076	9.4	—	47.2	2.4	41.0
1964	—	13,277	13.4	—	46.6	2.0	38.0
1965	—	16,550	18.7	—	46.5	3.2	31.6
Meat							
1958–60 average	—	716	34.7	0.5	9.6	16.9	38.3
1961	—	614	36.7	0.8	16.5	15.3	30.7
1962	—	705	36.7	0.4	16.6	15.9	30.4
1963	—	955	34.3	0.6	8.7	20.1	36.3
1964	—	1,144	31.6	0.4	10.8	14.2	43.0
1965	—	1,189	39.9	0.6	7.1	13.1	39.3

Source: U. N., *Commodity Trade Statistics.*
[a] Defined as SITC groups 0 (less 03), 1 (less 112.4 and 122), 211, 221, 261, 262, 263, 264, 265, 29, and 4.
[b] Excludes wheat flour imported into Belgium-Luxembourg.

$150 to $200 million is taken as an approximation of the consequences of the EEC for the United States during this period.

This estimate suggests that the United States alone absorbed about half of the total nonmember country impact of the CAP in 1964-65. This result is not surprising, since the United States is the largest supplier of temperate agricultural products for world markets. Aside from Denmark, the United States is the most vulnerable of all nonmember countries to the kind of agricultural protectionism involved in the CAP. The United States is the principal supplier of EEC coarse grains imports. It is also a large supplier of directly competitive wheat, unlike Canada, which sells mainly high quality hard wheat to the EEC.[21] The United States also became the principal supplier of poultry, only to have the EEC shut this market through very restrictive regulations. No wonder the United States, along with Denmark, viewed the CAP with alarm. Yet it is important to keep some perspective. This amount—$150 to $200 million—is only 3 to 4 percent of United States exports of agricultural products, and is very small in relation to overall sales of the agricultural sector of the U. S economy. The major interest in these figures lies in what they portend for the time when the CAP is completed.

Prospects for 1970

The agricultural decisions of December 1964 changed the strategy for achieving a single market for agricultural products within the Community. Rather than slowly converging on a single price for goods subject to variable levies, it was decided to move in one step to a unified pricing structure. The key pricing decision related to soft wheat. With wheat decided, it was possible to set the pricing structure for the rest of the grains, and subsequently for meat and poultry. The target prices selected in the December 1964 decision (see Table 3-8) indicate the necessity for increasing prices in France (except for maize), the Netherlands, and Belgium, and reducing prices in Germany and Luxembourg (except barley). In Italy, some prices must go up (barley and maize) and others down (soft wheat and durum wheat). Thus the indicated level is between the high German prices and lower French prices, but still 50 to 75 percent above the world prices of grains delivered to the EEC in 1964.

While subsequent decisions of the EEC will certainly alter the agricultural outlook, the setting of target prices for grains makes it possible to estimate the future impact of the CAP on nonmember countries. The year 1970 is a convenient reference point for such an estimate, since the transition period provided for in the Rome Treaty will then end. The estimate rests on a review of the prospects for grains, which occupy over 45 percent of the cropland of the EEC, and are a major input in the production of livestock and dairy products. Furthermore, the grains program has

[21] For a discussion of this point, see Sol Sinclair, *The Common Agricultural Policy of the EEC and Its Implications for Canada's Exports* (The Canadian Trade Committee, Private Planning Association of Canada, October 1964).

been chosen as the basis of the EEC farm income support policy. Thus grain prices are the primary determinant of the level of farm incomes and the level of consumer prices, and are very important in determining the volume of net imports of the Community from nonmember countries.

EUROPEAN GRAIN PROSPECTS. The major impact of the grain price decision is expected to be on French grain production. France already provides nearly half of total Community grain production and is the only member country with the potential for substantially increasing the amount of land devoted to grains. During the last fifty years, about 5 million hectares of land (12.4 million acres) have been retired from grain production in France. It was estimated to be technically possible to return to grains 1.5 to 1.6 million hectares, representing a 17 percent increase from current levels.[22] According to this estimate, it would require an increase of over 20 percent in grain prices to farmers to reach this result. The actual target prices will amount to an increase of 13 to 14 percent to French farmers, because they exceed the previous French support prices by 6 to 7 percent, and will also apply to the entire crop rather than to only one-half of it as under previous French policy. A reasonable estimate of the increase in land that might be devoted to grains, therefore, might range from 0.7 to 1 million hectares.[23]

A number of estimates have already been made of the potential for grain production in the EEC in 1970 and some of them reflect the consequences of the CAP target prices, as shown in Table 3-15. Using the estimate of the Food and Agricultural Organization (FAO) for 1970, Elmer Learn indicated the effects of the CAP under various assumptions about target prices.[24] One of his assumptions, identified as an average of German-French prices, is almost identical to the indicated target prices and therefore his analysis is of particular interest. He indicates that production of grains would be stimulated by 3 million (metric) tons with these prices. Accepting Learn's assumption that consumption would not be affected, the result would be a reduction of net imports of this amount

[22] Estimated by the EEC Commission and quoted in *France's Key Role in the Grain Sector of the European Common Market,* U. S. Department of Agriculture, Foreign Agriculture Service, FAS-122 (April 1963).
[23] A private study (unnamed) estimated this figure at about 0.7 million hectares. Cited in *Foreign Agriculture,* U. S. Department of Agriculture, November 15, 1965, p. 4.
[24] Elmer W. Learn, "Long-Term Effects of Common Market Grain Policies," *Foreign Agricultural Trade of the United States,* U. S. Department of Agriculture (January 1963).

TABLE 3-15

Estimates of EEC Potential for Grain Production in 1970

(In millions of metric tons)

Price Assumption	FAO–Learn Estimate	EEC Commission Estimate	Modified U.S. Dept. of Agriculture Estimate
No change			
Total grain	64.9[a]	63.4[b]	63.8[c]
Wheat	31.2	30.2	n.a.
Other	33.7	33.2	n.a.
1967 target			
Total grain	67.9[d]	68.0[e]	n.a.
Wheat	n.a.	32.0	n.a.
Other	n.a.	36.0	n.a.

n.a. Not available.

[a] FAO, *Agricultural Commodities Projections for 1970* (Rome, May 1962).

[b] EEC, *Perspectives 1970*.

[c] Estimated in part from the following publications of the Economic Research Service of the U. S. Department of Agriculture: *The World Food Budget, 1970*, October 1964; *Italian Agriculture*, January 1964; *Austria*, December 1963; and *United Kingdom*, 1962.

[d] Elmer W. Learn, in *Foreign Agricultural Trade of the United States*.

[e] EEC, "Europe: La Préparation de la Négociation Céréale au GATT Fait Apparaître Que la Production de la Communauté se Situera en 1970 à un Niveau Plus Elevé Que Prévu Initialement" (Press Release, Sept. 16, 1965).

from nonmember countries. Since the FAO estimated net import requirements of 8.8 million tons of grain (high-income assumption) by the EEC in 1970, the indicated level of EEC imports under CAP prices would be 5.8 million tons. The EEC Commission, under pricing assumptions similar to those used by FAO, estimated Community production in 1970 and then changed the estimate in the light of CAP target prices. The adjustment indicates an increase in production of 4 to 5 million tons due to the CAP. Since the Commission's study had originally estimated import needs of about 12 million tons in 1970, the adjustment reduces import needs to 7 to 8 million metric tons.

The estimates of EEC grain production in 1970 made by the FAO and the EEC Commission under a constant price assumption are similar to one another and close to an estimate constructed from various United States Department of Agriculture publications. The estimates by Elmer Learn and by the Commission of the stimulation coming from the CAP target prices are quite close to each other. It is instructive to note that in 1965 the French grain harvest already had reached a record 28.3 million tons—1.7 million tons above the original EEC estimate for 1970. Furthermore, the French yields per hectare for both wheat and coarse grains in the 1965 crop were above the expected 1970 yields (30qx/ha for wheat and 29.6qx/ha) for coarse grains.[25] If the lower estimate of the increase in land devoted to grains in France stimulated by the CAP (0.7 million hectares) proves correct, and the yields on this marginal land reach average yields now being obtained, then French grain production will increase by 2.1 million tons over the 1965 level to about 31 million tons in 1970. A figure of 31 million tons coincides with the amount of grain production anticipated in 1970 by the Fifth French Plan. With these prospects for French grain production in 1970, the EEC as a whole might well reach the revised figure of 68.0 million tons estimated by the Commission (up from 50.4 million tons in 1958/9 and 56.7 million tons in 1963/4). Since the FAO estimate of grain production without the CAP of 64.9 million tons in 1970 seems most reasonable, the stimulative effect of the CAP is estimated at about 3 million tons per year.

While shifting grain prices within the Community as a result of the CAP could have an impact on grain consumption, almost all observers investigating this question believe it will be negligible. Therefore, the production stimulus of the CAP is expected to have its full effect on imports, which implies a reduction of imports by the Community equal to 3 million tons per year. With total consumption for 1970 estimated by both FAO and the Commission at about 73.6 million tons of grain, the new higher level of domestic production expected under the CAP allows net imports of only 5.7 million tons (1958 level of about 10 million tons).

A level of net grain imports of 5.7 million tons in 1970, however, does not seem to be reasonable in view of the experience of the Community between 1958 and 1964. As noted in Table 3-14, EEC gross imports of grain have been rising, and not all of the increase has been balanced by larger EEC grain exports. What appears to have happened is that total consumption of grain within the Community has grown faster than had been expected. Part of the underestimation was due to the faster rate of growth of real income than expected, leading to a higher level of per capita utilization of grains. Part was also due to a higher rate of population growth. Both the FAO and the EEC Commission based their estimates on a rate of population growth between 1958 and 1970 of only 0.7 percent per year. But the actual growth rate between 1958 and 1965 was close to 1.2 percent, making the old 1970 forecast clearly unrealistic. If population grows at slightly more than 1.0 percent between 1965 and 1970, the level of population in 1970 will be 4.5 percent higher than originally esti-

[25] U. S. Department of Agriculture, *Foreign Agriculture,* Nov. 15, 1965, p. 4.

mated. Using 4.5 percent as a correction factor, total EEC consumption of grains in 1970 was reestimated at 76.9 million tons and net import requirements at 9.0 million tons.[26]

PROSPECTS FOR U. S. GRAIN EXPORTS. The prospects in 1970 for exports of U. S. grain to the EEC depend not only on net import requirements of the Community, but also on the distribution of gross imports between wheat and coarse grains and on the competitiveness of U. S. supplies. Both the recent trends in international trade and the structure of EEC target prices suggest that EEC gross imports will comprise mainly feed grains and high quality wheat. This suggests that U. S. wheat exports might be squeezed considerably, except in bad harvest years, but the expansion of feed grain needs will work to the advantage of the United States because of its dominant position in this world market. While a loss in market competitiveness could undermine the U. S. position, most economic factors point toward further improvement. Thus, the United States should continue to have a substantial market for grains in the EEC, even though considerably reduced from what it could be if the EEC were to adopt a liberal agricultural policy.

The estimated loss of trade due to the CAP of 3 million tons of grain per year will probably be shared by all grain-exporting nations. According to the analysis of the EEC Commission, half of the loss will be in wheat and half in coarse grains. The direct impact of larger wheat supplies within the EEC might well be felt by exporting nations through increased French competition in the markets of third countries, since the EEC has already achieved net self-sufficiency in wheat. Despite the fact that the United States supplies about 40 percent of total wheat moving in international trade, the U. S. share of wheat sold for cash in the mid-1960's has been only about 15 percent (with the remainder being P.L. 480 shipments).[27] Thus, the U. S. share of the loss of wheat sales might reasonably be expected to be only 15 percent of the total loss. In value terms, this would amount to about $15 million per year (at 1964 world prices).[28] In contrast, the loss of markets for coarse grains would be likely

---

[26] These more "optimistic" projections have been corroborated by a more recent study by the EEC. EEC Commission, *Comparison Entre les "Trends" Actuels de Production et de Consommation et Ceux Prévus dans l'Etude des Perspectives "1970"* (Brussels, June 1966).

[27] U. S. Department of Agriculture, *Foreign Agriculture,* Dec. 6, 1965, p. 11.

[28] This refers only to the direct loss. Indirect losses for the United States would also occur as other wheat exporters—notably Canada—suffered declines in shipments.

to be in direct sales to the EEC, since the EEC is a deficit area. Because the United States supplies close to 50 percent of coarse grain exports, the U. S. loss would be about one-half of the total, or $50 million per year (in 1964 world prices). Total grain loss for the United States would, therefore, be about $65 million per year.

PROSPECTS FOR OTHER PRODUCTS. An attempt to extend the analysis of the consequences of the CAP beyond grains runs into a host of problems. Not only are the policy decisions of the EEC for other products less complete; the economic impact of these measures is more ambiguous. It is certain that the CAP provides an institutional mechanism for isolating the market for any single agricultural product from international competition. Therefore, high price supports could stimulate output to the point of Community self-sufficiency or beyond, for practically any temperate product. However, the stimulation of one product is not identical to the stimulation of the agricultural sector as a whole. Stimulation of agriculture in the aggregate involves a decision to direct resources into agriculture, away from industry, and, of course, the industrial sector of the EEC is not insulated from foreign competition.

Overall agricultural policy is directly related to basic questions of sectoral resource allocation and therefore to aggregate economic growth. In an economy faced with labor shortages—the present and prospective situation in the EEC—the cost of maintaining labor in unproductive work is not only great, but quite visible. As noted previously, agricultural policy can be constrained by general economic conditions. From 1958 to 1964, agriculture within the EEC released 3.9 million workers for employment elsewhere, or approximately three-quarters of the total increase in the industrial labor force. This transfer made a substantial contribution to promoting economic growth.[29] While this migration has helped, it has not prevented excessive pressures in the labor market from forcing wage increases in excess of productivity growth, and some inflation has resulted. In the absence of this migration, however, income growth would clearly have been less and the inflation would have been greater.

It does not appear sensible from an economic point of view, nor reasonable from a political point of view, for the EEC to operate the CAP in a way which would make farming so attractive as to reverse the trend of

[29] Denison attributes to this factor a substantial portion of the growth of the member countries of the EEC in this period. See Edward F. Denison, assisted by Jean-Pierre Poullier, *Why Growth Rates Differ: Postwar Experience in Nine Western Countries* (Brookings Institution, 1967).

TABLE 3-16

Agricultural Employment as Percentage of Total Civilian Labor Force, EEC and EFTA Countries, 1958–64

Country	1958	1959	1960	1961	1962	1963	1964
EEC							
Belgium	7.9	7.5	7.3	7.1	6.7	6.4	6.0
Luxembourg	n.a.	n.a.	16.4	15.8	15.1	14.7	14.0
France	23.5	22.9	22.2	21.4	20.5	19.5	18.8
Germany[a]	15.9	15.2	14.1	13.4	12.7	12.1	11.5
Italy	32.7	32.4	31.5	29.9	28.5	26.5	24.9
Netherlands[b]	10.9	10.5	10.1	9.8	9.6	10.1	9.7
EFTA							
Austria	n.a.	n.a.	n.a.	22.9	21.9	20.8	n.a.
Denmark[c]	22.2	21.5	20.7	19.8	18.9	18.0	17.4
Norway	19.0	18.4	18.0	17.4	16.9	16.4	16.0
Portugal	n.a.	n.a.	43.1	n.a.	n.a.	n.a.	n.a.
Sweden[c]	n.a.	n.a.	n.a.	14.4	13.1	13.2	12.6
Switzerland	n.a.	n.a.	11.1	n.a.	n.a.	n.a.	n.a.
United Kingdom	4.5	4.4	4.3	4.1	4.0	3.9	3.7

Source: OECD, *Manpower Statistics, 1954–1964* (Paris, 1965).
n.a. Not available.
[a] Excludes West Berlin in 1958 and 1959; includes West Berlin in 1961–64. The year 1960 is an arithmetic average of the two figures.
[b] Figures based on old definitions used in 1950–62 volume of source cited.
[c] Total labor force, including military.

migration out of agriculture. Despite past migration, there are still substantial pools of workers left in agricultural employment. As seen in Table 3-16, Belgium had the lowest percentage of total civilian labor force in agriculture in 1964, 6.0 percent, but this was substantially above the 3.7 percent in the United Kingdom, indicating further room for reduction. It need not be stressed that the high percentages in Italy (24.9) and France (18.8) could be reduced as long as alternative employment is available and per capita agricultural incomes remain below nonagricultural incomes. It seems reasonable to assume that the CAP will not be used to change these income relationships.[30] Therefore, in the aggregate, it appears that the CAP will not be fundamentally different from national policies of the past, and that recent growth trends in aggregate agricultural output are indicative of future trends.

During recent years, the EEC countries have experienced an annual

[30] The requirements of the Rome Treaty could be met merely by equalizing the rates of growth of incomes.

rate of growth of agricultural output of 2 to 3 percent. Under the assumption that the EEC will follow protectionist policies with high price supports, John Coppock estimated conservatively that EEC output would continue to grow at a 2 percent rate.[31] Despite the fact that 2 percent falls at the low end of the range of recent experience, this estimate seems reasonable in view of the aggregate constraints on agricultural policy and the restricting pressures of lower producer prices in some countries.

With population growing at a rate slightly in excess of 1 percent, the per capita supply of domestically produced agricultural products in the EEC may increase by somewhat less than 1 percent per year until 1970. But this increase can easily be absorbed through continued upgrading of consumer diets as incomes rise. Therefore, the expected increase in EEC agricultural production could be absorbed without reducing the share of net imports in total consumption. Even if the estimated increase in agricultural output turns out to be low, the absolute size of net imports need not be reduced. Of course, demand-supply relationships will not be balanced for every crop. An imbalance has already been indicated for wheat, and milk, cheese, and poultry could be added. But increased self-sufficiency in one area should be balanced by increasing import needs in others such as feed grains and fresh meat.

To summarize briefly, the total impact of the Common Market for U. S. agriculture might be limited to the impact up to 1964-65—previously estimated at $150 to $200 million per year—plus the future impact on grains estimated at $65 million per year by 1970, or $215 to $265 million in total. For the world as a whole, a figure two to three times as large might be in order.

Agriculture in the
European Free Trade Association

Agriculture was treated separately in the Stockholm Convention, not because of the difficulty of unifying agriculture, as in the EEC, but because there was no desire to form a single market. The EFTA was viewed as a

[31] Coppock points out that his rate still greatly exceeds recent growth in the United States, where output has been restrained, and in Canada, which has had unfavorable weather. *Atlantic Agricultural Unity*.

means of obtaining free trade only for industrial products. The exclusion of agriculture followed partly from the British proposals for a European free trade area among all OEEC countries. The British thought it in their interest to exclude agriculture for three reasons. First, the United Kingdom is the world's largest cash customer for imported temperate zone agricultural products, and as such, would be greatly injured if it were necessary to purchase high-cost agricultural products from member countries instead of from lower-cost nonmember countries. Second, nonmember suppliers to the U. K. market were at that time primarily the Commonwealth countries and Ireland. Including agriculture in EFTA would have required removing Commonwealth preferences and forcing tariffs on these imports. This would not only have caused difficult problems of adjustment for these countries, but also might have seriously undermined the Commonwealth as a whole. Third, British farmers are protected by a unique scheme of deficiency payments. This mechanism has the advantage of keeping market prices low while adequately supporting farmers' income. An attempt to integrate this system with the market support policies found on the Continent would have been bound to lead to an inflationary increase in food prices, and possibly a misallocation of resources toward agriculture in the United Kingdom. (These problems are also involved in British attempts to join the Common Market.)

Britain was not alone in wanting to exclude agriculture from EFTA. The Norwegians recognized the high cost of their own agricultural production but wanted to keep a substantial number of workers on the farm for security reasons and also to prevent overcrowding in urban areas.[32] This has led to a level of price supports and subsidies in Norway which could not be maintained in a unified area. In similar fashion, Austria, Switzerland, and Sweden wanted to maintain national sovereignty over the size of their agricultural sectors for political reasons. Only Denmark and Portugal, of the seven, were anxious to have more freedom in agriculture as they foresaw the prospects of expanded export markets.

Given the disinclination for a general inclusion of agriculture within EFTA, special provisions of a limited nature were all that resulted. According to the Stockholm Convention (Articles 21 through 25), member governments in the pursuit of national agricultural policies are obliged to have "due regard" for the interests of other member countries. No firm commitments to take positive action to encourage agricultural interde-

[32] European Free Trade Association, *Agriculture in EFTA* (Geneva, October 1965).

pendence were included. Member countries were invited, but not required, to make bilateral agreements to spur agricultural trade among themselves. The convention did provide for an annual review of agricultural trade, with the presumption that if this trade did not develop satisfactorily, further bilateral agreements would be encouraged.

Consequences of EFTA for Agriculture

Three methods have been devised within EFTA to affect the agricultural trade of members. The first and most important device has been that of bilateral agreement. By mid-1966, nine major agreements had been concluded, the most notable being the United Kingdom-Danish agreement, whereby Danish butter and bacon obtained immediate duty-free entry into Britain, a concession of considerable value. The second device has been the classification of certain foods as industrial products, subjecting them to automatic internal tariff reductions. Sweden, for example, has eliminated its internal duty on goose-liver pâtés by this method. The third device has been the annual review of agricultural trade, which gives the agricultural exporting countries a forum for insisting upon liberalized treatment by the member countries. The meeting at Lisbon apparently was instrumental in encouraging certain member countries to conclude or expand bilateral agreements.

For EFTA to have a fundamental impact on agriculture in member countries, however, its influence must be felt upon national agricultural policies, since no institutional framework exists for influencing agriculture in the group as a whole. For all countries except the United Kingdom, prices paid to farmers are the most important element in agricultural policy and would reflect any adjustment being sought in EFTA obligations. As indicated in Table 3-17, EFTA producer prices since 1959 have varied considerably from country to country, although most exhibit a strong upward trend. If a generalization can be made, it is only that the several countries appear to be following their own national trends established in earlier periods, although still higher producer prices might have resulted without EFTA. The British, in particular, indicate that they take into account the interests of their EFTA partners when they set producer prices and deficiency payments. One must still conclude, however, that relatively little conscious effort has been made to accommodate agriculture to EFTA.

Referring to Table 3-2, agricultural output in EFTA has responded in

TABLE 3-17

Indexes of Current Agricultural Producer Prices, Deflated Prices,[a]
and Ratios of Prices Received to Prices Paid by Farmers,
EFTA Countries, Selected Years, 1947–65

(1957–59 = 100)

Type of Index and Country	1947	1951	1955	1957	1959	1961	1963	1965
Current Prices								
Austria	55[b]	88	93	99	103	102	106	119
Denmark	89	103	106	98	106	96	115	115
Norway	68	81	93	97	104	105	112	125
Portugal	97	100	87	89	107	101	101	104
Sweden	61	83	99	97	102	106	121	126
Switzerland	94	92	96	99	100	101	108	115
United Kingdom	75	92	103	102	96	97	96	99
Deflated Prices[a]								
Austria	n.a.	n.a.	101	100	102	95	92	95
Denmark	n.a.	n.a.	118	99	105	87	92	83
Norway	n.a.	n.a.	104	102	101	100	97	100
Portugal	n.a.	n.a.	92	90	105	94	90	87
Sweden	n.a.	n.a.	113	101	100	98	104	100
Switzerland	n.a.	n.a.	100	100	100	96	96	97
Ratios of Prices Received to Prices Paid								
Austria	n.a.	110	98	101	100	93	90	90
Norway	n.a.	n.a.	110	100	101	100	99	102
Switzerland	n.a.	104	103	101	99	95	92	89

Sources: FAO, *The State of Food and Agriculture, 1966,* and earlier annual volumes; OECD, *Agricultural and Food Statistics, 1959* and *Agricultural and Food Statistics, 1965;* Central Statistical Office, *Annual Abstract of Statistics,* No. 103 (London, 1966).
n.a. Not available.
[a] Current producer prices deflated by cost of living; not available for the United Kingdom.
[b] Estimated.

part to the price incentives noted above. Austria, Switzerland, and Portugal have moved to substantially higher levels of agricultural output since 1959. The United Kingdom has followed suit as a result of an incentive level of deficiency payments. While output in Sweden and Norway has not expanded appreciably, there is no evidence to suggest that this resulted from a conscious effort to allow more imports from EFTA partners. The stagnation of Danish agriculture reflects the inability to find profitable marketing outlets. Since Denmark is a net exporter of temperate agricultural products, its prices have primarily reflected market conditions in the United Kingdom and in EEC countries. Since these markets have not appeared encouraging, output has not been noticeably stimulated.

TABLE 3-18

Imports of Selected Agricultural Products by EFTA, by Source, 1958–65

Product and Year	EFTA Imports		Source of Imports (Percentage of total imports)			
	Millions of Dollars	Thousands of Metric Tons	Intra-EFTA	United States	EEC	Other
Total agricultural imports[a]						
1958–60 average	6,271	—	9.3	10.4	12.7	67.6
1961	6,156	—	9.9	10.4	14.1	65.6
1962	6,653	—	10.0	11.2	13.8	65.0
1963	7,097	—	10.7	9.7	14.3	65.3
1964	7,641	—	11.0	11.6	14.2	63.2
1965	7,675	—	12.1	9.6	15.5	62.8
Wheat and wheat flour						
1958–60 average	—	6,007	0.5	13.8	10.4	75.3
1961	—	5,624	0.8	14.9	6.8	77.5
1962	—	5,714	0.8	14.4	9.6	75.2
1963	—	5,475	1.6	9.5	13.1	75.8
1964	—	5,369	0.7	15.7	18.5	65.1
1965	—	5,937	2.1	9.6	21.9	66.4
Coarse grains						
1958–60 average	—	6,999	2.0	51.6	5.5	40.9
1961	—	6,621	1.8	41.7	14.3	42.2
1962	—	8,497	1.3	54.4	7.8	36.5
1963	—	6,389	1.8	43.5	12.5	42.2
1964	—	6,650	1.0	43.7	18.4	36.9
1965	—	6,745	2.0	44.4	22.2	31.4
Meat						
1958–60 average	—	1,542	22.5	1.4	4.9	71.2
1961	—	1,516	26.0	1.7	5.4	66.9
1962	—	1,523	25.6	2.2	5.8	66.4
1963	—	1,489	26.0	1.5	4.7	67.8
1964	—	1,602	26.2	2.1	5.2	66.5
1965	—	1,568	28.1	2.2	4.9	64.8

Source: U. N., *Commodity Trade Statistics.*
[a] Defined as SITC groups 0 (less 03), 1 (less 112.4 and 122), 211, 221, 261, 262, 263, 264, 265, 29, and 4.

Even though EFTA appears to have had little impact on agricultural output (and presumably consumption) in the member countries, it might still have had an effect upon agricultural trade if member countries had attempted to spur intra-EFTA trade at the expense of nonmembers. The annual reviews of agricultural trade might possibly have encouraged

TABLE 3-19

Foreign Trade in Food and Agricultural Products, EFTA Countries, 1950–65[a]

(Millions of dollars)

Country and Type of Trade	1950	1953	Average 1953–56	1957	1958	1959	1960	1961	1962	1963	1964	1965
Total EFTA												
Imports	4,480	5,324	5,683	6,171	6,103	6,267	6,444	6,156	6,653	7,097	7,641	7,619
Exports	1,295	1,542	1,665	1,922	1,916	1,996	1,988	2,058	2,164	2,459	2,617	2,862
Net imports	3,185	3,782	4,018	4,249	4,187	4,271	4,456	4,098	4,489	4,638	5,024	4,757
Austria												
Imports	160	160	184	219	207	222	237	208	249	258	273	333
Exports	16	14	19	43	47	50	53	58	64	107	70	89
Net imports	144	146	165	176	160	172	184	150	185	151	203	244
Denmark												
Imports	181	190	249	245	261	328	333	230	363	360	429	457
Exports	524	669	706	757	801	870	877	878	925	1,037	1,112	1,181
Net imports	−343	−479	−457	−512	−540	−542	−544	−648	−562	−677	−683	−724
Norway												
Imports	128	161	170	176	179	177	196	183	208	236	248	250
Exports	136	136	168	208	182	193	182	182	185	192	216	265
Net imports	− 8	25	2	− 32	− 3	− 16	14	1	23	44	32	− 15
Portugal												
Imports	80	58	64	72	66	66	81	97	87	107	128	157
Exports	62	76	86	90	97	91	87	98	109	113	127	152
Net imports	18	− 18	− 22	− 18	− 31	− 25	− 6	− 1	− 22	− 6	1	5
Sweden												
Imports	222	279	323	358	358	374	393	402	435	478	544	569
Exports	92	102	86	98	92	92	90	100	115	124	124	141
Net imports	130	177	237	260	266	282	303	302	320	354	420	428
Switzerland												
Imports	367	333	363	449	414	402	431	472	523	561	638	662
Exports	49	80	84	102	109	120	106	114	118	137	148	167
Net imports	318	253	279	347	305	282	325	358	405	424	490	495
United Kingdom												
Imports	3,342	4,143	4,329	4,652	4,618	4,698	4,773	4,564	4,788	5,097	5,381	5,191
Exports	416	465	516	624	588	580	593	628	648	749	820	867
Net imports	2,926	3,678	3,813	4,028	4,030	4,118	4,180	3,936	4,140	4,348	4,561	4,242

Sources: U.N., *Commodity Trade Statistics*; OECD, *Agricultural and Food Statistics, 1962.*
[a] Includes SITC groups 0, 1, 22, 29, and 4. Detail may not add to totals because of rounding.

114

such diversion since a member could escape criticism of its domestic policies if it could show an increasing trend of agricultural imports from
other members. Table 3-18 gives some superficial support to this hypothesis, since the percentage of agricultural imports of EFTA countries origi-
nating within the group increased steadily, from 9.3 percent in 1958-60 to
12.1 percent in 1965. An examination of the product details of Table
3-18, however, shows that only a few major products evidence this trend,
the most important being meat (22.5 percent in 1958-60 to 28.1 percent
in 1965). In meat, however, Denmark has had a comparative advantage,
and might have captured this trade in the absence of EFTA. Furthermore,
the countries suffering from a declining share (primarily Argentina) were
losing their competitive position everywhere, or were Commonwealth
countries whose position was weakened only to the extent that the margin
of preference they enjoyed in the United Kingdom market was being reduced. In any event, the overall diversion was quite small and was easily
absorbed through higher levels of trade.

The formation of EFTA does not appear to have affected the agricultural trade of the United States. While the value of U. S. agricultural exports to EFTA has not increased, this has resulted primarily from the slow
growth of EFTA's agricultural imports from all sources. (See Tables 3-13
and 3-19.) Where U.S. products have lost out (cotton, tobacco, and
coarse grains), they have not been displaced by EFTA producers. The
United Kingdom is the major market for the United States in EFTA, but
total agricultural imports of the United Kingdom have stagnated because
of rising domestic production, and not as a result of EFTA influences.
Despite this trend, EFTA still purchased about 13 percent of all U. S.
agricultural exports for dollars in 1965, and will probably continue to be
a market of great importance.

There seems to be very little evidence that EFTA has made an appre-
ciable impact on the agricultural sector of either member or nonmember
countries. Neither domestic production, consumption, nor the international trade in agricultural products have been noticeably disturbed. If,
however, EFTA continues its separate existence and is not absorbed into
a wider European regional arrangement, the difficult issues of unifying the
market for agricultural products will have to be faced, as they were in the
Common Market. Greater unification of markets for industrial products
generates pressure for unified treatment of factors that influence costs.
Agricultural prices are such a factor, and industrial goods producers in
"high-priced" agricultural countries and agricultural producers in "low-

priced" agricultural countries will all be pressing for intra-EFTA liberalization of trade in agricultural products. This economic pressure could be decisive in overcoming the obvious difficulties in negotiation.

Welfare Implications

This analysis has led to the conclusion that the agricultural policies of the EEC had caused a loss of agricultural exports by nonmember countries to the EEC of about $300 million per year by 1963-64, with the United States alone absorbing about one-half of the loss. Furthermore, the prospects for future trade diversion stemming from the CAP through stimulation of grain production within the EEC could amount to an additional $200 million per year by the end of the transition period, with $65 million being the U.S. share of the loss.

From a balance-of-payments point of view, if the CAP were abandoned, the potential increase of imports of one-half billion dollars per year by an area having a balance-of-payments surplus, such as the EEC, would be very important. It would mitigate the concern over the balance-of-payments deficits of many countries that developed during the 1960's. Furthermore, the welfare loss of stifling trade is greater in agriculture than for practically any other group of products because the differences between the real costs of production of potential exporters and the alternative domestic EEC suppliers are relatively much greater.

The whole dialogue over the adverse consequences of the CAP has an ironic aspect. While one group of experts is concerned with the problems caused by artificial stimulation of agricultural production, another group is worried about the growing insufficiency of agricultural production in the world. Yet these apparently contradictory problems can, in fact, coexist. The stimulation of agricultural production in a high-cost area will not help solve the world food shortage if that production merely replaces production that would have taken place elsewhere. Policies that raise internal prices in high-cost areas do discourage production in low-cost areas because they require import restrictions, and these restrictions in turn reduce demand and market prices for foreign production, thereby discouraging production by foreign farmers.

A major reason for the development of a world food shortage is that many less developed countries pursue policies which reduce returns to domestic farmers, discouraging agricultural output and investment. There are many well-known explanations for the tendency of less developed countries to favor industry over agriculture, and they need not be enumerated. However, one of the reasons is particularly relevant to this discussion. Because world agricultural prices have been depressed, rational policymakers in less developed countries have been discouraged from allocating investment to agriculture.[33] When these countries develop shortages of agricultural output, they are often unable to transform these needs into market demands for imported agricultural products because of a lack of foreign exchange. Thus, world prices are not driven up and a market solution to the shortage problem does not occur.

Two results of stimulating agriculture in high-cost areas can, therefore, be identified. One is that it displaces exports, and therefore production, of the low-cost areas. The second result occurs in countries which may not trade in agricultural products, but which do react to the depression of world market prices by diverting resources away from agriculture. This comes from distorting the international pricing mechanism.

Evaluating the Common Agricultural Policy of the EEC in the light of both of these results strengthens the case for condemning it, because the CAP, in addition to being protective, is damaging to the international market mechanism. The CAP prevents any changes which occur in the basic conditions of agricultural production from being translated into market prices within the Community. The reduction in these prices that could be expected to result from all improvements in productivity achieved outside the Community, for example, are prevented by increases in the variable levies on imports. All productivity gains occurring inside the Community are prevented from affecting prices by the rigidity of the support levels and the variability of the export subsidies. Under these circumstances, investment decisions both inside and outside the Community cannot be based on demand and real resource scarcities.

The EEC is not the only factor distorting the world market mechanism for agricultural products. Most agricultural importers and many exporters —including the United States—must share the blame. But in other countries the errors of this policy have been recognized in part, and in many countries—most noticeably the United States—policy changes have been introduced to reduce the degree of market distortion. The fact that such

---

[33] The extreme case occurs when agricultural products are given away—a unique American practice—which causes agricultural products to appear as practically free goods to the recipient government.

an important area as the EEC is moving in the opposite direction is disconcerting. Spokesmen for the EEC have pointed out that the Community is merely following the path of the United States in its agricultural policy. While this assertion is undoubtedly true, it is hardly a justification for repeating all the errors that have marked the U. S. experience.

The best thing that can be said for EFTA is that it has not made the agricultural situation of the world any worse than before it came on the scene. On the other hand, it has so far missed the opportunity to improve the world situation and to use agriculture as an internally unifying force. In an overall deficit area for agricultural products, it is possible to devise a policy for breaking down internal barriers while at the same time responding to changes in external factors. However, as long as countries continue to view agricultural production solely in national terms, this desirable path for agricultural policy will not be followed.

⋙ CHAPTER FOUR ⋘

Direct Foreign Investment

MANY AMERICANS first became aware of European integration when they learned that some American firm intended to establish or expand its manufacturing activity in one of the Common Market countries. Many such announcements have been made since 1958 and given wide publicity in the press. Some economists were quick to recognize the attraction of the European Economic Community for American investors and pointed this out as the first visible impact of the Common Market on the United States.[1] The first wave of American investment in the EEC came during a period of less than full employment in the United States and at a time of balance-of-payments weakness. It was, therefore, viewed with some alarm by observers who interpreted the foreign investment as a cause of unemployment at home and as a force weakening the U.S. dollar.

The increase in American investment in Europe was obvious, but the reasons for its occurrence were not at all clear. While not denying that the Common Market was an attraction, some observers believed that American direct investment would have increased in Europe in any event because of "economic dynamism" there, which was not the result of the EEC.[2] The mixture of economic motivations that is inevitably involved in a complicated investment decision makes it difficult to evaluate the conse-

[1] See in particular the testimony of Tibor Scitovsky and Emile Despres, *International Influences on the American Economy,* Hearings before the Joint Economic Committee, 86 Cong. 1 sess. (1959), Part 5.

[2] See the testimony of George W. Ball, *International Influences on the American Economy,* Hearings, Pt. 5.

119

quences of European integration for American direct investment. Yet the importance of this factor warrants the attempt.

American firms had many connections with the European economy prior to integration, including exports and direct investments.[3] The choice between these two business methods depends, in part, on their relative profitability. Exporting is preferred if American goods are able to meet the competition both of other foreign producers and of local producers who are protected by a national tariff. Direct investment is preferred if unit costs of production (including profits) in the local market at the required scale of operations are equal to, or less than, U.S. unit costs plus the tariff (and differential transport costs). Investment abroad might also be a means of producing for export to other European markets, but in that case unit costs must compare favorably with those in the United States directly, since no tariff savings are available on the output being exported.

How Integration Affects Direct Investment

The formation of the EEC and EFTA probably considerably altered the relative profitability of these approaches to the European market. Greater direct investment is encouraged by two factors. First, tariffs (now the common external tariff in the EEC) continue to inhibit U.S. exports, but no longer are applied to products coming from other member countries. Thus an American exporter, who previously could compete with German goods in the French market, might find the tariff discrimination too great to overcome and might decide to establish a plant in Germany or France to get within the tariff wall. Second, the enlargement of the market which the customs union allows may well permit economies of scale to be captured, thereby lowering unit costs of production and making direct investment more profitable. Thus, the same factors stimulating European growth would also be operating to attract U.S. direct investment into the market, whether the American firms were previous exporters or not.

Another aspect of the EEC makes it attractive for foreign investors. According to the Rome Treaty, member states are required to abolish obstacles to the free movement of capital among themselves and progres-

[3] Licensing arrangements should also be mentioned in this context, but they are of a somewhat special nature and require different analysis.

sively to allow companies of one member to establish operations in the territory of another. While obviously intended to encourage the flow of direct investment among member states, it also applies to American-owned subsidiaries incorporated in member countries. When implemented, these provisions will allow firms to rationalize their productive facilities within the EEC through further specialization, and will thereby encourage expansion. Also, firms are assured that they will be allowed to set up sales agencies and other distribution channels in the various member countries to accompany the free movement of goods, thus encouraging investment.

American firms apparently became aware of the benefits of European integration for direct investment, especially in the EEC. After reviewing several reasons for the increase in U.S. direct investment in Europe, Anthony Edwards concluded that "the most obvious reason has been the setting up of the EEC as such."[4] Reporting on a survey among firms investing in Europe during 1958-59, David Ashton noted that in response to questions concerning motivation, respondents indicated that the formation of the Common Market was the most important factor influencing the decision.[5] Other surveys (noted subsequently) also indicate that economic integration, in an all-pervasive way, influenced direct investment decisions.

These studies do not give a clear indication, however, of exactly what aspect of the Common Market has stimulated direct investment. Edwards suggests that the assumed price advantage of being inside the common external tariff was most important.[6] Tariff discrimination was found by Ashton to be of great importance. M. E. Kreinin, in a more recent survey, also noted that businessmen indicated that the tariff factor influenced their decision to invest in the EEC.[7] On the other hand, a survey by the McGraw-Hill Company found that the main stimulus for American direct investment came from the economic growth of the member countries rather than from the tariff factor.[8] This result can also be supported in part by

[4] Anthony Edwards, *Investment in the European Economic Community* (Praeger, 1964), p. 5.

[5] David J. Ashton, *New England Manufactures and European Investments,* Research Report of the Federal Reserve Bank of Boston, No. 23 (1963).

[6] Anthony Edwards, *op. cit.,* pp. 7 and 30.

[7] David Ashton, *op. cit.,* p. 25; M. E. Kreinin, "Freedom of Trade and Capital Movements, Some Empirical Evidence," *Economic Journal,* Vol. 65 (December 1965), pp. 748-58.

[8] McGraw-Hill Company, Department of Economics, *Foreign Operations of United States Industrial Companies* (1960).

the Ashton survey and was the conclusion reached by Bela Balassa in yet another study.[9]

Quantifying the Effects of Integration

If it were possible to identify exactly which of the economic factors was involved in the stimulation of American investment in the EEC and EFTA, then evaluation in quantitative terms would be easier. One would expect the tariff discrimination stimulus to be the more powerful, the higher the level of tariffs. The pattern of new direct foreign investment should, therefore, reflect the common external tariff schedule. If the stimulus came from the attraction of a fast-growing economy—due to the Common Market or other factors—then the pattern of new foreign direct investment should mirror, or even exaggerate, the structure of new investment in the economy in general. If both factors are important and intermingled, it may not be possible to detect a pattern in foreign investment, and little can be said about the consequences of integration for the aggregate of such investment.[10]

Making the analytical problem even more confusing, some observers have stated that the attraction of the Common Market for American investment cannot be traced to any single factor raising profit expectations, but instead is due to psychological factors. The Common Market dramatized the changes in the European economy that had occurred since the end of the war. The EEC may have merely drawn the attention of American businessmen to profitable investment opportunities that already existed and possibly had existed for some time. Furthermore, some American firms had been reluctant to invest abroad, fearing the reactions of the labor unions representing their workers and of the communities where their existing plants were located. The Common Market provided an "excuse" for these firms to invest abroad for seemingly defensive reasons. The psychological factors may not have been important for the very large American firms that have had a long history of direct investment in Eu-

[9] Bela Balassa, *Trade Liberalization Among Industrial Countries,* Council on Foreign Relations (McGraw-Hill, 1967), and "American Direct Investment in the Common Market," *Banca Nazionale Del Lavoro Quarterly Review* (June 1966).
[10] The lack of data prevents the use of multivariate techniques normally applied to measure the separate influences of two or more factors.

rope, and were in a position to make marginal calculations on investment opportunities, but for American firms with no previous European experience, such factors may have been decisive.[11] If these psychological factors are an important part of the Common Market stimulus, then the stimulus will clearly be impossible to quantify.[12]

Overview of American Direct Investment Experience

American direct investment increased very substantially in all foreign countries during the twelve years from 1953 to 1965, as shown in Table 4-1. The book value of this investment increased by $33 billion, or at a compound average annual rate of 9.6 percent. It can be seen that the total rate of growth of American investment abroad was decelerating slightly after the creation of the Common Market. (It declined from an annual rate of 10.8 percent in the 1953-58 period to 8.8 percent for 1958-1965.) For American investment in Europe, however, the growth rate was rising. In the five years preceding the EEC, American investment in the Common Market countries increased at an annual rate of 16.0 percent and then accelerated to 18.5 percent in the subsequent seven years. The same phenomenon is seen for U. S. direct investment in the EFTA countries, where the corresponding annual growth rates were 13.2 percent in the earlier period and 16.0 percent in the later one.[13] As a

[11] According to a survey done by E. R. Barlow and I. Wender in the mid-1950's, most American firms that did not have foreign investments had never made a decision against such ventures, but had merely never considered them. *Foreign Investment and Taxation* (Prentice-Hall, 1955).

[12] Adding to the difficulties noted above is a serious lack of appropriate statistics. A census of U. S. foreign investment conducted in 1957 provides a base for analysis, but no census data are now available for the post-integration period. (The next census is to be conducted in 1967, covering the year 1966.) While an annual sample survey is published on foreign investment, the data are not presented in sufficient detail because of disclosure and other problems, and the quality of the data is subject to serious doubt (being so far removed from a census bench mark). Furthermore, national investment data for European countries are generally not available with a sufficiently detailed industrial breakdown to allow rigorous analysis. Even when these data are available from national sources, comparability between countries is uncertain, making aggregation to EEC or EFTA totals very risky. Yet such summation is required to permit comparison with U.S. data. If for no other reason, the weakness of the statistical base should make one wary of accepting firm conclusions concerning any question dealing with foreign investment.

[13] Data have not been published in recent years for all EFTA countries; the figures exclude Austria and Portugal. However, these countries represented less than 4 percent of the EFTA total in 1953.

TABLE 4-1

Book Value of U. S. Direct Foreign Investment, Selected Years, 1953–65

(Dollar amounts in millions)

Area and Country	1953	1958	1965	Compound Annual Rate of Increase (Percent)	
				1953 to 1958	*1958 to 1965*
Total direct foreign investment	$16,329	$27,255	$49,217	*10.8*	*8.8*
EEC	908	1,908	6,254	*16.0*	*18.5*
Belgium-Luxembourg	108	208	585	*14.0*	*15.9*
France	304	546	1,584	*12.4*	*16.4*
Germany	276	666	2,417	*19.3*	*20.2*
Italy	95	280	972	*24.1*	*19.5*
Netherlands	125	207	698	*10.6*	*19.0*
EFTA[a]	1,309	2,438	6,881	*13.2*	*16.0*
Denmark	36	49	189	*6.4*	*21.3*
Norway	37	53	152	*7.5*	*16.2*
Sweden	74	107	305	*7.6*	*16.1*
Switzerland	31	82	1,116	*21.5*	*45.2*
United Kingdom	1,131	2,147	5,119	*13.7*	*13.2*
All other	14,112	22,879	36,082	*10.2*	*6.7*

Source: U. S. Department of Commerce, *Survey of Current Business*, August 1955, September 1960, September 1966.

[a] Excluding Austria and Portugal. Data for these countries are available only for 1953 and were $20 million and $23 million, respectively.

result, the combined EEC and EFTA shares in total U.S. direct investment increased from 15.9 percent in 1958 to 26.7 percent in 1965. The general presumption that European integration has been an important determinant of U.S. direct investment is, therefore, supported by these data.

American foreign investment is divided into three approximately equal parts: manufacturing, petroleum (including refining), and other (trade, mining, agriculture, public utilities, etc.). Some direct investment clearly could not be very sensitive to a stimulus such as economic integration. The pattern of investment in industries developing natural resources, such as metal ores and crude petroleum, is primarily determined by the location of these resources. While economic integration might speed up the search for such resources in member countries, this could be only marginally important.

Investment in Manufacturing

One would expect investment in manufacturing to be the most sensitive to the stimulus of economic integration. In Table 4-2 the data for manufac-

TABLE 4-2

*Book Value of U. S. Direct Foreign Investment,
by Major Subgroup, Selected Years, 1953–65*

(Dollar amounts in millions)

Area and Subgroup	1953	1958	1965	Compound Annual Rate of Increase (Percent)	
				1953 to 1958	*1958 to 1965*
Total direct foreign investment	$16,329	$27,255	$49,217	*10.8*	*8.8*
Manufacturing	5,226	8,485	19,280	*10.2*	*12.4*
EEC	908	1,908	6,254	*16.0*	*18.5*
Manufacturing	452	970	3,688	*16.5*	*21.0*
Petroleum	307	665	1,617	*16.7*	*13.5*
Other	149	273	949	*12.9*	*19.5*
EFTA[a]	1,309	2,438	6,881	*13.2*	*16.0*
Manufacturing	808	1,463	3,621	*12.6*	*13.8*
Petroleum	244	547	1,515	*17.5*	*15.6*
Other	257	428	1,745	*10.7*	*22.0*

Sources: U. S. Department of Commerce, *Survey of Current Business*, August 1955 and September 1966; *U. S. Business Investment in Foreign Countries*, Supplement to *Survey of Current Business*, 1960.
[a] Excluding Austria and Portugal.

turing investment are shown separately. Aggregate book value of U.S. direct foreign investment in manufacturing alone increased at a compound annual rate of 11.5 percent between 1953 and 1965 (by $14 billion), an annual rate of 10.2 percent in the first five years and 12.4 percent in the latter seven years, countering the trend of deceleration for direct investment as a whole. The acceleration of growth of investment in manufacturing in the EEC was, as expected, even more pronounced. From 1953 to 1958, U.S. manufacturing investment increased annually by 16.5 percent in the EEC countries, but accelerated to a remarkable 21.0 percent growth rate in the following seven years. The corresponding EFTA figures are 12.6 percent and 13.8 percent.

These figures seem to support the belief that a dramatic change did occur around 1958. American investment in manufacturing in the Common Market increased to such an extent that this became the prime area for new U.S. investment, rather than the previously-favored EFTA countries. In total book value the EFTA countries—mainly the United Kingdom—had substantially more United States manufacturing investment in 1958, but by 1965 the EEC figure was slightly greater. It should be remembered that U.S. manufacturing investment did increase in EFTA between 1958 and 1965 and at a slightly accelerated rate, but the EEC growth was much more spectacular.

COMMON EXTERNAL TARIFF AS STIMULUS TO INVESTMENT IN MANUFACTURING. While the aggregate data suggest that economic integration stimulated direct investment in manufacturing, particularly in the EEC, refined data are required to make the analysis more exact.[14] Some gross expenditure data for plant and equipment by manufacturing industries are shown in Table 4-3. These figures indicate a variety of responses among industries, although investment increased in every case. By comparing the sums of plant and equipment expenditures from 1959 through 1965, it is apparent that some industries, particularly transportation equipment and nonelectrical machinery, absorbed a great deal of investment; others, noticeably paper and paper products, rubber products, and food products took relatively little new investment.[15] This corresponds to the casual ob-

[14] The analyses in this and the following section are related only to the EEC because of the unavailability of meaningful data for EFTA. While data are available for the United Kingdom alone, using United Kingdom data as a surrogate for EFTA would probably miss the essence of the importance of economic integration. It is at this point that the deficiency of data is pronounced. Book value of U. S. investment in manufacturing, broken down into product subgroups by area, is available only for census years, and then in only eight usable categories at a very high degree of aggregation, for example, chemicals, nonelectrical machinery, etc. For noncensus years, the only data reported by subgroups of manufacturing are gross expenditures for plant and equipment. The plant and equipment series differs from the required investment data by excluding takeovers of existing enterprises and excluding working capital requirements, but including expenditures needed to replace depreciated assets and net additions to capital. The only way to proceed is to assume that the plant and equipment series is highly correlated with the missing investment data and to treat the former as the latter in the analysis.

[15] The basket category "other manufactures" includes many other industries, such as textiles and glass, where U.S. investment is presumably even smaller than in the categories that are reported separately.

TABLE 4-3

Plant and Equipment Expenditures in EEC Countries by
U. S. Manufacturing Companies, 1959–65

(Millions of dollars)

Year	Total Manufacturing	Food Products	Paper and Paper Products	Chemicals	Rubber Products	Metals	Nonelectrical Machinery	Electrical Machinery	Transportation Equipment	Other Manufacturing
Base[a]	997	43	33	103	27	71	263	115	239	104
1959	214	16	2	22	4	9	61	21	62	19
1960	370	17	2	44	11	10	114	21	128	23
1961	534	30	3	63	11	19	164	36	181	27
1962	619	30	4	54	26	25	156	44	245	35
1963	607	29	7	82	26	45	173	39	155	51
1964	707	26	11	121	26	78	184	46	161	55
1965	1,042	34	12	147	34	77	329	60	278	71
Total 1959–1965	4,093	182	41	533	138	263	1,181	267	1,210	281

Sources: U. S. Department of Commerce, *Survey of Current Business*, October 1960, September 1961, September 1965, September 1966; *U. S. Business Investment in Foreign Countries*, Supplement to *Survey of Current Business*, 1960.

[a] Book value in 1957 plus plant and equipment expenditure in 1958.

servation frequently made that U.S. investments are concentrated in a few European industries. Obviously the total size of these industries must be taken into account in interpreting these figures. The transportation industry, for example, which includes such high-value markets as automobiles and trucks, airplanes, and railroad equipment, is of an entirely different dimension than the rubber products industry. The adjustment for total industry size was accomplished by dividing the plant and equipment expenditures made in the whole period 1959-65 by the total value of U.S. investment in the same industry in the EEC countries in the base period (book values in 1957 plus plant and equipment expenditures in 1958). The results are shown in the first column of Table 4-4.

The rows of Table 4-4 are arranged in descending order of percentage growth of plant and equipment expenditures. This ranking puts chemicals, rubber products, and transport equipment in a cluster at the top, and paper products at the bottom. The second column of Table 4-4 shows the common external tariff rates in the EEC for the row industries.[16] While the tariff rates exhibit much less variability than the

[16] Since each of the row industries is made up of many products in different tariff classes, the recorded tariff rates in Table 4-4 are averages of many items. Averages of tariffs are always arbitrary, depending on the weighting system selected, and these are no exception. The only defense for using them is that they were already calculated for another purpose and therefore are not intentionally biased for this use.

TABLE 4-4

Indexes of Plant and Equipment Expenditures in the EEC by U. S.
Manufacturing Companies, and the Average Common
External Tariff, for the Period 1959–65

Manufacturing Subgroup	Index of U. S. Investment[a]	Average Common External Tariff (Percent)
Chemicals	517	15
Rubber products	511	18
Transportation equipment	506	22
Nonelectrical machinery	449	13
Food products	423	18
Metals	370	12
Electrical machinery	232	15
Paper and paper products	124	15

Sources: Data in Table 4-3 and Political and Economic Planning, *Atlantic Tariffs and Trade* (London, 1960).

[a] Index is sum of plant and equipment expenditures in 1959–65 divided by base (book value of investment in 1957 plus plant and equipment expenditure in 1958).

investment growth figures, there is some tendency for high tariff rates to be found at the top of the ranking, as one would expect from the earlier discussion of the CXT as a stimulant to direct investment.

RAPID GROWTH AS STIMULUS TO INVESTMENT IN MANUFACTURING. The second stimulus to direct investment by American firms is the attraction of rapid growth, either caused or permitted by economic integration. One would expect Americans to be attracted to those industries in Europe evidencing the greatest growth. To analyze the relationship between growth and direct foreign investments, either European investment data by subgroups of manufacturing for the Common Market as a whole or, alternatively, indexes of production, or both, would be useful. Since only the production data are published for these subgroups, there was no choice. The data for the EEC are shown in Table 4-5, along with comparable U.S. production indexes.

The production indexes are used as indicators of the desirability of investing. Therefore, the analysis assumes a one-year lag between the occurrence of the growth stimulus and the expected reaction of U.S. direct investments. As seen in Table 4-5, there was some variance in the growth of output among the subgroups of manufacturing between 1958 and 1964. Faster growth occurred for chemicals, transport equipment, and rubber products—industries favored by American investors—while the

TABLE 4-5

*Indexes of Output of Manufacturing Industries, by Subgroup,
EEC and United States, 1958–65*

(1958 = 100)

Area and Year	Food, Beverages, and Tobacco	Paper Products	Chemi-cals[a]	Rubber Products (Tires)	Metals	Non-electrical Machinery[b]	Electrical Machinery[b]	Transportation Equipment (Passenger Autos)
EEC								
1958	100	100	100	100	100	100	100	100
1959	102	108	114	113	105	104	109	117
1960	107	120	135	128	120	118	130	136
1961	112	125	148	144	131	130	145	137
1962	118	131	163	150	138	133	149	162
1963	124	139	179	166	145	129	152	188
1964	128	148	202	183	151	136	169	194
1965	131	154	216	194[e]	157	145	188	206
United States								
1958	100	100	100	100	100	100	100	100
1963	117	129	155	144	142	127	132	179
1964	122	137	167	164	152	142	141	183
1965	124	146	181	172	172	160	161	218

Sources: Statistical Office of the European Communities, *Industrial Statistics* (Brussels), various issues; and *General Statistical Bulletin*, No. 11 (1965), No. 12 (1966); OECD, *General Statistics* (Paris, September 1963); *Monthly Report* of the Deutsche Bundesbank (Frankfurt am Main), May 1965, December 1965, May 1966, December 1966; Board of Governors of the Federal Reserve System, *Federal Reserve Bulletin* (Washington, D. C.), July 1964, February 1966; U. S. Department of Commerce, *Overseas Business Reports*, December 1965, and *Survey of Current Business*, January 1967.
[a] For EEC, calculated with OECD weights. Index excludes the Netherlands.
[b] For EEC, Germany only.
[e] Estimated.

relatively laggard industries were food, nonelectrical machinery, and paper products. The figures for the percentage growth of output for the several industries in the EEC between 1958 and 1964 were entered in the second column of Table 4-6, in order to compare them with the pattern of growth of U.S. direct investment in these industries (Column 1). The rows of Table 4-6 are arranged in descending order of growth of U.S. investment in the same fashion as in Table 4-4.

ALTERNATIVE GROWTH HYPOTHESIS. An alternative form of the growth stimulus hypothesis is worth considering. One might think that the attraction for American direct investment would be greater in those industries in which Europe's growth rate contrasted more favorably with the corresponding industries in the United States. This form of the growth hypothesis would be plausible if, as some observers believe, investment by American firms is greatly affected by the availability of liquid funds. If firms are accumulating large amounts of liquid funds when the growth rate of domestic output does not require large investments (and U.S. antitrust laws prevent them from buying out competitors), the only way to invest those funds in the same business is to invest abroad. The alternative of increasing cash disbursements to stockholders may not appear important. In order to examine this hypothesis, the percentage growth of output in the EEC subgroup industries was divided by the corresponding figures for the United States to give a measure of relative growth, and entered as the third column in Table 4-6. Since the same industries tend to be growing rapidly everywhere, the variance of the relative growth factor is less than the other factors in Table 4-6.

TABLE 4-6

Indexes of U. S. Investment in Manufacturing in the EEC, Manufacturing Output in the EEC, and EEC Manufacturing Output as a Percentage of U. S. Manufacturing Output

(1958 = 100)

Manufacturing Subgroup	Index of U. S. Investment 1959–1965 (1)	Index of EEC Manufacturing Output 1964 (2)	EEC Output Index as Percent of U. S. Output Index, 1964 (3)
Chemicals	517	202	121
Rubber products	511	183	112
Transportation equipment	506	194	106
Nonelectrical machinery	449	136	96
Food products	423	128	105
Metals	370	151	99
Electrical machinery	232	169	120
Paper and paper products	124	148	108

Sources: Col. 1 is derived from data in Table 4-3; cols. 2 and 3 from Table 4-5.

Visual inspection of Table 4-6 gives some support to the original growth hypothesis as an important factor in attracting American capital. The high-growth industries are at the top of the list, although the rate of growth of output falls and then rises again (Column 2) rather than declining throughout. The alternative form of the growth hypothesis, that is, that the stimulus comes from the contrast in growth between the EEC and the United States, is not generally supported by the data of Table 4-6. This does not provide grounds for rejecting the hypothesis. Given the crudeness of the measure, it is not surprising that it could not be supported. Later data will provide a better test of this hypothesis. In more recent years, some industries have been growing faster in the United States than in the EEC and possibly could have a more profound effect upon the pattern and the aggregate amount of American direct investment.[17]

TARIFF VERSUS GROWTH STIMULI. The tariff and growth hypotheses are competitive, but not mutually exclusive, explanations of American direct investment. The two relationships described above may be additive, in the sense that they may supplement each other as explanations, or one may replace the other because of its greater importance. This question must remain unsettled until better data become available.

Other Factors Affecting
Direct Investment in Manufacturing

There are additional factors that bear on prospective earnings of American direct investment in manufacturing, and although they may not be related to economic integration, they need to be considered in evaluating the stimulus of integration. Some economists, notably Stephen Hymer,[18] have viewed foreign investment in the context of an extension of the theory of the firm. Such an approach includes some factors that affect profits only through the market position of particular firms. Some firms, for instance, might make a direct investment in order to buy out a foreign competitor, thereby reducing competition in international markets and earning greater monopoly profits. Further, a firm might enjoy a preferred market position through ownership and control of new advanced technology. It may be difficult to earn large profits from sales in foreign markets by exporting be-

[17] The analysis would be strengthened considerably if it were possible to employ multivariate techniques. They would permit simultaneous testing of the importance of tariff rates, growth measures, and possibly other variables as explanations of direct investment. Furthermore, they would permit measurements relating changes in the explanatory variables to expected changes in the pattern and amount of direct investment. With only eight observations, which may not be fully independent, this approach is ruled out.

The difficulty would not be alleviated merely by another census of direct investment of the type made in 1957. A much finer breakdown of manufacturing by subgroup, possibly similar to the components of the Federal Reserve Board's index of industrial production, would be needed. A historical record of direct investment by geographic area, including earnings, incomes, and sales as well as the amount of investment for each subgroup, would significantly improve the quality of analysis of a host of questions of great public interest.

[18] "The International Operations of National Firms: A Study of Direct Investment" (unpublished Ph.D. dissertation, Massachusetts Institute of Technology, 1960).

cause of heavy transportation costs, high tariffs, preferences in government procurements, or because of a natural reluctance to buy imports. In such a case, direct investment would appear very attractive even though profits presently being earned by local producers are not very great. The advantage to the American firm comes from the relative backwardness of existing producers.

Analysis of data is not likely to shed much light on such motivations for investment, nor are business executives in interviews likely to point to these factors in their decisions. Yet situations of this kind could exist. Technological backwardness in particular is an accusation that has been leveled at European business since the start of the Marshall Plan. While this charge is probably exaggerated, especially in view of the rapid changes in the European economy in recent years, the condition might still persist in some industries. The French food-processing industry, for instance, was often chastized during the 1950's for its lack of initiative and change, and subsequently attracted a great deal of American investment. It would be surprising if a cause-and-effect relationship were not involved. The formation of the Common Market might have highlighted such opportunities, even though the benefits to the investing American firms were expected to come primarily from serving the French market alone and thus were unrelated to integration as such. The same description might apply to other industries, especially those that have invested heavily in research in the United States.

Another factor that must have been influential in the evaluation of prospective earnings by firms was the actual level of earnings and the rates of return on existing direct investment in Europe. Tables 4-7 and 4-8 contain relevant data. Table 4-7 shows that in 1958 the rates of return on American investment in Europe were quite substantial by most absolute standards. Of primary interest are the figures for manufacturing alone.[19] Earnings for U.S. direct investment enterprises in manufacturing in the EEC countries in 1953 were only half as much as Americans obtained in the EFTA countries, and represented a smaller return on invested capital. However, by 1958 the average rate of return on investment in manufacturing in EFTA had declined, while the rate of return in the EEC increased to a level above that of EFTA. This may have encouraged Americans to direct more of their new investments to the EEC and away from EFTA.

By looking at the rates of return by subgroups of manufacturing in

---

[19] Because of some peculiarities of the petroleum industry, the figures for the rates of return on petroleum investment should be disregarded.

TABLE 4-7

Earnings[a] *of U. S. Direct Investments in EEC and EFTA,*
by Industry Group, Selected Years, 1953–65

(Dollar amounts in millions)

Area and Industry Group	1953	1958	1965	Rate of Return on Book Value (Percent)		
				1953	*1958*	*1965*
Total EEC	$ 97	$201	$394	*10.7*	*10.5*	*6.3*
Manufacturing	57	145	362	*12.6*	*14.9*	*9.8*
Petroleum[b]	23	13	−32	*7.5*	*2.0*	—
Other	17	43	64	*11.4*	*15.8*	*6.7*
Total EFTA[c]	201	372	678	*15.4*	*15.3*	*9.9*
Manufacturing	122	199	458	*15.1*	*13.6*	*12.7*
Petroleum[b]	46	102	−26	*18.9*	*18.7*	—
Other	33	71	246	*12.8*	*16.6*	*14.1*

Sources: U. S. Department of Commerce, *Survey of Current Business*, August 1955 and September 1966; and Supplement to the *Survey of Current Business*, 1960.
[a] After all local taxes, but before U. S. income taxes, if any.
[b] See discussion on rates of return on petroleum investment, p. 134, and footnote 19, p. 132.
[c] In 1953 EFTA includes only Sweden and the United Kingdom. In 1958 and 1965 all EFTA is included except Austria and Portugal.

Table 4-8, it is possible to speculate on the effect of existing profit levels on the subsequent pattern of investment. The rows of Table 4-8 (like those in Tables 4-4 and 4-6) are arranged by descending order of growth

TABLE 4-8

Rates of Return[a] *on U. S. Direct Foreign Investments in*
Manufacturing, by Subgroup and Area, 1957

(In percentages)

Manufacturing Subgroup	Europe	Canada	Latin America
Chemicals	23.2	9.4	10.3
Rubber products	16.9	8.3	14.3
Transportation equipment	13.5	17.1	19.4
Nonelectrical machinery	11.9	10.1	11.5
Food products	24.8	10.3	10.0
Primary metals	21.9	8.5	13.3
Electrical machinery	15.4	10.0	8.1
Paper and paper products	[b]	8.0	7.7

Source: U. S. Department of Commerce, Supplement to *Survey of Current Business*, 1960.
[a] Calculated after local taxes but before U. S. income taxes, if any. Rates exaggerated somewhat through inclusion of total earnings of direct investment enterprises, not just the share of U. S. ownership.
[b] One percent or less.

of investment in the EEC. Unfortunately, only figures for 1957 are available, and these are not given in sufficient detail to identify EEC and EFTA countries. Comparable figures for Canada and Latin America for 1957 are also shown to give some idea of competitive foreign investment opportunities of U.S. investors. One striking conclusion that emerges is that rates of return were higher in Europe than in either Canada or Latin America for every product subgroup, except paper and transport equipment. The very low rate of earnings in paper products in Europe may well explain why little American investment was attracted. On the positive side, the high rates of return on investment in food-processing and chemicals may have been important in encouraging the substantial increase of U.S. investment in those industries. It should be noted, as shown in Table 4-7, that the average rates of return in manufacturing in 1965 had been reduced considerably in the EEC and slightly in EFTA. This probably reflects the large inflow of investment and the general European profits squeeze often observed. If past earnings experience is an important determinant of future investment, then a reduction of investment growth in the EEC may be expected in subsequent years.

Investment in Petroleum

The special nature of direct investment expenditures in the petroleum industry requires a separate discussion. Next to manufacturing, the petroleum industry is the most important recipient of U.S. direct investment in Europe, representing 26 percent of the total American commitment in the EEC in 1965 and 22 percent in EFTA. The special nature of petroleum investment comes from a number of factors. First, it includes investment for exploration and production of crude petroleum and natural gas as well as investment in refineries (and possibly even some petrochemical installations). Since motivations for investment differ among the stages of the production process, one's ability to analyze the data is reduced. Second, the world market for crude petroleum and petroleum products is dominated by a few international companies to a greater degree than most other markets. For this reason, it is subject to oligopolistic influences which make general analysis of investment behavior very difficult, particularly because most firms in the industry are vertically integrated. For instance, the calculated rates of return on petroleum investment in Europe have little meaning since the companies can shift the site of reported earnings for tax or other reasons merely through internal accounting practices in pricing crude petroleum. Third, there is a much greater degree of government interference in this industry than in most of the others, possibly a reflection of the market structure of the industry. In France and Italy, government-owned enterprises are major producers. The German government levies special taxes on petroleum to protect coal interests, and thereby distorts investment. Further, many governments give special inducements to investment in refinery capacity in their country or in particular regions. Certainly the significant amount of government involvement alters the prospects for profitable investment in many different ways.

The pure economics of the petroleum industry suggests that economic integration would provide a strong stimulus to new foreign investment. There are extensive economies of scale in refining and ancillary activities. One would expect the free trade in petroleum products among members to encourage investment in order to concentrate production in a few large facilities. However, the special factors discussed above militate against such a development. The impact of government regulation tends to promote national rather than regional development of the industry, particularly in the EEC. For instance, a company might be prevented from serving the French market from German refineries by a requirement that a certain percentage of crude oil come from Algeria—which has not been the cheapest source of crude oil. Also, foreign companies might be hesitant to expand vigorously, or they might actually be prevented from increasing their share of the market because of government participation. Since American firms have had direct investments in this industry for many years, there is every reason to expect a continued flow of direct investment to Europe. But this follows merely from the growth of consumption in the market and would appear to be only slightly affected by economic integration.

There is an aspect of the EEC, however, that could have considerable importance for American direct investment in petroleum. It has been proposed that the Common Market adopt a unified energy policy in which petroleum would receive much attention.[20] While these proposals are still far from complete, there is a good chance that ownership of energy-generating facilities as well as their location will become subject to further government action. Also, since allocation among energy materials cannot be discussed independently of relative prices, it would appear that the operation of the industry would be fundamentally altered. If such a policy were to be adopted, U.S. direct investment would undoubtedly be affected.

[20] See Chap. 5, p. 158 ff, for further discussion.

Evaluation

In view of the evidence considered—both subjective and empirical—there does seem to be some basis for believing that the amount of U.S. direct investment in Europe is greater than it would have been in the absence of economic integration. However, the amount of investment that may properly be attributed to the stimulation of integration is difficult to estimate. From the analysis of the structure of tariff rates and the structure of investment in manufacturing, some evidence of a relationship was uncovered for the EEC. But the limitations of data restricted the analysis to such crude observations that it was not possible to distinguish between the stimulation that came from establishing a common tariff wall around a large economic market and the stimulus that the old national tariffs would have provided to direct investment without integration. Also, a relationship was suspected between the structure of direct investment in manufacturing and the structure of growth of output in the EEC. But it was not possible to distinguish the stimulus that might have come from the general growth of output from a more narrowly defined stimulus that would arise only from the marginal increase in output attributable directly to integration. Furthermore, some other factors that are not directly related to integration, such as the pre-existing pattern of rates of return on U.S. direct investment, also appear to be related to new U.S. direct investment. It is clearly impossible to relate in any precise way an observed increase in American investment to a particular motivating factor, since the factors are not mutually exclusive, and they interact with each other.

It is possible, however, to define some limits to the amount of stimulation that can be attributed to economic integration. Some industries receiving American investment can be excluded entirely because integration is unlikely to be very important to them. Thus mining (and smelting), public utilities, trade, and petroleum (for reasons previously discussed) could be excluded, along with the basket category "other industries."[21] This leaves only investment in manufacturing as responsive to the integration stimulus.

[21] One industry included in "other," insurance and finance, clearly is affected by integration through provisions for the free movement of services and capital within the EEC. Unfortunately, data for it are not separately available. In any event, it could not be quantitatively very important.

With respect to manufacturing, it is clear that some increase in U.S. direct investment in European production facilities would have occurred in the absence of economic integration. Difficulties arise in trying to estimate the amount of investment that would appear to be "normal." A number of different hypotheses were considered for this purpose. They are all of the "naive" type, in that it is assumed, without evidence, that U.S. direct investment would have followed a growth path analogous to the variable that is highlighted in the hypothesis. The estimate of the stimulus of economic integration comes from subtracting the "normal investment" expected from the particular hypothesis from the actual growth of investment between 1958 and 1965.

The naive hypotheses considered are as follows:

1. The growth of American investment in Europe between 1958 and 1965 would have been the same as the growth of U.S. investment in the rest of the world. In this case, the stimulus of integration affects both the total amount and the regional distribution of U.S. direct investment in manufacturing.

2. The rate of growth of American investment in Europe would have been the same as that for the total of U.S. direct investment and implies that only the regional distribution would be affected. Here the growth rate of U.S. investment in the world as a whole between 1958 and 1965 was applied to the European base to estimate normal investment.

3. Since Europe is different from other regions, apart from the aspect of integration, U.S. investment in Europe in the pre-integration period may be a better guide than the preceding hypotheses for estimating normal investment. Thus, the rate of growth of U.S. investment in Europe between 1953 and 1958 was applied to the 1958 base to calculate normal investment.

4. In this hypothesis Europe's pre-integration experience is considered normal, as in the third hypothesis, but an adjustment is made for differences in rates of return. Since the rate of return on manufacturing in 1958 was greater in the EEC than in EFTA, the normal investment growth in the EEC would be expected to be greater than in EFTA. The rate of return in 1958 for the EEC was almost identical to that for EFTA in 1953 and the same is true for the EFTA rate in 1958 in comparison with the earlier EEC rate. Thus, the growth rate of EFTA between 1953 and 1958 was applied to the 1958 base of the EEC, and the EEC rate to the EFTA base.

5. Americans might have wanted to maintain, but not increase, their

1958 share of European industry in the absence of economic integration. The normal growth of U.S. investment would be expected to follow the general growth of investment in European manufacturing. Since Americans have interests in only a few product lines, the product distribution needs to be taken into account. Thus, the growth rate of output of European manufacturing by product subgroup between 1958 and 1965 was applied to the base value of U.S. investment in the subgroup to calculate normal investment. Additional assumptions about production functions are implied, that is, that marginal capital-output ratios equal average ratios in each industry and that these ratios have not changed over time. Data are available to make this calculation only for the EEC.

These are not all the hypotheses that one could imagine. Some observers have noted, for instance, that American foreign investment is related to American domestic investment and a hypothesis might be obtained from this relationship. Appropriate data under a reasonably close classification system were not available, however, so such a hypothesis was not formulated. Also, a hypothesis based upon a stock adjustment mechanism would be interesting. This would imply a tapering off of American investment in Europe as target levels of investment are approached. Since this model depends on the time-pattern of investment, about which little has been or can be said, this hypothesis was not tested.

Estimates for these hypotheses are shown in Table 4-9. The totals for the combined European effects over the period range from $1 billion to $2.5 billion (or from $150 million to $375 million per year). All of the estimates indicate that the EEC was the more stimulating. These figures imply that 20 to 30 percent of the increase in U.S. investment in Europe since 1958 was motivated by economic integration, and for the EEC alone 20 to 45 percent.

It is hard to judge the reasonableness of these figures. The highest estimate results from the first hypothesis and may be a reasonable upper bound in that an even larger figure would not *a priori* seem sensible. During this period, Europe was a very attractive area for American investment quite apart from integration and, therefore, the first hypothesis is extreme. The lowest estimate comes from the third hypothesis but commands less respect as a reasonable lower limit. If European countries in 1958 had only ended exchange controls and dollar discriminations, liberalized controls over their economies, achieved rapid growth, and elected conservative governments, American investors would have been attracted even without economic integration. The third and fourth hy-

TABLE 4-9

Estimates of the Stimulation to U. S. Direct Investment in Europe from European Economic Integration for the Period 1958–65, "Naive Models"

(In millions of dollars)

Hypothesis	EEC Effect	EFTA Effect	Effect of Total Europe
Hypothesis 1: Europe investment same rate as rest of world	1,770	730	2,500
Hypothesis 2: Europe investment same rate as total world	1,480	300	1,780
Hypothesis 3: Europe investment same as Europe's previous experience	860	260	1,120
Hypothesis 4: Europe investment corrected for earnings effect	1,460	—	1,460
Hypothesis 5: Europe investment same as growth of EEC industries	1,950	n.a.	n.a.

n.a. Not available.

potheses seem more like "best guess" estimates than lower limits. A longer historical perspective would also elevate the third and fourth hypotheses over the first and second, in that the former pair would allow Europe eventually to regain the share of U.S. investment it commanded before the Great Depression, while the latter would freeze 1958 geographical patterns of investment. A safe characterization of these estimates might be that the stimulus was no greater than $2 billion, and may have been $1 billion or less.

Welfare Implications for the United States

The widespread belief that European integration, particularly the Common Market, was attracting American firms to build plants abroad caused some concern among Americans. As previously noted, fears were expressed that this investment would reduce the U.S. domestic rate of growth, increase unemployment in the United States, and worsen the already precarious balance of payments. It is a matter of some dispute, however, whether foreign direct investment does any or all of these things.[22] The issues are very involved and a definitive answer is yet to be given. If a firm establishes a plant abroad to produce products that could have been exported from the United States, and reinvests most of its earnings in new foreign ventures, then adverse effects on the U.S. economy might occur.[23] On the other hand, if the investment encourages exports that would not otherwise be made, leads to the fairly prompt repatriation of sizable earnings, and does not sacrifice domestic investment, then diametrically opposite results could occur.

With respect to domestic growth and unemployment, direct investment cannot be given much "real income weight" because of its relative unimportance, regardless of whether it is positively or negatively related. Foreign investment could not be a major causative factor either of the slow rate of growth of the U.S. economy or of the high level of unemployment when those conditions occurred in the late 1950's and early 1960's. Nor would one consider employing policy instruments which act on foreign investment to affect domestic growth or unemployment. More traditional monetary and fiscal measures are clearly dominant in this field.

In contrast, the importance of direct investment for the balance of payments is very great. The magnitude of the stimulus to U.S. direct investment from European integration, as discussed above, is large in relation to the deficit in the U.S. balance of payments during the years 1958-1965. The uncertainty about the relationship between direct investment and the balance of payments is so great, however, that it permits honest disagreement as to the balance-of-payments consequences. Some of the links between direct investment and the balance of payments are observable and partially measurable, for example, direct exports to and imports from subsidiaries, capital flows to and earnings and royalty fees from subsidiaries. However, some factors which may be equally important are not measurable, such as related export stimulation and import and export displacement. Furthermore, to measure the balance-of-payments consequences of the stimulation of direct investment from econom-

[22] These issues were discussed by Lawrence B. Krause and Kenneth W. Dam in *Federal Tax Treatment of Foreign Income* (Brookings Institution, 1964). See also Judd Polk, Irene W. Meister, and Lawrence A. Veit, *U.S. Production Abroad and the Balance of Payments* (National Industrial Conference Board, 1966).

[23] The adverse consequences are still not certain to occur, because the reaction to the investment of the rest of the economy in the United States and abroad might be offsetting.

ic integration, the time pattern of the stimulation as well as the cumulative amounts are of very great importance, and the previous analysis did not and could not estimate them.[24] Given the degree of uncertainty in this economic relationship, further discussion of its implications does not appear to be fruitful.

European Views of U.S. Direct Investment

The welfare implications of the increased flow of U.S. direct investment must also be viewed from the side of the recipient countries, as consequences abroad can reflect upon the United States. The large influx of American investment since 1958 has been viewed with mixed emotions by European governments and by the European public. In earlier years, the predominant European opinion seemed to be overwhelmingly favorable to U.S. investment. Recently, however, the critics have become more numerous and certainly more vocal. While the distinction between fact and fiction in this public discussion has often been blurred, the impact has nonetheless been quite real.

The beneficial effects of American direct investment have long been recognized by European governments, who have encouraged further investments through tax and other incentives. Indeed, the enhanced ability to attract American investment was one of the reasons given by some countries for wanting to join the EEC or EFTA. American investment has made a positive contribution to achieving and maintaining high rates of economic growth in Europe. American subsidiaries have often introduced new products and new processes into the European market. As a result, Europe has benefited from the extensive research efforts of American parent firms. Also, the level of productivity in the European economy has been raised directly by U.S. subsidiaries and indirectly through the force of their competition on European-owned firms. Desirable American competition has come to some industries that were previously nearly monopolized, such as those producing automobiles, tires, boilers, and mar-

[24] For example, utilizing the illustrative models developed in Krause and Dam, *op. cit.,* the time required to turn the cumulative balance-of-payments consequences from negative to positive would be about eight years if the stimulus yielded the same increase in net investment per year (meaning a declining share of new capital from the United States), but ten years or longer if the stimulus led to an accelerating increase in investment over time (depending on the growth path followed).

garine.[25] Furthermore, American investment has been very responsive to the regional development schemes of European governments and has made an important contribution to their success. In particular, new American investment has gone to the northeast of Britain, the coal regions of Belgium, the lower Rhone Valley of France, and southern Italy.

The ability of American firms to be lured by incentives underscores a more general difference between U.S. enterprises and their European-owned competitors, a difference which is both admired and condemned in Europe. The typical American business firm has prospered in a more competitive, less tradition-bound atmosphere than is found in Europe. Its behavior is more likely to follow rules of short-run profit maximization. It is more mobile because it has few geographical preconceptions and lacks corporate roots in any particular European country. It is, therefore, quicker to grasp the profit potential of location and relocation. American subsidiaries were among the first to recognize and obtain some of the benefits from interrelated corporate activities across national lines within the EEC.[26] The ability of American firms to respond quickly to the stimulus of European integration is also related to the fact that, with few exceptions, only American corporations had production facilities in more than one EEC country and, therefore, could begin rationalization of production immediately. In addition, American firms had experience in the large-scale techniques needed to produce for a continent-wide market of high-income earners, had the financial strength to expand rapidly, and were not intimidated by having to operate according to six different bodies of corporate law, since they had to deal with almost fifty varieties at home.

As one would expect, the aggressive behavior of American firms has led to a substantial amount of criticism by competitors, by governments, and by certain journalists.[27] While these criticisms have risen in intensity in recent years, it is important to note that public opinion in France and Germany showed some resentment of foreign investment as early as 1959.

[25] John H. Dunning, *American Investment in British Manufacturing Industries* (London: Allen and Unwin, Ltd., 1958).

[26] Christopher Layton describes American firms as the only true "Europeans" in the Common Market. For a detailed discussion of these issues, see his *Foreign Investment in Europe* (The Atlantic Institute, 1965). This apparently is also true in the Latin American Free Trade Area.

[27] Many newspaper articles have been written raising fears of domination by American "giants" in Europe. They have appeared mainly, but not exclusively, in France. Many have been based upon Michel Drancourt, *Les Clés du Pouvoir* (Paris: Fayard, 1964).

Public opinion polls indicated that the majority of the public in France and Germany favored imposing special taxes on the profits and transferred dividends of non-EEC-owned firms, restricting their right to buy established trademarks, forcing majority control by domestic interests, and forcing these firms to invest part of their profits in public welfare projects.[28] Thus there existed a climate of opinion in which fears of foreign-owned ventures could be nurtured.

The particular criticisms of the European business community can be grouped under two headings: dislike of certain aspects of American business behavior; and resentment of factors believed to discriminate in favor of American firms in the competitive struggle. The first category includes such things as irritation at American advertising methods, concern over the way American firms lure workers in tight labor markets, and a dislike of the way American managers fraternize with lower echelons of management and remain clannish and withdrawn in their personal lives. American firms have been sensitive to some of these criticisms and have "Europeanized" much of their senior management, but usually not their management methods.

The second category of criticism by European business is more serious and some of the points may be well-taken. It is claimed that American subsidiaries have an unfair advantage in the market for research-intensive products because the costs of the research have been borne by the U.S. government through military development or space research contracts or other government grants to parent firms. European governments provide little or no corresponding help to their nationals. Unlike the case of American subsidiaries, the cost of research done by European firms must be recovered through market sales, which puts them at a competitive disadvantage in the pricing of their products. Furthermore, European firms claim that the financial strength of the American parents gives the subsidiaries a tremendous competitive advantage in Europe. American subsidiaries can even lose money for a number of years without feeling severe liquidity pressures, while the same firm, if European-owned, would probably be forced into bankruptcy. Because most European governments rely on monetary policy as their main anti-inflationary weapon and inflationary pressures have predominanted in recent years, money has been costly and very difficult to borrow in Europe. Many European firms,

[28] "How European Consumers React to American Firms and Brands in the European Common Market," *Public Opinion Index for Industry* (Opinion Research Corporation, August 1959), cited in Emile Benoit, *Europe at Sixes and Sevens* (Columbia University Press, 1961).

when short of money, have been forced to liquidate, and only American firms have sufficient financial strength to take over such enterprises. Also, some European firms claim that they are discriminated against by European banks in the allocation of what little funds are available for loan. When given the choice of lending to a small European firm or a subsidiary of an American "giant," a European bank might well choose the latter because of its greater ability to surmount adverse market developments. Added to this feeling of discrimination is the fact that American parent firms can borrow money, destined for their subsidiaries, in the United States at the going interest rate, while European firms, when borrowing in the United States, are forced to pay the Interest Equalization Tax as well as the interest rate and, consequently, are lucky to be able to borrow at all. Finally, the U.S. government, through its Voluntary Balance of Payments Program, has encouraged American firms to raise a greater percentage of their capital needs for foreign expansion in Europe, thus making it even more difficult for Europeans to borrow money.

European firms may well have a twofold purpose in raising these criticisms of American subsidiaries. They certainly would like to limit the increase of American subsidiary competition. With profit margins generally narrowing and wages rising, a slowing down of U.S. direct investment would relieve European firms of some of the pressures on them. They hope through their vocal criticisms to dampen some of the enthusiasm of American firms for new ventures. Second, they want to persuade their own governments not to enforce national antitrust laws very vigorously and, more important, they want to influence the evolution of EEC antitrust laws toward "liberal" views of mergers and near-mergers.[29]

European governments have also been critical of what they consider to be some excesses of American direct investment. Clearly, in the aggregate, American investment need not be feared, as it is a small part of total investment in all of the European countries.[30] European governments have continued to welcome new U.S. direct investment, particularly when new technologies are introduced and when it leads to the construction of

[29] See Chap. 5 for a further discussion of EEC antitrust policy.

[30] While the figures leave much room for doubt, the book value of U.S. direct investment relative to total investment in manufacturing in 1963 was about 2.85 percent in Britain, 1.25 percent in France, 1.15 percent in Germany, and 1.30 percent for the EEC as a whole. C. Layton, *op. cit.* Even if these figures are substantial underestimates, as Gervais suggests is the case for France, his figure of 5 percent is still not large. Jacques Gervais, *La France Face aux Investissements Étrangers, Analyse par Secteurs* (Paris: Editions de l'Entreprise Modern, 1963). Also, a

new plants rather than the takeover of existing facilities. But still a number of criticisms have been forthcoming.

Some governmental criticisms have been nothing more than reactions to U.S. business practices. The French government, for instance, was angered when some American subsidiaries closed entire plants and laid off workers without trying to work out a solution with the government, preventing immediate absorption of the workers into alternative employment. In a labor-short economy, of course, these workers were not long unemployed, but the adjustment could have been made easier.

Other criticisms are more serious, however, since they indicate a belief that American firms interfere with some basic goals of public policy. Parents of American subsidiaries have been accused of deciding questions for their subsidiaries concerning pricing of products and kinds of products to be made. Making these decisions outside the country is thought to lead to possible conflicts with the needs of the host country.[31] Also, subsidiaries may be prevented from exporting to areas in competition with the parent company or to areas such as Cuba, China, or North Vietnam that are embargoed by U.S. laws but not by those of the host country.

American firms are accused of concentrating their investments in a few industries and thereby taking almost complete control. Many of these industries, such as automobiles, aircraft, computers, and electronics, are considered essential for national defense. The ability to provide for an independent defense force can be undermined if crucial segments of domestic industry are foreign-owned and if this allows a foreign government, through action on the parent firm, to interfere with the development, production, or sale of important ingredients of a weapons system. In a related vein, it is argued that the industrial and military strength of a country in the future will be determined by its ability to develop new products and processes through research. If American firms dominate these research-intensive industries, then the research is carried on in the United States, often by European-trained scientists whose education was supported by European governments.[32] Some of these industries in Europe are domi-

---

figure of 3.4 percent for U.S. participation in German industry was suggested in "Foreign Ownership in German Enterprises," *Monthly Report of the Deutsche Bundesbank*, Vol. 17 (May 1965).

[31] Allan W. Johnstone, *United States Direct Investment in France: An Investigation of the French Charges* (Massachusetts Institute of Technology Press, 1965).

[32] For a discussion of the wider politico-military aspects of this problem, see William R. Kintner and Robert L. Pfaltzgraff, Jr., "Prospects for Western Science and Technology," *Orbis* (Fall 1965).

nated by single American firms to a degree that would not be permitted in the United States under the antitrust laws.

Some European governments complain that their ability to operate anti-inflationary monetary policy is undermined as long as American subsidiaries can escape tight money by drawing upon foreign funds. They argue that they must either accept inflation or accumulate unwanted dollars in their official reserves or both. In countries such as France that utilize controls over credit to direct the structure as well as the aggregate pace of their economy, foreign investment can be even more disruptive of desired goals. Furthermore, because of economic integration, these governments feel constrained in the use of other policy measures to control the "excesses" of American direct investment. If the French government, for instance, would disallow a certain investment in France, it knows that some other EEC country will welcome it and France will have to face the competition from the investment without obtaining any of the benefits. This may well be a rather frustrating situation for a government.

The implications of the growing opposition to American direct investment could be far-reaching. The immediate reaction of European business has been a movement toward mergers among companies in order to reach a scale of operation closer to that of the American firms with which they compete. The merger movement has been sanctioned and almost insisted upon by European governments. Some of the pressure to merge can be attributed to other factors, but the challenge of U.S. competition has clearly been the most dramatic. Also, the type of mergers occurring may be changing.[33] Mergers in the past have been mainly among firms of the same nationality or between national firms and the large international firms—usually American-based.[34] But recently within the Common Market there have been some faint signs that the transnational mergers that have long been expected are finally beginning. Since the competitive American firms are transnational, this trend might be strengthened. There is the obvious danger that if this movement goes too far, competition could be severely undermined in Europe and elsewhere. Given the previously dem-

[33] For a contrary view, see Charles P. Kindleberger, "European Integration and the International Corporation," *Columbia Journal of World Business*, Vol. 1 (Winter 1966), pp. 65-76.

[34] As reported by J. A. Bakker, the State Secretary for Economic Affairs of the Netherlands, there were 258 mergers in the Netherlands between 1958 and 1965. Of these, 175 involved only Dutch companies, 75 were with U.S. or British concerns, and only 8 were with companies of other EEC countries. *New York Times*, March 22, 1966.

onstrated proclivity of European firms to join cartels, it is not unreasonable to believe that the merger movement could go beyond socially desirable limits.

It is interesting to speculate on how European governments might react in the future if the inflow of U.S. direct investment does not abate and especially if it accelerates. One reaction might be a reversal of the liberalization of capital movements of recent years. This would be damaging not only to U.S.-European relations, but also to intra-EEC and intra-EFTA relations, as most of the criticisms of U.S. investment can be applied to all foreign investment. There is a further danger to economic integration from the frustration felt by some member countries which could lead them to demand more control over trade flows among themselves.

European governments could, however, react in an opposite fashion, and try to enhance closer economic integration by spurring capital flows among themselves in order to foster countervailing power. Other reactions that would improve international economic relations are also possible. Since some foreign investment is attracted by the external tariff wall, EEC and EFTA countries might be encouraged to reduce tariffs in order to undermine this inducement. Also, member countries might be encouraged to use fiscal policy more flexibly as a stabilization measure and thereby avoid attracting foreign capital by tight money. This would free monetary policy for use in countering balance-of-payments disequilibria, as has often been recommended. Further, European governments might promote research and development expenditure and encourage capital markets to provide facilities for their nationals equal to those available to Americans. This development would also have desirable international implications.

The most important impact of the large flow of American direct investment to Europe, attracted in part by economic integration, has been the change in the business climate that it has caused. Organic links have been forged between the economies of the United States and Europe through truly international business enterprises. This has had consequences on both sides of the Atlantic. The concept of a national market loses its meaning when business enterprises have no single nationality. While such a loss is anathema to "economic nationalists," it is generally applauded by those in Europe and elsewhere who believe that world economic welfare and even world peace are enhanced through its development.

-»» CHAPTER FIVE ««-

Internal Issues

ONE PREDICTION that can be made with certainty is that the European Economic Community and the European Free Trade Association will not remain as they are today, but will continue to evolve, with significant consequences for nonmember countries. Some developing areas of economic integration are not sufficiently advanced to warrant detailed analysis, but are important enough to require recognition and the identification of nonmember interest in them.

Many aspects of economic integration could be singled out for separate treatment. In this chapter, only a portion of the internal issues affecting members are discussed. The choice was based on their economic importance and the prospects for their further development. The guide for the latter consideration comes from the Rome Treaty. If it calls for unified treatment of an issue, such as antitrust policy, it is presumed that something significant will happen in that area. Further, if some movement toward unified action has already begun, such as in the area of a common energy policy, then the subject warrants some investigation. The chapter deals first with issues affecting competition—antitrust problems, unified patents, tax harmonization, and energy problems. These are followed by a discussion of the general economic policies of the member countries: problems of internal and external balance, and issues such as economic planning.

This chapter is focused on the Common Market for pragmatic reasons. Since the EEC from its inception was intended to reach a more complete form of integration, it has given more consideration to the issues discussed here. While EFTA will have to deal with many of the same issues, discussions have not yet reached an advanced stage. Some of the implications of the analysis, however, probably will be applicable to EFTA as

148

well as the EEC, even though the institutional form of the solutions will certainly be different.

Antitrust Problems

The antitrust question is probably the most important issue affecting competition. The authors of the Rome Treaty recognized that the expected benefits of the EEC would not be realized if private restrictions on trade replaced the governmental tariff and quota restrictions that were to be dismantled. Therefore, measures to guarantee the maintenance of competition through an antitrust policy were thought to be as essential to the Common Market as they had been to the European Coal and Steel Community (ECSC). If there were little concern for maintaining competition within the Community, then competition coming from the outside in the form of goods or investments might not be welcome. The interest of the United States in European antitrust questions arises from its role as a trading partner of the EEC and from the reciprocal ties of ownership of industrial enterprises.

Although the Rome Treaty includes antitrust provisions and an institution exists for enforcement, the main outlines of the EEC antitrust policy are incomplete. Numerous administrative regulations and interpretive legal decisions are required before the real policy will be defined, and it will always be subject to change. Therefore any analysis must be speculative. Speculation in this area is difficult because there is little antitrust tradition in Europe from which to draw analogies. Before 1958, only Germany had reasonably strong antitrust enforcement and this was a postwar development stemming directly from U.S. encouragement. The other countries of the Continent either had no antitrust laws, as in Italy, Belgium, Luxembourg, and the Netherlands, or did little to enforce them, as in France.[1]

European Attitudes

There is little evidence that popular support exists among European populations for strong antitrust enforcement. Understandably, business-

---

[1] In the Netherlands before 1958, a pro-cartel law existed, which allowed members of a cartel to obtain legal enforcement of cartel decisions against recalcitrant business firms.

men are not enthusiastic about antitrust legislation since it is against them that the regulations would be directed. One might think that small firms would desire protection from predatory actions of large firms or combinations of firms, but the very existence of small firms in Europe often depends upon the lack of real competition in the marketplace. European commercial banks have also been suspicious of antitrust laws, since one bank may lend to many firms in the same industry and thereby influence market decisions. Antitrust examiners might interpret this as an implicit cartel. It is only with the advent of economic integration that European businessmen have begun to recognize the virtues of competition (in speeches if not in practice). Previously, the adjectives "ruinous" and "wasteful" were likely to be used to describe competition. If a transformation in ideas has occurred, it is indeed a significant shift.

Areas of European society where support for an antitrust policy might be found are at present either ineffective or indifferent to the problem. European consumers are as poorly organized as consumers elsewhere in the world. Representation has been made in Brussels by consumer groups in support of vigorous antitrust policies, but the support for these movements is so narrow that it does not constitute a political force in any EEC country. Organized labor has not supported antitrust legislation in the past. Labor unions have been more interested in maintaining organized labor markets and stabilizing employment practices than in competition in product markets. They have often viewed cartels as beneficial to their basic needs and have frequently been the force pushing hesitant firms into cartels. European unions have typically looked to the government to control abuses of market power by firms acting alone or in combination. They have felt that the government's power need not and preferably should not come through antitrust laws, but through the myriad other controls that European governments have over private industry. In this way, the practices of labor unions themselves would not come under scrutiny.

European governments, with the exception of Germany, have not supported vigorous antitrust prosecution. The prevailing opinion has been that antitrust policy is unnecessary, since any proclivity toward antisocial behavior on the part of business firms could be controlled without explicit legislation. Attention has been directed toward the abuse of market power rather than toward the existence of power as such. In this it differs substantially from U. S. antitrust policy and the trend in its administration. Furthermore, there is less interest in Europe than in the United States in protecting small businesses from corporate giants. Presumably it is hard to become protective about something that does not appear to be endangered. In France, where an antitrust law did precede the Rome Treaty, the practice had been to maintain a constant dialogue between government and powerful business forces to prevent abuses, rather than to provide harsh administration of the law.[2] It is even likely that the French government has initiated concerted action among competitors in the same industry by its planning procedure of bringing together the major firms to discuss investment decisions and other aspects of business behavior. Aggressive price competition would be difficult to maintain under such conditions.

Provisions of the Rome Treaty

It was against this rather unpromising background that the antitrust provisions of the Rome Treaty were drawn. The authors recognized that the removal of tariff and quota barriers would encourage private restrictions to the flow of trade, and were aware that the methods used on the national level to control antisocial business behavior were not available to the EEC as a whole. Even the most optimistic "Europeans" did not expect the rapid development of a strong central government in the EEC which could enter into the kind of dialogue with business firms necessary to control private actions. This situation seemed to require a legal basis for antitrust enforcement. Fortunately a precedent had been set by the antitrust provisions of the European Coal and Steel Community and these became the basis of Articles 85 through 90 of the Rome Treaty.

Article 85 prohibits restrictive business practices unless they are specifically exempt. The kinds of activities considered undesirable are agreements among firms to set prices, restrict output, or allocate markets. Exemptions might be given if the agreement could be shown to contribute to the improvement of production or distribution of goods or to the promotion of economic efficiency through rationalization of industry. It was made clear that a rule of reason would prevail in antitrust administration; the goal of policy would be the promotion of meaningful competition, even if it were to result in fewer competitors. The prohibitions relate only to agreements affecting trade among EEC countries and therefore do not inhibit the formation or operation of cartels for exporting outside the Community.

[2] *Antitrust Developments in the European Common Market,* Subcommittee on Antitrust and Monopoly, U. S. Senate, 88 Cong. 2 sess. (1964).

Article 86 deals with the monopoly problem. It is significant that control by a single firm over an exceptionally large portion of an industry is not prohibited; only the abuse of that market power is illegal. In this respect, the Rome Treaty differs not only from U.S. practices, but also from the European Coal and Steel Community Treaty. There is in fact little guidance in the Rome Treaty as to what constitutes an abuse of power other than practices prohibited under Article 85. In explaining Article 86, all member governments and the Commission have emphasized that bigness alone is not being opposed and that mergers are not undesirable. On the contrary, most of the countries actively encourage mergers to form larger and stronger business units.

Implementing Antitrust Policy

The step from accepting competition as an abstract goal to the implementation of an effective antitrust program is obviously a very great one. In addition to the somewhat hostile attitude of many segments of European society, the actions required by the EEC to enforce an antitrust policy are different from and more difficult than those required in forming a customs union. Eliminating tariffs and quotas is relatively simple because the barriers themselves are government-made, and their removal requires only a reversal of public policy. Private barriers to trade occur, however, because governments do not prevent them, and their elimination requires the creation of new policies.[3] The fact that there is little administrative or judicial experience in Europe in this area is bound to lengthen the time required to evolve a workable policy. Furthermore, the effectiveness of the Community's policy will depend upon the reinforcement of national policies, which differ greatly if they exist at all. Finally, the inherent conflict between the concept of antitrust regulation and national economic planning of the French variety will somehow have to be resolved.

As expected, the EEC antitrust policy has progressed at a slow pace. Implementation began with the approval of Regulation 17 by the Council of Ministers in December 1961. This regulation requires the registration of all cartel-like agreements under penalty of heavy fines. Tens of thousands of agreements were registered, and each required investigation to

[3] Jesse W. Markham, "Competition in the European Common Market," in *Factors Affecting the United States Balance of Payments,* Joint Economic Committee, 87 Cong. 2 sess. (1962).

see whether it qualified for exemption. Some agreements have been approved (given negative clearances), while others, for example, those dealing with the sale of sand, cement, other building materials, detergents, and an exclusive dealership contract in the electronics equipment field, have been ruled in violation of the treaty.[4] Some others have yet to be acted upon and presumably some time will be required to investigate all of them, although much of the backlog of original submissions was handled by means of blanket exemptions.

EFTA Policy

EFTA has faced the antitrust question in characteristic fashion. The Stockholm Convention recognizes the problem, but puts responsibility on the member states to deal with the issue when it arises. No special powers were granted to the Council of EFTA, although it was directed to review the whole question in the future. Two working parties have been appointed to help member countries carry out their obligations.[5]

U.S. Interest in European Antitrust Policy

The United States has a considerable interest in the European antitrust question because of its impact on competitive conditions in the United States and its effects on European subsidiaries of American companies. The United States has long recognized that domestic market conditions can be influenced by actions taken outside its borders and, therefore, U.S. antitrust laws have certain extraterritorial applications. In practice, however, it is very difficult to enforce this aspect of the law without the cooperation of foreign governments and courts. Investigations can be stymied if business records are kept outside of U.S. jurisdiction and judgments can be frustrated if the guilty party maintains all its assets and business activities outside the United States. In the past, foreign governments and courts have frequently been less than cooperative and often have obstructed the work of U.S. antitrust authorities on the grounds of national sovereignty.

[4] As reported in various issues of the *European Community Bulletin,* Information Service of the European Communities, Washington, D.C.
[5] Secretariat of the European Free Trade Association, *Stockholm Convention Examined* (Geneva, 1963), and "Comparative Study of Development in the EFTA and the EEC" (January 1967, mimeographed).

If a real antitrust tradition develops in Europe, then greater cooperation with the United States might be possible.

A specific problem could arise if the Common Market develops a very liberal attitude in granting exemptions under Article 85. If a European cartel agreement (allocating production) in which two or more American subsidiaries took part were given a negative clearance on the grounds that it contributed to the rationalization of an industry or to general economic efficiency, then a legal conflict might occur. Competition in the U.S. market among the parent firms might be considered in jeopardy because of the cooperation of the subsidiaries, and the parent firms might be judged to be in violation of U.S. laws. Indeed, the U.S. Department of Justice might feel compelled to pursue the case because of the public declaration of the cartel agreement, even though it recognized the difficult position of the American firms. Furthermore, a European export cartel in which American subsidiaries were involved might operate in a way detrimental to American parent firms regardless of whether the goods were destined for the United States or for other countries where U.S. firms have an export interest.

It is also possible that if cartels are tolerated in the EEC or EFTA, foreign competition will be kept from undermining the cartel through high tariffs or other restrictions. Similarly, if cartel arrangements prevent competitive price changes inside the EEC or EFTA, firms in member countries might be encouraged to dump products in third-country markets.

The interests of the United States might also be hurt by zealous enforcement of the EEC antitrust laws. In the unlikely event that a tough stand is taken against exclusive dealership arrangements, American exports to the EEC might suffer. Exclusive dealerships help firms far removed from the country to maintain close contact with the market through an agent having vital economic interests in it. Also, smaller firms that cannot afford their own distribution network find exclusive dealerships very useful. If the use of these restrictive contracts is greatly limited, then some U.S. exports might be lost.

The prohibition of the abuse of market power under Article 86 of the Rome Treaty could conceivably become a tool for limiting the competitiveness of American subsidiaries, if that should become the goal of EEC policy. Given the lack of explicit guides as to what constitutes an abuse of market power, much leeway exists for interpretation. The Commission, in a memorandum issued in January 1966, endorsed the need for some mergers in the EEC, but felt compelled to warn against violations of the treaty.[6] It noted that the ability of a firm to oust competitors could indicate excessive market power even if the firm controlled only a small part of the market. The power could come from production, distribution, and financial strength and, therefore, the company's entire activities and relationship to the market would be pertinent, presumably including any tie to an American parent firm. The activities that would indicate abuse of dominant position include cutting prices below a competitor's costs to force him out of business, into a merger, or to accept other unfavorable terms. While such motivations would be illegal under U.S. laws, the act of price-cutting is very hard to distinguish from normal competitive business practice and could inhibit American firms from establishing themselves in the market.[7]

There are legitimate reasons for the Common Market countries' concern over the market position of American subsidiaries. One reason is that, in many cases, mergers of European firms are a defensive response to the competitive challenge of American investment. If European observers are correct, this concentration of power is generally desirable. The interests of both the United States and the EEC are furthered, however, if the movement toward concentration is not allowed to destroy competition and if all competitors in the market are treated equally.

Patents and Trademark Problems

An issue closely related to antitrust problems is the granting of patents and trademarks. There is a natural conflict between the desire to protect the property rights of individuals and the need to prevent licensing agreements from becoming a means of allocating national markets among producers. Unlike the area of antitrust policy, the Rome Treaty does not suggest that a Community approach is needed. Quite early in the process of

[6] European Economic Community Commission, *Concentration of Firms in the Common Market* (Brussels, January 1966). This represents an elaboration of an earlier speech by Commissioner Hans van der Groeben to the European Parliament and was summarized in *European Community Bulletin,* No. 89, February 1966.

[7] It is hard to see how a firm could avoid this kind of violation when making a price cut, since, in order to do so, it must know the details of its competitors' cost functions, which are presumably not available to it.

moving toward internal free trade in goods, however, the need was felt for more coordination in the field of patents. One reason is that, for patent rights to be fully protected, producers have to take out patents in every country to which their goods are shipped. Thus the expense and difficulty involved constitute a substantial barrier to commerce. Second, national differences as to the obligations of patentholders are so substantial that clarification is needed to prevent the complexity of the patenting process itself from disrupting the flow of knowledge among countries.

The problems involved in forming a coordinated patent policy within the EEC stem from the great diversity of national laws in the member countries. Important differences exist in what constitutes a patentable invention, in the procedure for obtaining a patent, in the obligations of the patentholder, and in enforcibility.[8] Most countries require an invention to be novel and to have some industrial utility to be patentable, but Germany requires in addition a demonstration of a certain amount of inventiveness. Under Italian laws, it is impossible to patent pharmaceuticals, much to the distress of all foreign and some Italian chemical companies. Patents may be obtained almost immediately upon application in France, Italy, Belgium, and Luxembourg, leaving the questions of patentability and prior claims to be settled by the courts in the event that a patent is contested. However, Germany and the Netherlands require different degrees of prior examination before a patent is granted. In France and Italy, the patentholder is required to develop the invention on an industrial scale. The Italian law is somewhat more stringent, requiring a patent to be used within three years. Other differences exist in compulsory licensing regulations in the event that a patentholder attempts to maintain a monopoly over the use of an invention. These national differences did not occur by accident, and there are vested interests in maintaining national peculiarities even though there is a general desire for uniformity.

Coordinating Patent Policy

In an effort to formulate a coordinated patent policy, a working party on patents was established in November 1959, with representatives of the member countries and the EEC Commission. After three years, this working party published a draft law for an EEC patent system, but the

---

[8] *European Community Bulletin,* No. 87, November 1965.

law has never been adopted. The original proposal advocated the establishment of a Community patent system to complement the individual national systems. Inventors could apply to the proposed EEC patent office (as well as to national offices) and obtain protection in the entire EEC area. The EEC system would have its own administration and would be adjudicated in Community courts. One weakness of the proposal was the limitation of the Community patent to citizens of member countries. This would discriminate against nonmember countries and would be in violation of the existing International Patent Agreement to which all EEC countries adhere.

In November 1964, the EEC Commission submitted to the member governments a report on a possible European patent law similar to the 1962 proposal, but without the discriminatory feature. There has been very little action on this proposal.

The 1964 proposal of the EEC Commission is not necessarily limited to Community countries; some or all of the EFTA countries might join in such an endeavor. The concept of a multinational approach to patent problems had been considered as early as 1950 in some of the EFTA countries. In that year, a plan for a Scandinavian patent system was studied by the Nordic Council. The EFTA countries have since taken part in many discussions in the Council of Europe on this subject and have indicated a willingness to consider a transnational approach to patent protection. Just as in the case of the narrower EEC proposal, however, little concrete action has resulted.

U.S. Interest in a European Patent System

The United States is concerned that the rights of its citizens to equivalent national treatment under the International Patent Union be recognized in any European patent agreement. In a nondiscriminatory situation, both Americans and Europeans would benefit from being able to obtain a continent-wide patent. International trade of research-intensive products would be encouraged and the utilization of inventions through direct investments would be made easier. It would facilitate the cooperation of the U.S. government and American firms with European research undertakings as has already been accomplished in the European Atomic Energy Community (Euratom). With proper guarantees of industrial property rights, there would be less hesitancy to share new developments in nuclear energy technology from which both Europeans and Americans would benefit. A continent-wide system would provide for central clearing and examination of patents and might lead eventually to an international patent system. Finally, the United States patent system itself is far from ideally suited to the needs of a rapidly changing industrial society. If the Europeans are able to settle their differences and arrive at a modern patent system, the United States would do well to emulate this development.

Energy Problems

In the negotiations leading to the EEC, a unified energy policy was discussed, but it was not incorporated into the Rome Treaty. The issue was dropped because, at the time, agreement was not possible. Yet the importance of energy has kept the issue under almost constant discussion since 1958. There are several reasons for considering a common energy policy to be desirable. First, energy poses an important institutional problem, since jurisdiction is divided among the three European Communities. The EEC is responsible for natural gas and petroleum, the European Coal and Steel Community is responsible for coal, and Euratom is responsible for nuclear energy. The diffusion of responsibility has led to different market conditions for the separate fuels. The commercial policy for oil and gas is (almost) unified, but the internal market remains somewhat separated. For coal, the reverse situation exists; the internal market is unified, but the member countries have different import controls. Each Community has difficulty in devising an independent policy for its fuel because of the competition in end-use among the fuels. The problem will be alleviated, but not solved, by the unification of the executives of the three Communities, since the treaties themselves will not be unified.

Second, the existence of segmented energy markets has led to differing energy prices in the member countries. In France, for instance, oil prices have been 20 to 30 percent higher than in Germany, and coal prices have been significantly lower in Italy and the Netherlands than in Belgium or Germany. These differences in fuel prices can distort competition in those products that require significant amounts of energy in their manufacture. For products such as steel, aluminum, certain chemicals, and stone, clay and glass products, energy input amounts to 20 to 30 percent of value added in manufacture. The countries with low energy prices will have a competitive advantage in the intra-Community trade of energy-intensive products.[9] A unified energy market would prevent such distortions.

The third factor is of less immediate interest and concerns the geographic-industrial structure of the petroleum industry. The strong trend since the war toward greater reliance on imported crude petroleum in Europe is unlikely to be reversed in the foreseeable future. This growing dependency has made Europeans aware of the risks of both physical interruption of supplies and very high petroleum prices. Physical interruption of supply is more than a theoretical possibility, as demonstrated during the Middle East crises. The possibility of high petroleum prices comes from the oligopolistic market structure of the petroleum industry in which a few international companies control a substantial portion of crude petroleum exports. The newly-formed Organization of Petroleum Exporting Countries (OPEC), whose purpose is to raise the revenues of the crude-petroleum-producing countries, contributes to the possibility of high petroleum prices.[10] Guarding against these risks may involve substantial costs and thus require a Community approach.

The major obstacle to a Community approach to energy is coal. If a unified price for coal is to exist, Germany, France, and Belgium want it to be high enough to prevent wholesale closures of their national coal mines. But the competitive position of European coal has been very weak in relation to practically all competing fuels and promises to remain that way or deteriorate in the future.[11] As seen in Table 5-1, EEC coal production declined from a Suez Crisis peak of over 250 million metric tons to a level of about 230 million metric tons and within recent years has declined much further. Imports of coal followed this trend for a while, but because of cheaper prices in recent years, they have generally stabilized in value and

[9] Within the ECSC, the fastest growing steel industry is in Italy, the country which depends most on cheap imported coal for its fuel needs. The dissatisfaction of some German steel producers over being forced to purchase high-cost domestic coal has led to a threat of foreign investment in steel facilities in order to take advantage of cheaper energy costs.

[10] For a discussion of the OPEC issue, see Leslie Emery Grayson, "Economic Considerations of a Common Energy Policy in the European Economic Community" (unpublished doctoral dissertation, University of Michigan, 1965).

[11] The competitive position of the German coal industry—the most efficient in the Community—has been weak in relation to petroleum during the entire postwar period, especially since 1958. German coal has been decidedly more expensive than American coal since 1962-63; not competitive with natural gas following large discoveries in the Netherlands and in the North Sea; and more expensive than atomic energy since about 1965. The degree of competitiveness differs depending upon end-use.

TABLE 5-1

*EEC Production of Hard Coal and Imports of Coal,
Coke, and Briquettes, 1955–66*

Year	Production Imports (Millions of metric tons)		Imports as Percentage of Production	Total Imports	Imports from United States (Millions of dollars)	Imports from United States as Percentage of Total Imports[a]
1955	250	54	21.6	807	169	20.9
1956	252	66	26.2	999	455	45.6
1957	251	76	30.3	1,433	644	45.0
1958	249	58	23.3	1,266	560	44.2
1959	238	47	19.7	1,012	342	33.8
1960	237	48	20.3	1,027	271	26.4
1961	233	49	21.0	870	173	19.9
1962	231	51	22.1	926	199	21.5
1963	227	63	27.8	1,171	295	25.2
1964	235	62	26.4	1,110	285	25.7
1965	224	57	25.4	1,004	278	27.7
1966	210	—	—	—	—	—

Sources: Statistical Office of the European Communities, *Statistics of Energy, 1964*, and *General Statistical Bulletin*, No. 12 (Brussels, 1966), No. 2 (1967); United Nations, *Commodity Trade Statistics*, Ser D (New York), various years.
[a] By value.

grown in volume. In order to obtain a market price for coal that would keep most EEC mines in production, a very restrictive policy toward imported fuels would be necessary or, alternatively, massive subsidies to coal producers. For Italy and the Netherlands, such a policy would be very costly without yielding any benefits, and they have not been willing to cooperate. There are also some secondary issues obstructing agreement involving French preferences for Algerian crude petroleum.

Frequent consultations over energy policy among the member countries have had some effect. In the April 1964 Protocol on Energy Policy, general agreement was reached on what the goals of policy should be and some suggestions were made for coordinating national policies. The goals are simply security of supply, a single price for energy in the entire EEC, and the coordination of member government policies toward oil and natural gas industries. From the EEC point of view, the need for a coordinated energy policy increases as imported fuels grow in relation to total energy consumption. In 1965, imports provided 54.1 percent of internal energy consumption, up from 31.2 percent in 1958. A degree of urgency has been added to the issue by the rate at which imports have replaced domestic sources of supply. Yet little concrete action has resulted. The ECSC has approved national subsidies to coal mines, but this reflects little more than the recognition and approval of previously-enacted national policies.

U.S. Interest in a Common Energy Policy

The United States is affected by the proposed Common Energy Policy through its role as principal nonmember coal supplier to the Community, and through the operations of American firms providing energy in Europe. As seen in Table 5-1, imports of U.S. coal by the EEC have fluctuated greatly in recent years, reaching a peak of $644 million in 1957 during the Suez Crisis and a low of $173 million in 1961 when a major adjustment to an oversupply of coal was occurring. U.S. coal has been subject to import quotas in some EEC countries, but the quantity of imports from the United States has increased slightly. The United States is somewhat more interested in expanding trade in coal than in other products because coal is produced in a depressed area of the United States. If a unified market price for coal were established at a low level, then thermal energy would continue to have some role in the competitive electricity market. Otherwise the use of coal will decrease in favor of residual fuel oil and nuclear energy.

American firms play a major role in both the petroleum and natural gas industries in the EEC. Since most of the fears with regard to security of supply concern petroleum, American interests are likely to be affected by any solution to that problem. Most observers believe that diversification of sources and a high level of local inventories would provide sufficient defense against a sudden cessation of supplies. Both of these measures entail increasing costs for producers. If the burdens are shared equitably by all participants in the market, then little distortion could result among individual firms, but much care will be needed to ensure this result. As the market for nuclear energy expands, American firms will be affected as suppliers of equipment. While there is no present indication that this role would be altered by a common energy policy, pressures favoring Community suppliers exist and might well find expression in such a policy.

Tax Harmonization

Tax harmonization is appropriately the last of the issues affecting competition to be discussed because it not only affects competitive conditions among the member countries, but is also involved in general economic policy (as an ingredient in fiscal policy) and therefore belongs as well in the following section of this chapter.

It has long been recognized that tariffs are not the only fiscal charges that can influence international trade. The total flow of imports can be influenced by high retail sales taxes, for instance, if they are applied only to products that are primarily imported. Obviously changes in fiscal charges for the purpose of influencing import trade would be inconsistent with the intentions of a customs union. Of even greater immediate interest is the problem of border tax adjustments of internal indirect taxes.[12] Discussions concerning the problem of border tax adjustments in a customs union were started before the EEC came into existence. The issue arose during the early years of the European Coal and Steel Community and is yet to be fully settled. Two major difficulties with border tax adjustments have created pressures for tax harmonization within the Common Market. The first difficulty is the determination of the exact amount of border tax adjustment needed to compensate for internal indirect taxes. If it is known, for example, that the total amount of indirect taxes paid on an item represents 10 percent of its wholesale value, then it is a simple matter to rebate this amount to exporters and to levy it on importers. However, all EEC countries other than France have been using a "cascading" type of turnover tax which prevents an exact determination of taxes paid on many products.[13] If the border tax adjustment is below the effective tax

---

[12] Based on the belief that indirect taxes are shifted forward in higher prices, most countries rebate indirect taxes on export sales and levy compensating indirect taxes on imported products. This practice is sanctioned by the General Agreement on Tariffs and Trade.

[13] Under a cascading type of turnover tax, a tax is levied on every market transaction regardless of whether an intermediate or a final good is involved, and no credit is allowed for taxes paid on inputs at an earlier stage in the production process. Thus, on barbed wire produced by nonintegrated firms, a tax is collected when coal, iron ore, and steel scrap are purchased by the basic steel producer; when the steel ingot is sold to the wire rod producer; when the wire rod is sold to the wire drawer; and when the barbed wire is sold to the ultimate user. However, if barbed wire is produced by a partially or fully integrated firm, some or all of the tax payments on intermediate goods are avoided as internal company transfers

rate on domestically-produced goods, then imports are given a competitive advantage and exports are penalized. If, on the other hand, the border tax adjustment is greater than the effective domestic tax rate, imports are discriminated against and exports are subsidized. Over- and under-adjustment at the border for indirect taxes will not be uniform among products, resulting in a distortion of the structure of production.[14] When border tax adjustments are altered—whether defensibly or not in terms of tax equity—the change is equivalent to changes in tariffs and in export subsidies. Such changes are, therefore, of particular concern to the member countries of a customs union.

The second difficulty with border tax adjustments is that they will require the maintenance of fiscal frontiers between the members of the EEC even after all tariffs on intra-Community trade will have been eliminated. The advantages of the removal of fiscal frontiers are both economic and psychological. If products do not need to be inspected when they cross national borders among the member countries, transport time and costs will be reduced. Also, administrative economies will be obtained, since customs houses will be required only at points where products enter the Community from nonmember countries. Further, the very existence of a customs house, even when not engaged in the collection of tariffs, increases the possibility of a resumption of tariff charges and is thus an inhibiting factor in the development of intra-Community trade. For these reasons, it is thought desirable to eliminate fiscal frontiers.

In addition to indirect taxes, benefits may be derived from the harmonization of certain direct taxes. If factors of production such as labor and capital are free to move among members of a customs union as provided for in the Rome Treaty, then differences in direct taxes can affect the distribution of these factors among countries. Private capital, for instance, is expected to flow to the area with prospects for the highest after-tax rate of return. If the structure of these rates among countries differs from the

---

replace market sales. There is no single compensating tax rate on imported barbed wire that would equalize the burden on the identical item produced domestically. As a practical matter, an average border tax adjustment is determined from studying typical production patterns, but there is room for error and manipulation. This is only one of many possible illustrations of the difficulties involved in determining the actual tax burden under a cascading type of tax.

[14] If errors of adjustment were uniform among products, then they would be equivalent to an adjustment in the exchange rate for merchandise and would not be a serious problem in themselves. Exchange rates, of course, may require adjustment, but this is a much broader issue.

pre-tax profit rates, then capital flows could be distorted, resulting in a loss of economic welfare.[15]

Proposals for Change

When the border tax problem arose following the formation of the ECSC, a committee of experts was appointed, under the chairmanship of Professor Jan Tinbergen, to investigate the issue.[16] The report of this committee indicated that border tax adjustments were necessary among the members because these adjustments would reduce the distortion of production caused by differing tax systems. Furthermore, if the existence of border tax adjustments did cause some distortion of competitive conditions, the committee felt that the exchange rates of the member countries had probably adjusted to this factor in the past—along with other factors influencing competition—and further corrections were not required. The Tinbergen Committee recognized that they were faced only with the problem of integrating the coal and steel industries and that their conclusion might be different if the entire economy were involved.

Subsequently, the border tax issue was discussed at some length in the preparation of the Rome Treaty, and articles 95 through 99 reflect this work. The difficulty of determining the proper amount of adjustment was implicitly recognized and the treaty directed the Commission to consider ways of harmonizing the tax systems of the member countries. The Commission was to submit proposals to the Council of Ministers for this purpose. Another committee was appointed, this time under the chairmanship of Professor Fritz Neumark.[17] The Neumark Committee recommended that tax harmonization be approached in three stages. In the first stage, all member countries would replace their turnover tax system with a tax levied on value added.[18] Since the French had already adopted such

[15] The same theoretical issue is discussed at some length in Lawrence B. Krause and Kenneth Dam, *Federal Taxation of Foreign Income* (Brookings Institution, 1964).

[16] European Coal and Steel Community, *Rapport sur les Problèmes Posés par les Taxes sur le Chiffre d'Affaires dans le Marché Commun* (Tinbergen Report) (Luxembourg, 1953).

[17] European Economic Community, *Report of the Fiscal and Financial Committee* (Neumark Report) (Brussels, 1963).

[18] A value-added tax is similar to a turnover tax in that it is calculated whenever there is a market sale of a product, but it differs by allowing a tax credit for taxes paid on inputs into the production process. Except for some minor difficulties, this allows an exact calculation of the tax burden on every product.

a system, the suggestion applied to the other member countries. In the second stage, member countries would equalize their tax rates on value added. This would eliminate the necessity of maintaining fiscal frontiers between the members since all products would be carrying the same burden of taxation.[19] In the third stage, member countries would begin to harmonize other fiscal charges, including direct taxes.

The Commission accepted the findings of the Neumark Committee and submitted two recommendations to the Council of Ministers containing the essential ingredients of the first stage of the report.[20] These proposals were accepted by the Council on February 9, 1967, but some time will be needed for all the member countries to enact the required implementing legislation. Most tax experts believe that a tax on value added is technically superior to a cascading turnover tax and, therefore, national governments began examining their own systems even without a Council directive.[21] The process has gone farthest in Germany. Legislation has been passed and is due to take effect in 1968. In the Netherlands and Belgium, where some resistance had appeared to ending the turnover tax, the climate for the change seems much improved—in part because of the German example. Only in Italy was the change really questioned, but Italy is certain to follow the Council directive in time.

U.S. Interest in Tax Harmonization

The interest of nonmember countries in the proposals for tax harmonization within the Common Market results from their possible consequences for international trade. The mere change from a turnover tax to a value-added tax could affect trade. It has long been argued by business interests in Germany and elsewhere in the EEC that the existing level of

[19] Certain problems of distribution of tax revenues would arise under such a system. Without fiscal frontiers, taxes would be collected according to the origin principle (that is, when a product remained within the Community, the country of origin of the product would keep the tax revenue regardless of where the product was consumed in the Community). Countries whose exports are oriented toward member countries and away from third countries gain more revenue than they would under a full border tax adjustment system. Less revenue would be received by member countries whose exports are directed more to nonmember countries.

[20] The first recommendation was submitted to the Council in 1963 and the second one in 1966.

[21] In addition to the increased accuracy noted above, a tax on value added does not promote tax-induced vertical integrations as does a turnover tax. It is much more equitable, therefore, in the competition between large and small firms.

border tax adjustments is inadequate to compensate for the indirect tax burden on traded commodities.[22] If this is the case, then the changing of the tax system will, on the average, increase the amount of border adjustments allowed and thereby reduce the competitiveness of all products entering these markets from nonmember countries.[23]

If the second stage of tax harmonization were also to come about, then additional trade effects might occur, depending on a number of factors, including the common tax rate decided upon. Taking an extreme example, if the high French rate were to be adopted, then the other member countries would substantially change their fiscal systems. If we assume that these countries did not want to add to total governmental revenues, the increase in indirect taxes subject to border adjustments would be matched by a decrease in direct taxes such as corporate income taxes, for which border tax adjustments are not allowed.[24] While public finance experts disagree on the possible consequences of such a change in a tax system, businessmen almost universally believe that the international competitive position of a country making such a change would improve. The competitive improvement would certainly occur if the government used the occasion of the change in tax systems to increase governmental revenues—without a corresponding increase in expenditures—or if the monetary authorities would not allow a sufficient increase in the money supply

[22] In Germany the argument stemmed from the inability to calculate the adjustment accurately. In Italy, however, the excess burden comes from having some very high excise taxes which cannot be rebated under the present system (that is, excise taxes on electricity and petroleum products).

[23] While the border tax adjustment applies to imports from both member and nonmember countries, a change in the adjustment bears more heavily on nonmember country goods. This results from the common practice of applying the ad valorem tariff rates against the value of the landed imports including the border tax adjustment. Thus if the c.i.f. price of an import were $1.00, and the border tax and tariff rate 10 percent each, the imported product would first be assessed a border tax of 10c and a tariff charge of 11c (10 percent of $1.10). If the border tax were raised to 20 percent while the tariff rate remains 10 percent, the charges become 20c for the border tax and 12c for the tariff (10 percent of $1.20). In essence, the nominal ad valorem tariff rate is raised by a factor equal to one plus the border tax and, of course, only nonmember countries are required to pay tariffs.

[24] The rules for border tax adjustment come from the General Agreement on Tariffs and Trade. Indirect taxes are compensated for at the border because of the belief that they increase product prices by the full amount of the tax (that is, they are shifted forward). Direct taxes, however, are believed not to affect product prices, and therefore, do not require border adjustments. The theory of tax incidence, however, is in dispute among public finance experts. If indirect taxes are not fully shifted forward, and/or direct taxes are partially or wholly passed on in higher prices, the GATT rule leads to some trade distortion.

to permit prices to rise by the full amount of the indirect tax increase.

Because of the uncertainties both as to possible events and their consequences, the analysis in this area is speculative. However, it is safe to say that any profound change in a country's tax system would be likely to affect market prices and thereby influence the trade of other countries. A full implementation of the Neumark Committee recommendations would influence international flows of capital as well as trade. Developments in tax harmonization within the EEC will therefore command a great deal of attention from nonmember countries.

General Economic Policies

Because the Rome Treaty envisioned the development of the EEC beyond a simple customs union, provision was made for joint consideration of broader issues of economic policy. Institutional arrangements have evolved for this purpose, including a monetary committee, a fiscal committee, and a Medium Term Economic Policy Committee. Nonmember countries have an interest in this work of the Common Market since it could affect such things as the Community's balance of payments and the evolution of international monetary arrangements.

Internal and External Balance

By design, a customs union leads to the closer integration of the economies of the member countries. The consequences of this for short-term economic stabilization objectives are profound. Inflationary or deflationary impulses emanating from one country quickly spread to other member countries via trade and movements of labor and capital.[25] The

[25] An attempt has been made by Stephen Resnick to measure empirically some of these linkages and feedbacks. Using a very simplified model, he estimated, for instance, that a 5 percent increase in government spending in Germany would lead to a percentage increase in gross national product in France of almost the same amount as in Germany (1.53 compared to 1.64 percent). Thus if France was suffering from inflation when Germany was faced with deflation, a conflict of policy measures would be likely to ensue. Because of the simplicity of the model employed and certain unavoidable statistical difficulties, Resnick warns that little faith should be put in his numerical estimates. Nevertheless, the closeness of the relationship is suggestive. *An Econometric Study of the Common Market* (Unpublished Ph.D. thesis, Massachusetts Institute of Technology, 1964).

mutual interest of the member countries in avoiding extremes of inflation or deflation in partner countries has heightened the interest of all members in current economic conditions in the Community. Meetings of the monetary and fiscal committees have provided the forum for frank and open discussions of the economic situation in each member country and the policy measures being used by the national governments.[26] The major policy problems which have been discussed concern the achievement and maintenance of internal and external balance (that is, avoidance of inflation and deflation while maintaining balance-of-payments equilibrium). Achieving these policy goals is important for all countries and the problems involved do not differ fundamentally for members of a customs union. Choosing policy instruments and assigning them to their appropriate policy goals are the core of the problem.[27] Members of the Common Market, however, must recognize the institutional limitations brought about by the obligations of the Rome Treaty and by the logic of a customs union.

The institutional limitations include the obligation to liberalize intra-Community movements of goods and capital. Among other things, this means that member governments cannot artificially restrict the inflow of imported goods for balance-of-payments reasons or put limits on the inflow of short-term capital to counter inflationary tendencies. The logic of an integrated market implies the fixity of exchange rates among members. Given these conditions, it is generally believed that the job of internal stabilization is best performed by fiscal policy, and external balance is best achieved by monetary policy.[28] If a country is suffering from inflation, for instance, restrictive monetary policy alone is unlikely to prove a very

[26] These discussions are reported to be much more "intensive" than the confrontations at the Organization for Economic Cooperation and Development in Paris. Each member country is represented by two delegates in order to get a diversity of views about conditions within the countries. Policies of the governments are critically appraised and alternatives are suggested if appropriate.

[27] A great deal of research has been done on this problem in recent years. In particular, see Robert Mundell, "Capital Mobility and Stabilization Policy under Fixed and Flexible Exchange Rates," *Canadian Journal of Economics and Political Science,* Vol. 29 (November 1963), pp. 475-85.

[28] The theory of economic policy indicates that at least one policy instrument is needed for every policy goal. If countries desire goals in addition to internal and external balance—such as a high rate of economic growth or a limitation on the net inflow of foreign capital—other policy instruments will be required. Changes in tax structure, incomes policy, or price and wage controls are a few possible instruments. J. Tinbergen, *On the Theory of Economic Policy* (Amsterdam: North-Holland, 1952).

effective policy instrument. As domestic money supply is contracted to limit domestic expenditures, short-term interest rates will be forced up. Capital inflows from other countries will be attracted, which will restore the liquidity in the domestic market and give an unwanted stimulus to domestic expenditures. The more fully the capital markets of the member countries are integrated, the less effective monetary policy is in controlling inflation and deflation. Fiscal policy, however, is not subject to external offsets to the same degree, and therefore can be used for domestic stabilization purposes. An increase in taxes (or a reduction in governmental expenditures) can be an effective tool for reducing inflationary pressures, even though some of the force of the policy is dissipated as expenditures on imports are reduced along with expenditures on domestic goods. On the other hand, because of the responsiveness of capital movements to interest rate differentials among countries, monetary policy is a very effective means of overcoming balance-of-payments problems. Thus, if a member country is suffering from a balance-of-payments deficit, it need only raise interest rates, as noted above, to attract foreign capital and finance the deficit. This suggests the proper role for each policy.

The member countries require a reasonable degree of flexibility in their fiscal policies if excesses of inflation and recession are to be avoided. At any point in time, however, the degree of restraint or stimulation required to maintain internal balance will differ among the countries. Therefore, members will need to have independent, but coordinated, fiscal policies. From the tax side, however, the need for independent fiscal policies runs counter to the need and desire for tax harmonization. If the Neumark Committee recommendations were adopted in their entirety, the only variance allowed among countries would be in the level of retail sales taxes, and some practical limitation exists on differentials even here.[29] While the dilemma could be solved by making governmental expenditures fluctuate according to stabilization needs, the political difficulties involved are obviously very great. Meaningful reductions in government expenditures are almost impossible when a large share of such expenditures is devoted to social welfare programs and another large share is required to

---

[29] With automobile ownership becoming more widespread, many consumers will be induced to travel the short distances required to cross national frontiers to avoid paying high retail sales taxes. Already a considerable number of Belgians and Germans make regular trips to the Netherlands to buy items such as butter for which retail prices differ greatly. The amount of cigarette sales in New Jersey and Connecticut to residents of New York City because of high sales taxes in that city is suggestive of possible consumer reaction to retail tax differentials.

meet contractual obligations such as interest payments on the public debt.

The actual use of fiscal policy in the member countries since the start of the EEC has been disappointing. The growth of governmental expenditures has slowed during periods of intense inflationary pressure in some countries, but not in others. Also, tax changes seem to have been used as frequently to influence elections as to stabilize the domestic economy. As a result, monetary policy has been forced to bear almost the full burden of policy needs. Since the deviations from stability have more frequently been toward inflation than deflation, tight money conditions have frequently prevailed.[30] Monetary policy has been effective in containing inflation in the member countries despite the limitations noted previously, but only to the extent that interest rates have risen in the entire Community, and, through the EEC, in some nonmember countries. At times, interest rates in certain member countries have been higher than necessary for either internal or external balance.

Turning now to the question of external balance, the conditions needed for balance-of-payments equilibrium are the same whether or not a country is a member of a customs union. Equilibrium is achieved when overall inpayments equal overall outpayments exclusive of settlement items. For a member in such a situation, a deficit with other members will be matched by an identical surplus with nonmember countries, or the reverse. The customs union as a whole must be in equilibrium if all members are in equilibrium. When a member has a deficit in its balance of payments, being part of a customs union does make a difference. It is prevented from interfering with trade or capital flows by its treaty commitments, it must not depreciate its currency unless unable to avoid doing so, and, therefore, it is forced to use internal policy measures to adjust the external situation.

There are many reasons why exchange rate adjustments among member countries of a common market should be avoided. First, fixed exchange rates promote the closer integration of member countries by encouraging intra-Community trade and factor movements, just as among regions of a single country. To achieve a truly integrated capital market,

---

[30] The predominance of inflationary pressures can be traced to the European labor market. The shortage of new entrants into the market, combined with the decline in the average number of hours worked, only partially offset by inflows of foreign workers, has meant an excess of job openings and pressure for higher wages. For a more detailed analysis, see Walter S. Salant and others, *The United States Balance of Payments in 1968* (Brookings Institution, 1963).

for instance, investors of one member country must be confident that the value of their investment in another member country will not be undermined by a currency devaluation. Confidence in the stability of exchange rates grows primarily when currency values are kept unaltered in the face of balance-of-payments difficulties.

Second, with free internal markets, exchange rate changes would have such large direct income effects on other member countries that depreciations would be intolerable. In the goods market, the impact would probably be concentrated on those industries close to the competitive margin, causing sudden distress. In the labor market, foreign workers in the depreciating country would suffer particular hardships unless their money incomes were increased to offset the loss of purchasing power in their home markets. Retired workers would lose real income in that portion of their retirement credits earned in the depreciating currency unless compensating provisions were made.

Third, undesirable shifts in resource allocation could occur because some prices within the depreciating country are fixed in terms of community units and would change automatically with the devaluation. Thus within the EEC, most agricultural prices are fixed in EEC "Units of Account." In the event of a devaluation, the farmers in the depreciating country would obtain an immediate increase in prices equal to the devaluation, which would encourage more investment in agriculture (and less elsewhere), and would also cause undesirable inflationary pressures. Thus, the internal policies which were to be avoided by the currency devaluation would be required nonetheless to control the inflation.

The internal policies referred to are the familiar monetary and fiscal measures. Since monetary policy is best suited for balance-of-payments adjustments and more easily available to policymakers, it will undoubtedly be used. But raising interest rates to obtain private financing of balance-of-payments deficits is not a long-run solution to external disequilibrium. Countries cannot remain indifferent to a growing amount of external indebtedness or to a level of interest rates that for long periods of time is higher than required for internal economic needs. Both the distribution and growth of national income would be adversely affected. A more basic mechanism is required to adjust the competitive positions of member countries, such as the vigorous use of incomes policy. If a member country incurs a deficit in its balance of payments, in addition to raising interest rates to finance the deficit, it could enforce guidelines on wages and prices to insure a competitive improvement relative to other member countries. Likewise, surplus countries could be more lenient in allowing wage and price increases.

The difficulty with this prescription is that incomes policy has not been notably successful in the past in helping industrial countries contain inflation. It has been used in varying degrees in the United Kingdom, the Netherlands, France, Germany, and the United States. The only successes claimed for incomes policy have occurred in countries where only modest objectives were being sought and when general economic conditions were not tending to counter the policy. It is fairly certain that incomes policy alone cannot reduce money wages and prices or hold the line against their increase in the face of strong inflationary pressures. Thus, if a large fundamental disequilibrium occurs in the balance of payments of member countries, a painful dose of deflation for deficit countries appears unavoidable. This conclusion has led to the search for methods of preventing major maladjustments in addition to the investigation of adjustment mechanisms. Prevention, however, requires a broader policy horizon than is implied by short-term stabilization objectives. It is for this reason that medium-term policy has been accepted as a necessary part of the Common Market.

Medium-Term Economic Policy

No specific provision was made for medium-term economic policy by the Rome Treaty. Indeed, because of its close association with economic planning, it was opposed by Germany on ideological grounds. Eventually, German policymakers recognized the need for a longer time period for the determination of sound economic policy. Background work was begun within the EEC Commission and it has been expanded by the operations of the Medium Term Economic Policy Committee.[31] While indicative planning of the French type may have been envisioned by some experts as the proper model for the EEC to follow, the conditions of the Community as a whole are so different from the conditions of any single country that new departures in this area are likely to occur.

The primary task undertaken by medium-term policy was the formation of a series of projections of the aggregate economic performance of the

[31] The technical difficulties involved in such work are tremendous. Theoretical work was required to incorporate several countries into a single model. Existing information systems had to be correlated and new data obtained. Much of this work broke new ground in economics and will be useful elsewhere. It is anticipated that these difficulties will take many years to overcome.

member countries for a five-year period assuming a "reasonable" economic environment.[32] These projections are constantly revised as new and improved data become available and in the light of actual experience. The projections serve as a bench mark for private and government planning within the member countries. Individual entrepreneurs can presumably make better investment decisions if they have a guide to the market potential of the entire EEC. Member governments will also be better able to estimate variables such as export demand and external labor supply which aid them in planning for internal and external stability. The Medium Term Economic Policy Committee can issue guidelines for noninflationary increases in government spending on the basis of the projections. All of these yardsticks for behavior are meant to prevent the excesses of inflation and deflation in member countries which could upset the economic stability of the Community and require painful internal adjustments.

Medium-term economic policy could conceivably develop into a full-fledged planning apparatus. This would require a mechanism for achieving the projected or desired rate of economic growth. The possibility of such a development is quite remote for the foreseeable future. It would not only require a change in basic economic philosophy in some countries, but also a substantial divestiture of national sovereignty by all countries. For quite a while, the major achievements in medium-term policy will probably be the provision of economic information rather than the formulation of "action programs" to which member governments must adhere.

U.S. Interest in EEC Economic Policy

Since the Common Market is the largest trading complex in the world, its economic policies affect all nonmember countries. While the United States is less susceptible than most countries to inflationary and deflationary impulses from abroad because of its relatively slight involvement in international trade (low ratios of imports and exports to gross national product), the U.S. economy nevertheless is affected directly and indirectly by European conditions. If, for instance, the major countries of the EEC go into an economic recession, the United States would feel the loss of export sales directly and would suffer indirectly through the

[32] The Council of Ministers adopted the EEC's first medium-term economic program on February 8, 1967, which implies an acceptance of the growth projections.

(probable) deterioration in the U.S. balance of payments. Since the "excesses" of the EEC have tended to be on the inflationary side, the stimulus provided to U.S. exports has been welcomed for its effect on economic growth and its presumed favorable effect on the U.S. balance of payments. The situation did not develop as well as might have been expected, however, because of the excessive use of monetary policy as an anti-inflationary device. With interest rates relatively high on the Continent despite balance-of-payments surpluses, the United States was inhibited from using monetary policy for its own balance-of-payments difficulties by the fear that tighter money would choke off economic expansion.[33]

In a broader context, EEC policies have a tremendous influence on world capital markets. Europe as a whole is the largest source and destination of short-term and long-term international capital movements and the EEC represents the major share of Europe. The importance of this influence goes beyond balance-of-payments consequences to include effects on economic growth. The tight money policies pursued by the EEC countries have drawn funds from the money markets in the United Kingdom, Japan, and the United States, making borrowing more difficult and expensive everywhere. As a result, restrictive influences have been transmitted to some countries at times when it was inappropriate from their point of view. The development of more flexible fiscal measures within the EEC would relieve EEC monetary policy (that is, the task of controlling inflation would allow a lower level of interest rates to prevail in the world, and would give more scope to monetary policy to solve short-term balance-of-payments problems in all countries). Thus the U.S. has a direct interest in policy formation within the EEC.

Looking into the future, if the EEC actually developed fully integrated capital markets in which long-term and short-term money could be raised, the U.S. would be greatly affected. On the one hand, the profits of U.S. financial intermediaries in underwriting and distributing financial assets would be reduced because of greater competition from the EEC. On the other hand, the greater supply of savings that would be mobilized in Europe for long-term investment would relieve the strain on the U.S. capital market. If integration within the EEC went even further, to include the adoption of a single currency, then the entire international monetary

[33] This inhibition was strengthened by the belief that it was necessary to create an interest rate differential in favor of the United States, and by the lack of any assurance that a differential could be created, since an increase in U.S. interest rates might be matched by further increases in Europe.

system would be fundamentally altered. The new currency would compete with the U.S. dollar as the world's primary medium of exchange. Already the EEC has had an influence on the deliberations for changes in the international liquidity mechanism. While not always reaching agreement, the EEC countries have consulted among themselves in order to present a more unified position in the "Group of Ten" meetings and, in the final agreement, obtained the power of veto over the use of the new credit facilities. Finally, in the unlikely event that the medium-term economic policy of the EEC developed into a full-fledged central planning mechanism, serious consequences would occur for the U.S. because of the basic incompatibility of planning with a market-determined allocation of goods, services, and capital.

This chapter has considered many of the factors within the EEC that have recognizable external consequences. The analysis necessarily has been tentative because of the constantly changing nature of the EEC and the incompleteness of its policies. Of the issues discussed in the first sections, tax harmonization seems to be the most pressing. The Germans have taken the lead in implementing the Neumark Committee recommendations and the others may follow, now that action has been taken within the Council of Ministers. With respect to general economic policy, it is again the Germans who may be leading the way toward more responsive policy. The Federal Republic is attempting to bring some sort of central direction over total governmental expenditures. If granted new legislative powers, the Bonn government would for the first time have the instruments needed to pursue fiscal policy. Government tax and expenditure policies are areas in which most countries are deficient and in which improvement is clearly needed.

≫ CHAPTER SIX ≪

Foreign Relations

BOTH THE European Economic Community and the European Free
Trade Association have devoted much attention to their bilateral relations
and their relations with other countries. Despite the failure of attempts to
alter radically the membership of the two groups, changes have taken place
since their inception. EFTA expanded shortly after birth through the association of Finland. After the colonial territories of the Common Market
countries obtained independence, they formed an association with the
EEC. Greece and Turkey have negotiated EEC Association Agreements
with the intention of ultimately becoming full members. These developments were not unexpected, since both groups wanted to avoid becoming
closed societies by forever excluding all countries unable to take part in
the original venture.

The Rome Treaty provides a number of ways in which countries can
establish special relationships with the EEC. Part Four of the treaty (Articles 131-36), Annex IV, and a special Implementing Convention all relate to the association of dependent overseas countries and territories. Article 237 provides for the full membership of other European countries,
and Article 238 deals with the association of European or non-European
countries with the Community. Furthermore, the treaty anticipates that
the EEC would want to conclude commercial treaties with nonmember
countries, and makes provision for this in Articles 110-16. The treaty
even requires that members harmonize their national commercial treaties,
which are most important in regulating trade with communist countries.

The European Free Trade Association provided for the accession of
new members in Article 41 of the Stockholm Convention. The provision
indicates that any state is eligible to join as a full member and also allows

176

for association agreements with other countries or with any "union of states or international organization." This last phrase was intended specifically to give EFTA flexibility in reaching its objective of promoting wider economic integration in Europe. Recalling that EFTA grew out of the inability of other European countries to negotiate with the EEC, the authors of this provision intended to point to one possible solution to the problem—a negotiation between EFTA and the EEC. Being a free trade area rather than a customs union, EFTA does not interfere with the ability of member countries, either individually or jointly, to negotiate commercial treaties with other countries.

According to the theory of customs unions, the geographical expansion of customs unions has interesting economic welfare implications for nonmember countries. On the positive side, the larger a customs union is or becomes, the more likely it is that the lowest-cost producer of goods will be found among the members, thus increasing the possibility that all the forthcoming expansion in trade will be trade-creating rather than trade-diverting.[1] Going to the extreme, a customs union comprising the entire world would be identical to a pure free-trade system and therefore would be desirable, according to classical reasoning.

From the point of view of a nonmember country, however, the expansion of a customs union does not look desirable. The larger the customs union becomes, the wider is the area of discrimination against the outsider's products, and the more likely it is that a serious competitor will obtain membership status. Again taking an extreme example, if all countries but one were part of a customs union, the economic welfare of the excluded country would necessarily deteriorate. There may, of course, be dominant political or other reasons why the expansion of a customs union would be welcomed by nonmember countries.[2]

Finland's Association with EFTA

The ink was hardly dry on the Stockholm Convention when efforts began toward associating Finland with EFTA. Indeed, Finland even had an ob-

[1] This assumes that new members are drawn at random. If only high-cost countries are accepted into membership, then the positive result will not occur.

[2] It is even possible that nonmember countries could gain in economic welfare through the expansion of a customs union. This would occur, for example, if serious obstacles to rational economic policy exist in individual countries and these are removed through membership in a customs union.

server present during the original negotiations. Finland represents a classic case of the economic difficulties facing a nonmember country upon the formation of an integrated area. International trade is very important to Finland, as exports absorb about 20 percent of its gross national product, and a disruption of export markets could seriously affect its national well-being. Finnish exports are concentrated to an uncomfortable extent in a single product line—70 percent of export earnings come from forest products. These goods are in direct competition with those from Sweden, Norway, Denmark, and, to a small degree, Austria. Furthermore, fully 20 percent of Finnish exports go to the United Kingdom. If Finland had remained outside of EFTA, which includes both its prime customer (the United Kingdom) and its major competitors (the Scandinavian countries), trade diversion would have been inevitable and very painful. To associate with EFTA would prevent trade diversion, but it would at the same time cause Finland other difficulties. Unlike the Scandinavian countries, Finland had high national tariffs, which were needed to protect a relatively inefficient manufacturing sector against foreign competition. Faced with the necessity of paying reparations to the Soviet Union following the Second World War, Finland developed a wide-ranging but small-scale secondary manufacturing sector to provide the goods sought by the Russians. High tariffs helped to protect these industries and to provide the needed goods surplus to cover the unrequited capital flow in the Finnish balance of payments. Association with EFTA would expose these industries to competition from the nearby Scandinavian countries and the United Kingdom.

The close economic and geographic ties of Finland with the Soviet Union meant that political factors would be of great importance in any accommodation between Finland and EFTA. After the war, Finland was able to establish its independence from the Soviet Union, but was scrupulously careful to follow both internal and external policies that were not in conflict with the interests of the USSR. This delicate balancing of mutual interests was universally recognized as a desirable state of affairs. With 20 to 25 percent of its trade involved, the Finnish economy developed some dependence upon the Eastern bloc. The Soviet Union recognized that an association between EFTA and Finland would reduce this dependence and might well violate the terms of the Soviet-Finnish Friendship and Trade Agreements, which grant the Soviets "most-favored-nation" treatment in the Finnish market. During the original Stockholm negotiations, the Soviet position was communicated to Finland through a warning that participation in EFTA would put Finland "under the influence of powers concerned only with the strengthening of their (own) political and economic positions."[3] The Soviets expressed satisfaction with the economic relationship developing between themselves and Finland, and were not anxious to see it undermined. However, the Russians were mindful of the economic difficulties facing Finland because of EFTA and presumably did not want to see Finland suffer unnecessarily.

In early 1960, negotiations were begun between representatives of Finland and the permanent delegates to EFTA. The technical problems of association were rather quickly resolved and a draft agreement was ready by spring. In order to overcome the political obstacles to agreement, the Finns held exploratory talks with the Russians in May 1960. In September, the Soviet Union agreed to negotiate with Finland to clear the way for a Finland-EFTA association. These negotiations were completed by the end of November, with an understanding which protected Soviet trading interests. The terms of this understanding were made known to the EFTA members, and a renegotiation between Finland and EFTA followed. By the end of March 1961, the final agreement was ready, and the signing took place in Helsinki, with the agreement to go into effect on July 1, 1961, after parliamentary approval.

The terms of the agreement set up a new free trade area, FINEFTA, with EFTA as one member and Finland the other. Exports from Finland to EFTA benefit from the internal tariff reductions according to the same schedule as products from the original member countries. Because of the difficult adjustment problem of Finnish industry, Finland was allowed a somewhat stretched-out schedule for reducing its tariffs against its EFTA partners. Since FINEFTA is a free trade area, Finland is also permitted to eliminate its tariffs against Russian imports and to treat them in the same manner as EFTA goods, thereby fulfilling its obligations to the Soviet Union. Furthermore, the administrative and other technical details of FINEFTA were worked out in a way which would maintain the sovereignty of Finland and avoid difficulties with the USSR.

While Finland had mainly defensive economic motives in mind, it also hoped that association with EFTA would lead to product diversification of its exports. Loss of protection might force Finnish industry to make the adjustments required to meet all competitors. This improved competitive position, combined with easier access to EFTA markets, might pave the way for a rapid expansion of exports of industrial products. The major outline of Finnish trade is shown in Table 6-1. The total value of Finnish

[3] *New York Times,* July 20, 1959.

TABLE 6-1

Trade of Finland, Selected Years, 1953-65

Type of Trade and Area	Value (In millions of dollars)						Percentage Distribution					
	1953	1959	1962	1963	1964	1965	1953	1959	1962	1963	1964	1965
Total imports	528	830	1,221	1,201	1,505	1,646	100.0	100.0	100.0	100.0	100.0	100.0
EFTA	119	237	390	393	482	565	22.5	28.6	31.9	32.7	32.0	34.3
EEC	116	261	424	362	447	508	22.0	31.4	34.7	30.1	29.7	30.9
Soviet bloc	181	208	236	261	336	310	34.3	25.1	19.3	21.7	22.3	18.8
United States	28	43	63	74	92	101	5.3	5.2	5.2	6.2	6.1	6.1
Other	84	81	108	111	148	162	15.9	9.7	8.9	9.3	9.9	9.9
Total exports	570	830	1,097	1,142	1,291	1,427	100.0	100.0	100.0	100.0	100.0	100.0
EFTA	164	248	334	357	442	473	28.8	29.9	30.4	31.3	34.2	33.2
EEC	111	218	317	342	395	400	19.5	26.3	28.9	29.9	30.6	28.0
Soviet bloc	174	197	248	242	229	301	30.5	23.7	22.6	21.2	17.7	21.1
United States	41	49	59	60	74	86	7.2	5.9	5.4	5.3	5.7	6.0
Other	80	118	139	141	151	167	14.0	14.2	12.7	12.3	11.8	11.7

Sources: European Free Trade Association, *EFTA Trade 1959–64* (Geneva, February 1966); International Monetary Fund-International Bank for Reconstruction and Development, *Direction of Trade, Annual 1958–62* (Washington, D. C., 1963) and *Annual 1960–64* (Washington, D. C., 1965); U. N. — IMF-IBRD, *Direction of International Trade Annual Issue 1938, 1948, 1953–1956*, Series T, Vol. VIII, No. 7 (New York, 1957).

exports and imports has been increasing quite rapidly in recent years. Comparing 1959 to 1965, exports increased by 71 percent and imports by 98 percent. The association with EFTA appears to have had some effect on Finnish trade. Exports to EFTA partners have risen by 91 percent and imports by 138 percent, both increasing more than total trade. As a result of Finland's membership, EFTA has replaced the EEC as the major provider of Finnish imports and improved its position as the major recipient of Finnish exports. The good performance of Finnish exports in EFTA markets indicates that Finnish hopes for "defensive" gains in associating with EFTA were fulfilled. While the reorientation of Finnish trade was primarily at the expense of the Soviet bloc, the shift did not reduce the absolute values of trade with this area, and was accomplished gradually, so that there have been no political repercussions. Since the Soviet Union itself was not subject to tariff discrimination by Finland, the reorientation of trade might well be explained by general economic trends in the Nordic area or by a relative loss of competitiveness by the Russians.

The secondary Finnish motive for association—product diversification of exports—may also have been served by FINEFTA. As expected, many Finnish industries went through a period of retrenchment following the liberalization of trade, but most industries recovered, and some developed a thriving export business. Exports of manufactured products doubled between 1959 and 1965, increasing from 50.5 percent to 58.9 percent of total exports. Even more striking is the fact that manufactured goods made up only 33.7 percent of Finnish exports to EFTA in 1959 but grew to 53.1 percent of a much larger total in 1965. Even within the forest products group, Finland processed the natural products of rough logs and wood pulp before exporting into wooden products and paper to a greater extent in 1965 than in 1959. Illustrations of successful export expansion include cutlery and building hardware of advanced design, paper and pulp machines, hydroelectric plants, electrical instruments, and machinery components produced in new engineering shops under contract to the Swedish engineering industry. The last-mentioned development would not have been possible without FINEFTA.

The United States and FINEFTA

There is little ambiguity in the appraisal of FINEFTA from the point of view of the United States. The United States has gained indirectly on both economic and political grounds. On the economic side, Finland has avoided loss through trade diversion, and has maintained its rapid pace of growth with expanded international trade. These results imply favorable consequences for its nonmember trading partners. The United States has managed not only to increase the absolute value of its exports to Finland (Table 6-1), but also to increase its share of the market despite the tariff discrimination in favor of EFTA. While it is possible that the United States might have increased its penetration of the Finnish market to an even greater extent without FINEFTA, it is also probable that total Finnish imports would have been much less in the absence of the EFTA association. Since Finnish exports in general do not compete directly with U.S. goods, the privileged position of Finland in EFTA markets should not be detrimental to the United States. In any event, the amount of trade diversion disadvantageous to the United States would be small, if it existed at all.

The political aspects of FINEFTA are possibly even more important for the United States. Stability has been reinforced on the northwestern border of the Soviet Union through economic unity in the Nordic area. The economic dependence of Finland on the Soviet Union has been reduced without the unleashing of pent-up nationalistic feelings. These developments must be considered desirable from the United States point of view.

The EEC and the Associated Overseas Countries

The first "expansion" issue faced by the EEC was its relationship with the dependent overseas territories of the member countries.[4] Unless the basic philosophy of the customs union was to be breached, these areas had to sever their privileged trade ties to individual member countries. France, the major colonial power, insisted that these territories be given some status in the Common Market. The other powers reluctantly agreed. The

[4] The Rome Treaty specified the following areas: French West Africa including Senegal, Sudan, Guinea, Ivory Coast, Dahomey, Mauretania, Niger, and Upper Volta; French Equatorial Africa including the Middle Congo, Ubangi-Shari, Chad, and Gabon; St. Pierre et Miquelon, the Comoro Archipelago, Madagascar and dependencies, the French Somali Coast, New Caledonia and dependencies, the French Settlements in Oceania, the Southern and Antarctic Territories; the Autonomous Republic of Togoland; the French Trusteeship Territory in the Cameroons; the Belgian Congo and Ruanda-Urundi; the Italian Trusteeship Territory in Somaliland; and Netherlands New Guinea.

original association was limited to a five-year term because the member countries recognized that the dependent territories would want to negotiate treaties for themselves after they had achieved independence. When the original agreement expired in 1963, a new five-year association agreement, to take effect on July 1, 1964, was signed at Yaounde.

The nature of the association was not radically altered in the Yaounde Convention. The associated overseas countries (AOC's) obtain trade preferences and financial and technical aid from the EEC, and in return grant conditional trade preferences to the EEC. Exports from the AOC's to the metropolitan EEC countries receive the same treatment as other intra-Community exports and have thus shared in all the internal tariff reductions. In addition, the EEC immediately eliminated internal tariffs on some tropical products of special interest to the African countries.[5] Furthermore, the EEC promises funds for a transitional period to support the prices of certain commodity exports of the AOC's. These trade arrangements should not be thought of as totally new concessions to the African countries since, to some degree, they replace concessions previously granted by France to its African dependencies. The reciprocal concessions given by the AOC's to the EEC require them to reduce their tariffs against EEC products according to a prearranged schedule. The AOC's have been permitted, however, to maintain tariffs for fiscal purposes or to protect infant industries. It is hard to think of more permissive exceptions than these.[6] The AOC's are further required either to remove all quantitative restrictions to trade, or to generalize them so as not to favor one member country over another or any nonmember over a member. EEC enterprises are also granted certain favored rights of establishment within the AOC's. According to the letter of the Yaounde Convention, the AOC's can undermine the economic implications of the concessions to the EEC by forming new customs unions or free trade areas with other African countries.

The consequences of the association for trade can be seen in Table 6-2. The value of EEC imports from the AOC's increased between 1958 and 1965 by 32 percent, or at the unspectacular growth rate of 4.5 percent per year. This is substantially below the growth rate for all EEC imports and, perhaps more surprisingly, below the growth of EEC imports from nonassociated African countries. While these figures do not prove that as-

---

[5] Products include cocoa beans, coconuts, coffee, pineapples, tea, unground cloves, nutmeg, pepper, vanilla, and certain tropical woods.

[6] In view of these exceptions, it is questionable whether the association arrangement qualifies under the GATT exception to "most favored nation" treatment for customs unions or free trade areas.

TABLE 6-2

EEC Trade with Associated Overseas Countries and Nonassociated African Countries, 1958–65

(In millions of dollars)

Type of Trade and Area	1958	1959	1960	1961	1962	1963	1964	1965
Imports								
Associated overseas								
countries[a]	1,546	1,352	1,663	1,771	1,850	1,902	2,059	2,046
Algeria	473	354	549	663	756	666	703	665
Other	1,073	998	1,114	1,108	1,094	1,236	1,356	1,381
Nonassociated								
African countries[b]	1,048	1,121	1,158	1,160	1,302	1,610	1,939	2,196
Exports								
Associated overseas								
countries[a]	1,860	1,699	1,882	1,764	1,433	1,547	1,653	1,733
Algeria	1,012	991	1,130	917	586	585	539	564
Other	848	708	752	847	847	962	1,114	1,169
Nonassociated								
African countries[b]	941	980	1,212	1,151	1,148	1,287	1,324	1,523

Source: Statistical Office of the European Communities, *Foreign Trade Monthly Statistics, 1966*, No. 12 (Brussels, 1967).
[a] 1958–1962 includes Surinam and Netherlands Antilles, excludes West New Guinea.
[b] Class 2.

sociation has been meaningless from a trade point of view, they do suggest strongly that tariff preferences are not a panacea for all the ills confronting less developed countries in their efforts to expand international trade. Another aspect of the stagnating trade relations between the EEC and the AOC's is illustrated by the decline of EEC exports to the AOC's between 1958 and 1965, although there has been a steady recovery from the low point in 1962. In view of the rapid economic expansion experienced by the EEC countries during this period, the stagnation of trade can be traced to general economic developments within the AOC's themselves.

The stagnating trade relationship with the EEC has commanded the attention of the AOC's. Because of their criticism, a study was undertaken by the European Parliament.[7] The report issued at the conclusion of the

[7] A report was prepared by Georges Spenale, French Socialist member of the parliamentary committee for cooperation with developing countries and was presented to the Assembly in November 1965. The report was summarized in the publication of the Information Service of the European Community, *European Community Bulletin*, No. 90 (Washington, D.C., March 1966).

study discussed some of the factors which tended to hide the value of the trade stimulus coming from the association agreement. In the first place, much of the overall trade stagnation was due to the fact that the political turmoil in the Congo (Kinshasa) had interrupted its normal international trade. In normal times Congolese exports to the Community were almost 40 percent of the total. Second, the full advantage of the tariff preferences for African tropical products will not be felt until the external tariff wall is fully erected in mid-1968.

These factors cannot completely account for the observed situation. Even if the trade of the Congo were eliminated, the growth of exports to the EEC of the seventeen remaining associated countries would not match that of the nonassociated African countries. The AOC's point to two conditions which they believe limit their export growth to the Community. The first problem, as previously pointed out by a GATT study,[8] is that the excise taxes charged by many EEC countries on tropical products such as coffee seriously limit final demand for them. Member countries have so far been unwilling to reduce these charges. The second criticism voiced by the AOC's is that Germany has continued to import a very large share of its bananas from Latin America under a tariff-free quota authorized by the Rome Treaty.[9] Since the quota prevents trade diversion, it is highly desirable from the point of view of nonmember countries, but it does limit some of the advantages of association.

While all of these factors may be significant, general economic developments within the AOC's must still be held mainly responsible for the stagnation of trade. Because the AOC's previously had markets which were protected through their former metropole ties, increases in exports to the EEC had to come primarily from expanded production or reduced domestic absorption. The required expansion of supply potential has not developed fast enough to provide for more exports. Reducing barriers to trade is not enough. Aside from tropical goods, AOC products must compete in EEC markets with the domestic production of member countries and, therefore, productive efficiency is of prime importance. For this reason, only a slow growth of manufactured goods exports can be anticipated. As industrialization proceeds in the AOC's, the advantages of association will increase through the avoidance of the tariff discrimination that would otherwise occur.

[8] General Agreement on Tariffs and Trade, *Trends in International Trade* (Geneva, 1958).

[9] This was one of several such arrangements worked out so as not to disturb seriously the trading relations that member countries had before the Rome Treaty.

The United States and the EEC-AOC Association

There are both direct and indirect economic consequences for the United States in the association of African states with the Common Market. Since the United States is itself a producer and exporter of certain semitropical products such as cotton, tobacco, and oilseeds, the United States is in direct competition with the AOC's. For other tropical products such as coffee and cocoa several Latin American countries are major exporters to the EEC and thus compete with products from the AOC's. The United States becomes involved indirectly since the export earnings of the Latin American countries greatly determine their imports, which, to a large degree, come from the United States. Looking at the association from the other side, the United States is not likely to be greatly concerned on economic grounds with the preferences given by the African states to the EEC, since the United States has not been a major exporter to them. However, some U.S. direct investment may have been attracted to Europe to take advantage of these preferences. In general, the United States has supported efforts of developed countries to help less developed countries, but it has objected to having this stimulus to growth come at the expense of other less developed countries, particularly those in Latin America.

Traditionally, the United States has been a major supplier to the EEC of many semitropical products subject to direct competition from the AOC's. During the years 1958 to 1960, the United States supplied an average of 39 percent of EEC imports of raw tobacco, 37 percent of all imports of cotton, and 27 percent of EEC imports of vegetable fats and oils (mainly through oilseeds). The possible loss of this market to associated countries would depend in part on the height of the common external tariff (CXT). Because there were no European producers to protect, the CXT was set at very modest levels for some commodities, and duty-free entry was permitted for cotton and oilseeds. Thus, tariff discrimination has been small, and has not provided much incentive for trade diversion. Furthermore, in order to replace U.S. products in the market, the AOC's must build up supply potential, which they have not been able to do.

In Table 6-3, data on EEC imports of certain semitropical commodities are shown. The trend in individual commodity shares provided by the AOC's mirrors the aggregate trade totals fairly closely. The AOC shares have declined noticeably for all products except fats and oils (not in-

TABLE 6-3

EEC Imports of Selected Semitropical Commodities,
Selected Years, 1958–65

(Dollar amounts in millions)

Commodity and Year	Total Imports	Imports from Associated Overseas Countries	
		Value	*Percent of Total Imports*
Tobacco			
1958	$216	$ 15	*6.8*
1959	205	10	*5.1*
1963	313	8	*2.6*
1964	331	9	*2.8*
1965	333	7	*2.2*
Cotton			
1958	661	54	*8.1*
1959	549	49	*9.0*
1963	641	36	*5.6*
1964	666	36	*5.4*
1965	576	28	*4.9*
Oilseeds			
1958	478	141	*29.4*
1959	502	119	*23.7*
1963	601	100	*16.6*
1964	668	96	*14.4*
1965	705	87	*12.4*
Fats and oils			
1958	372	87	*23.4*
1959	401	83	*20.8*
1963	472	84	*17.8*
1964	455	100	*21.9*
1965	522	94	*18.1*

Source: Statistical Office of the European Communities, *Foreign Trade Statistics, 1958* (Brussels, 1958) and subsequent annual issues.

cluding oilseeds). While the CXT on fats and oils does not appear particularly high—generally 10 percent—the real protective effect of the tariff is very large, because the value added in processing oil from oilseeds is small and oilseeds enter duty-free. This protection may be aiding AOC exports. However, U.S. exports are at a disadvantage mainly because they must compete with domestic EEC vegetable-oil producers. The addition of AOC competition cannot be very serious. For the other products there is no evidence of trade diversion. This has not, however, guaranteed the United States its traditional position in EEC markets. If its competitive position deteriorates as it has in cotton and tobacco, then the United States will suffer. If, on the other hand, the United States has an ample supply of a commodity at a competitive price, soybeans, for example, and there is no tariff barrier, then U.S. exports can expand and capture a larger share of the market.

The indirect economic effects of the AOC's on the United States are somewhat harder to appraise. From the start of the association arrangement, the Latin American countries and the nonassociated African countries have been very concerned over their future markets in the EEC.[10] While most attention has been directed to coffee and cocoa, other products including tea, bananas, and tropical woods have been examined. The Latin Americans were particularly concerned with the possibility that the AOC's would displace their coffee exports to Europe. The result would be an accumulation of unsold stocks because of the general condition of excess coffee supplies in the world. This would cause a loss of foreign exchange earnings and subsequently reduce Latin American imports from the United States. The Latin Americans were among the first to send diplomatic representatives to Brussels to make their concern known to the members. In recognition of the economic importance of coffee and cocoa, and because of the intense displeasure of nonassociated suppliers, the EEC reduced the CXT on coffee from 16 percent to 9 percent and on cocoa from 9 percent to 5 percent. Trade in tropical products between the EEC and the AOC's, as seen in Table 6-4, follows the pattern already observed. The AOC's saw their share of EEC imports of coffee and bananas decline somewhat, but they were able to increase their share of EEC imports in the cocoa market.

The Nigerian Association

The African ties of the EEC were expanded in an important way through the negotiation of a separate association with Nigeria in 1966. Nigeria is the first African country to become associated that had not previously

[10] Economic Commission for Latin America, *Economic Bulletin for Latin America,* Vol. III, No. 1 (Santiago, March 1958), pp. 9-50.

TABLE 6-4

EEC Imports of Selected Tropical Commodities, Selected Years, 1958–65

(Dollar amounts in millions)

Commodity and Year	Total Imports	Imports from Associated Overseas Countries		Imports from Latin America	
		Value	Percent of Total Imports	Value	Percent of Total Imports
Bananas					
1958	$163	$ 93	56.8	$ 67	41.1
1959	141	70	49.9	63	45.0
1961	159	84	52.9	70	43.8
1962	164	90	54.5	67	40.7
1963	175	97	55.6	70	39.9
1964	167	80	48.1	78	47.0
1965	244	125	51.3	108	44.3
Coffee					
1958	563	164	29.0	300	53.2
1959	507	122	24.0	294	58.1
1961	508	118	23.3	304	59.8
1962	516	122	23.6	315	61.1
1963	526	125	23.8	315	59.9
1964	667	167	25.1	382	57.2
1965	690	138	20.0	420	61.0
Cocoa					
1958	233	82	35.3	39	16.8
1959	240	70	29.2	36	15.2
1961	199	62	31.2	25	12.7
1962	195	65	33.3	21	10.6
1963	208	80	38.2	15	7.4
1964	218	83	38.2	17	7.7
1965	198	83	42.0	13	6.7

Source: Statistical Office of the European Communities, *Foreign Trade Statistics*.

had a colonial relationship to a member country. It is also the most popu-
lous country in Africa, with substantial economic and political importance
on that continent and beyond. The association grew out of Britain's abortive attempt to join the Common Market in 1962-63. During those negotiations, Britain tried to convince her Commonwealth partners in Africa
that their trading interests would be protected through association with an
expanded Community. While Nigeria, along with Ghana, rejected the idea
at that time, many Nigerians were convinced that association with the
EEC was worthwhile whether or not Britain joined. Thus in September

1963, Nigeria requested the opening of discussions which eventually led to association.

The Nigerians had several economic and political motives for associating with the EEC. First of all, they were particularly concerned over the tariff discrimination faced by their traditional exports to the Common Market—cocoa, oil and oilseeds, and tropical hardwood—compared to competitive products coming from the AOC's. As seen in Table 6-5, Ni-

TABLE 6-5

Trade of Nigeria, Selected Years, 1958–65

(Dollar amounts in millions)

Year	Imports			Exports		
	Total	From EEC		Total	To EEC	
		Value	*Percent of Total Imports*		Value	*Percent of Total Exports*
1958	$467	$ 85	*18.2*	$380	$118	*31.1*
1959	503	93	*18.5*	458	156	*34.1*
1962	568	110	*19.4*	472	159	*33.9*
1963	581	126	*21.7*	531	195	*36.7*
1964	712	165	*23.2*	601	215	*35.8*
1965	766	191	*24.9*	750	271	*36.1*

Source: U.N., *Commodity Trade Statistics*, Series D, Vol. VIII (New York, 1959) and subsequent years.

geria was relying increasingly on the EEC market, and it wanted to be assured of continued access. Second, Nigeria hoped to become the industrial leader of black Africa and looked to the EEC and the AOC's as natural export markets. Third, the Nigerians thought that through the association they might obtain some of the development aid distributed by the Overseas Investment Fund of the EEC. Among political considerations, the Nigerians hoped that their relationships with the former French states in Africa would improve with association. The economic division of Europe has been mirrored in Africa, since most commerce has been between the African states and their former European metropole countries. Nigeria has long desired the development of pan-Africanism for both political and economic reasons, and saw its association with the EEC as a way of developing closer ties with the AOC's. As a counterweight to these motives, some Nigerians were fearful that economic association might involve too close a political relationship with Europe and undermine the nation's professed foreign policy of nonalignment.[11]

The motives of the member countries for wanting Nigeria to become associated with the EEC were also a mixture of economics and politics. For five members (other than France), an African association seemed to offer, for the first time, some prospect of economic gain. Nigeria is an expanding and lucrative market by African standards, and EEC exports could gain through tariff concessions granted by Nigeria. This gain would come primarily at the expense of the United Kingdom, which has benefited in the past from Commonwealth preferences. Some political advantage was seen in opening the Community to many less developed countries, not just the ones that happened to be former dependencies. Such a step would also relieve the EEC from the charge of being a barrier to pan-Africanism. France also had political motives in supporting the association, viewing it as a means of spreading French influence over the English-speaking parts of Africa. On the other hand, the French ran some political risk in supporting Nigerian association, as their ties to the existing AOC's could be weakened by granting EEC status to a major competitor of the AOC's.

The substance of the association agreement negotiated between Nigeria and the EEC did not satisfy all of the objectives of either side in the short run. While Nigeria obtained Community status for many of its exports, the four products of particular concern to it—cocoa beans, peanut oil, palm oil, and plywood—were treated as exceptions. Under a quota system, only a limited amount of these products is allowed duty-free entrance. The quotas have been set at current levels of trade with only a modest allowance for future growth. Thus, the existing AOC exports are protected from severe Nigerian competition. Also, Nigeria is not to receive any development assistance under the agreement.

Nigeria, for its part, granted only limited tariff concessions to the EEC. On twenty-six products of relatively minor importance, EEC exports receive customs preferences of 2 to 10 percent. Even on these products Nigeria may impose quantitative restrictions if required for development or for the balance of payments. Nigeria is obliged to treat EEC commerce and enterprises in a nondiscriminatory manner under a number of circumstances. The agreement provides for an Association Council for

[11] Claude S. Philips, Jr., *The Development of Nigerian Foreign Policy* (Northwestern University Press, 1964).

Administration and will continue in operation only until May 31, 1969. Subsequently the Nigerian Association and the Yaounde Convention of the AOC's can be brought into harmony, since they both expire on the same day and presumably will be jointly renegotiated.

The U.S. Interest in the Nigerian Association

In view of the rather limited economic importance of the association, the amount of U.S. hostility aroused by the agreement may be somewhat surprising. Both the United States and Great Britain objected strenuously while the details of the Nigerian Association were being worked out. On the economic side, this extension of regionalism does not appear desirable from the point of view of the United States. The association of Nigeria introduces a new preference scheme to the disadvantage of U.S. exports rather than liberalizing an existing preferential agreement, as was the case with the original AOC agreement. The preferential arrangement is clearly not covered by the GATT exemption for free trade areas, and therefore is another element weakening the "most favored nation" principle in international trade. Also, the association of Nigeria will put increased competitive pressure on the remaining nonassociated less developed countries such as Ghana, which are poorly equipped to deal with it.

The United States feels that the political implications of the agreement are undesirable. The association portends the development of "sphere of influence" diplomacy or neocolonialism, with continental Europe staking out Africa as its own preserve. Again, this association differs from the original AOC agreement in that metropole influence was already dominant in those countries. While the United States is not convinced that the influence of France in its former dependencies is in the U.S. interest, it has not been in any position to challenge French leadership or to accept the burdens which leadership requires. On the other hand, Nigeria as a member of the Commonwealth seemed to have found its place in the world and the association agreement may be a step backward from political maturity, a step which could bring with it a more hostile attitude toward the United States. This could lead to another outbreak of anticolonial extremism, which would increase the instability of international relations.

Two significant counterarguments to the political objections noted above must be considered in making an overall evaluation. It could be argued that a much greater danger to U.S. interests than the spread of continental European influence in Africa would be the further develop-

...

ment of European provincialism—a refusal to accept any responsibilities outside their own continent. Interest in Africa, after all, does broaden Europe's horizon, and identification of European interests with those of Africa may lead some day to concern for Latin America and even Asia. The ambivalent position of the United States on this point reflects the leader-partner conflict long evidenced in other aspects of U.S. foreign policy. The second argument concerns the question of political instability in less developed countries. While the formation of regional ties between developed and less developed countries may add to potential instability in the LDC's, it also may reduce the instability that already exists. The image of Nigeria as an evolving nonviolent democracy has been fully shattered by its civil war. The EEC association may be too unimportant to cool passionate tribal conflicts, but it does act in the direction of holding the country together by increasing the gains to be derived from maintaining a large cohesive unit. A potential source of instability is present in the further "balkanization" of Africa and the association with the EEC works against this tendency.

Other Possible African-EEC Associations

Two other groups of possible African associations with the EEC need to be mentioned: the Mahgreb countries, and the English-speaking East African countries. The Mahgreb countries (Morocco, Algeria, and Tunisia) are in a position similar to the original AOC's in that each of them benefits from preferences granted bilaterally by France. If the customs union principle is to be kept intact, these bilateral arrangements must be superseded by EEC agreements or ended completely. They were not provided for in the Rome Treaty, as were the AOC's, because Tunisia and Morocco had already become independent states and Algeria was still an overseas department of France, whose eventual independence was not officially anticipated. However, a declaration indicating the willingness of the EEC to negotiate association agreements with independent nations of the French franc area was attached to the Rome Treaty, and this invitation was subsequently accepted by the Mahgreb countries.

The EEC-Mahgreb negotiations have not been concluded for a number of reasons. The Council of Ministers of the EEC invariably finds it difficult to reach a unanimous decision when an issue before it is of greater interest to one member (in this case France) than to the others. The other members are likely to withhold agreement until adequately compensated by the interested member. This means that the granting of a negotiating mandate by the Council to the Commission is always confused with other matters. This is particularly onerous because numerous sequential decisions by the Council are required to bring the negotiation to fruition. Also, the other member countries have not been in any hurry to accept the "Frenchman's burden" in North Africa. They had no choice with respect to the original AOC's, since France insisted upon an agreement as a condition for signing the Rome Treaty. But, for the Mahgreb, they made no such binding promise, and feel no pressure for immediate agreement. The Italians, furthermore, have a special reason for not wanting to see an immediate association. The Mahgreb countries produce citrus fruit, wine, and vegetables that compete directly with Italian output. The Italians insist that the proposed Mahgreb association be considered part of a general policy for Mediterranean countries (including Spain and Israel) in which Italy's special interests would be recognized and protected. Finally, the relations between France and the Mahgreb countries have not always permitted negotiations, and the relations between Germany and the Mahgreb countries have been strained as a result of the recent Arab-Israeli war. For these reasons negotiations have languished.

The proposed association between the EEC and the East African countries of Kenya, Uganda, and Tanzania is similar to the Nigerian association in that it grew out of the breakdown of negotiations between the United Kingdom and the EEC. If concluded, it will probably be patterned after the Nigerian agreement. East Africa began exploratory talks with the EEC at about the same time as Nigeria, but negotiations were shunted aside until the Nigerian agreement was reached. The Council has given the Commission a mandate to negotiate and no insuperable barrier to agreement is known to exist. Once the EEC proved that an association was possible with an English-speaking Commonwealth country, however, the pressure for further agreements seemed to abate. It would no doubt be desirable to conclude the negotiations before the expiration of the Yaounde Convention, but no other deadline is apparent.

Along with the prospects for further EEC-African association agreements, it is necessary to examine the possibility that the trend will be in the opposite direction. Even the original AOC's are associated by an agreement with a limited life and it is possible that one of the periodic renewals will not succeed. Intuition suggests that the probability is small, but certainly not zero. As noted before, from the point of view of the AOC's, the association has not worked out as well as anticipated. Trade with the EEC did not expand appreciably even when association was fairly exclusive and the CXT was fairly high. Now that more countries are being allowed to associate and the CXT has been reduced, the weak stimulus of the trade preferences will probably be even further diluted. While the AOC's have benefited from the aid granted under the Yaounde Convention, the risk that development aid will be completely terminated is small. World pressures will force the Europeans into giving aid, and the African countries are natural recipients of their aid. The political leaders of the AOC's might also see some benefit in converting their relationships with the advanced countries of Europe from one of obvious dependency to a more subtle one between apparent equals. The existing association does provide a would-be demagogue with a plausible argument of neocolonialism and, if the economic benefits of association are not clearly observable to the populace, a disruptive opposition might become popular.

The member countries still have reservations about the advantages of continuing the EEC-African association. Germany, in particular, has publicly expressed its position. While agreeing to the 1964 renewal of the association, Dr. Gerhard Schroeder, then Minister for Foreign Affairs, indicated that Germany considered the association a special sacrifice on its part, since Germany had certain reservations "both on the basis of its own interest or lack of special interest in continuing ties based on the past and because the Treaty's drawback is that it brings out again dividing lines in Africa which have been considered out of date."[12] The member countries could possibly gain a great deal of influence in international relations if they generalized the trade preferences of association to all less developed countries as suggested at the first United Nations Conference on Trade and Development. This would, of course, effectively end special African associations. Even France could become disenchanted with the association if it were forced to make continual concessions to its EEC partners as a price for the periodic renewals. While none of the above suggests that the associations are doomed, their continuation can certainly not be taken for granted.

[12] *European Community Bulletin,* No. 63, June 1963, p. 5.

The U.S. Interest in Changing
African-EEC Associations

The United States has many and conflicting interests in the associations between African and European states. From the economic point of view, the United States would benefit if those discriminations were ended which favor African over Latin American commodities in the EEC market, and EEC over U.S. products in the African markets. But the United States does not wish to assume the burden of development aid now assumed by the EEC in Africa. Viewing these associations politically, the United States would like to see a reduction of political instability in Africa with a corresponding maturing of indigenous leadership, but it is not clear whether that goal is furthered or retarded through association. On the institutional side, the United States sees a danger in the proliferation of special councils that administer EEC agreements with other countries (AOC, Nigeria, Greece, and Turkey). The awkwardness of the procedures which these multiple arrangements cause when, for instance, tariff negotiations are conducted with the EEC, may substantially affect the ability of the EEC to have a flexible policy vis-à-vis nonmembers. However, the institutional structure could be improved by uniting the several African associations into a single entity.

There may be a more deep-seated reason why the United States should be interested in a continuation and expansion of the EEC association with African countries. It can be argued that only a highly emotional conflict could ever lead to use of nuclear weapons, since a rational calculation would indicate that there would be no victors after a nuclear exchange. Such emotions could arise if political differences corresponded to divisions along racial or religious lines. All multinational agreements which create an identity of interests among peoples of different races can therefore be considered as desirable for world peace. Technological advances in the future will make possible the development of nuclear weapons in today's less developed countries. Future peace may depend on how well the foundations for international relations are prepared today. It is an open question, of course, whether the EEC-AOC association is the best of all possible types of multiracial ties between Europe and Africa, but the existence of some kind of tie seems highly desirable.

EEC Agreements with European Countries

The EEC has made some effort to ease the problems of intra-European trade that were caused by its own creation. Articles 237 and 238 of the Rome Treaty are both available to European countries which desire an institutional connection with the Community. It was anticipated that Article 237 (full membership) would be the favored vehicle, but this has not been the case. Only Greece and Turkey have been able to complete a successful negotiation with the EEC, and in both cases the special provisions of Article 238 were employed. Greece applied for association in June 1959, an agreement was signed in July 1961, and the association became effective in November 1962. Turkey applied for association in July 1959, but did not reach agreement with the EEC until June 1963 (signed in September). This became effective in December 1964.

The Greek and Turkish associations, while similar, do have important differences. They both take the form of a customs union, viewed as a transitional stage toward full membership. In the Greek case, customs duties were scheduled to be abolished over a twelve-year period, with the member countries giving Greek products immediate Community status. Greece, however, was allowed some exceptions from the timetable for certain strategic products, representing about one-third of Greek imports from the EEC. Tariffs on these goods would be reduced over a period of twenty-two years. Greece was also allowed to institute temporary new duties or raise existing ones on EEC products if needed to protect infant industries. Agriculture was treated separately, with Greece accepting the obligation to harmonize its policies with the Common Agricultural Policy (CAP) over twenty-two years. In recognition of the great importance of agriculture to the Greek economy in general, and to Greek export receipts in particular, the EEC immediately extended duty benefits already in operation among the members, and lowered tariffs ahead of schedule on the crucial Greek products, tobacco and raisins. But it insisted upon safeguards against Greek products that are competitive with member country products such as citrus fruit, table grapes, peaches, and wine.

Other aspects of the Rome Treaty were incorporated into the agreement with Greece. Free movement of workers was provided for, but only at the end of the twelve-year transition period. Schedules were also drawn up for the development of the free right of establishment and the right to supply services. Capital market restrictions were also to be eliminated. Furthermore, $125 million from the European Investment Bank was set aside for loans to Greece during the first five years and a continuation of the program was implied.

Greece was given special treatment because of the relatively underdeveloped state of its economy compared with the member countries. The contrast in development is even greater with respect to Turkey. The Turkish-EEC agreement provides for three distinct stages in the association, the last two (transitional period and the definitive phase) paralleling the Greek agreement. The first stage or preparatory phase was scheduled to last five years. Its purpose is to promote Turkish economic development with EEC aid so that Turkey will be able to make the adjustments involved in forming a customs union without disruption. Turkish exports are to be stimulated by trade preferences such as tariff quotas on tobacco, raisins, dried figs, and nuts, products which represent 37 percent of Turkish exports to the EEC. Other trade-promoting concessions may be subsequently added. During this phase, Turkey will also receive financial assistance of $175 million from the European Investment Bank. Other aspects

TABLE 6-6

Trade of Greece and Turkey, Selected Years, 1958–65

(Dollar amounts in millions)

Country and Year		Imports				Exports				
		From EEC		From United States			To EEC		To United States	
	Total	Value	Percent of Total Imports	Value	Percent of Total Imports	Total	Value	Percent of Total Exports	Value	Percent of Total Exports
Greece										
1958	$ 565	$241	42.7	$ 78	13.8	$232	$ 98	42.2	$ 32	13.8
1959	564	215	38.1	59	10.5	204	81	39.7	26	12.8
1962	701	304	43.4	67	9.6	248	89	35.9	19	7.7
1963	804	320	39.8	85	10.6	290	95	32.8	55	19.0
1964	885	375	42.4	101	11.4	309	116	37.5	45	14.6
1965	1,134	469	41.4	113	10.0	328	122	37.2	31	9.5
Turkey										
1958	315	102	32.4	88	27.9	247	86	34.8	48	19.4
1959	442	157	35.5	96	21.7	354	140	39.5	63	17.8
1962	622	188	30.2	181	29.1	381	154	40.4	75	19.7
1963	691	197	28.5	212	30.7	368	140	38.0	50	13.6
1964	542	156	28.8	156	28.8	411	138	33.6	73	17.8
1965	577	164	28.4	162	28.1	459	155	33.8	82	17.9

Source: U.N., *Commodity Trade Statistics.*

TABLE 6-7

Selected Commodity Exports of Greece and Turkey to EEC as Percentage of Total Exports of Those Commodities, Selected Years, 1957–65

Country and Commodity	1957	1958	1959	1964	1965
Greece					
Tobacco	52.4	45.3	44.7	39.3	41.2
Cotton	49.5	38.3	44.3	17.7	6.0
Fats and oils	45.5	31.6	65.3	—	18.7
Oilseeds	95.5	62.9	48.8	—	46.6
Turkey					
Tobacco	15.8	17.6	16.7	14.2	12.1
Cotton	79.2	74.4	64.6	43.5	34.4
Fats and oils	—	—	—	76.3	58.7
Oilseeds	16.1	24.7	29.4	18.3	21.2
Coarse grains	54.4	88.1	79.0	54.2	48.4

Sources: U. N., *Commodity Trade Statistics;* Organization for Economic Cooperation and Development, *Trade by Commodities*, Series C (Paris, 1966).

of association will be considered during the first phase but will not come into operation until the customs union is formed. From that point on, the Turkish and Greek associations would be identical. Special EEC-Turkish and EEC-Greek Association Councils are provided to administer the respective association agreements.

It is too early to appraise the consequences of the agreements for the participating countries. As seen in Tables 6-6 and 6-7, a substantial portion of total Greek and Turkish trade, and an overwhelming portion of their trade in some strategic products, is with the EEC. These countries obviously had strong defensive reasons for joining the Common Market. But the strongest attraction must surely have been the prospects for developing new large-scale manufacturing industries to serve the entire European market. However, the trade figures thus far show no sign that the agreements have been effective. While this was fully expected with respect to Turkey because of the time factor, the Greek result is more surprising. In 1958 and 1959, Greece sent roughly 40 percent of all its exports to the EEC and by 1964-65 this figure had declined slightly to about 37 percent. Neither do the import figures indicate a rising trend. While some dissatisfaction over these results has been expressed by Greek observers, in all fairness it must be emphasized that sufficient time to make an appraisal has not elapsed.

The U.S. Interest in the Greek and Turkish Associations

The United States has the same general interest in the expansion of the EEC to include Greece and Turkey that it has in the inclusion of other countries. The area of potential tariff discrimination against U.S. exports has been widened. While Greece and Turkey are not major recipients of U.S. exports, their markets are not inconsequential. Roughly $65 million of U.S. exports went to Greece in 1958-59, and this grew to $105 million by 1964-65. The corresponding increase for Turkey was from $90 million to $160 million. Shipments to both countries include those financed by U.S. aid. A substantial reduction in these exports would, therefore, have a noticeable effect on the U.S. balance of payments unless matched by a reduction in aid-grants. In the EEC market, Greek and Turkish exports are more a potential than an actual threat to U.S. exports. The United States does export a significant amount of tobacco to the EEC, but it is generally of a different variety than that coming from the associates. In fact the United States itself is a major importer of Greek and Turkish tobaccos for use in blending with milder U.S. varieties. Greek and Turkish cotton exports are directly competitive with U.S. products but with the common external tariff at zero, no tariff discrimination is involved. Turkish coarse grain exports could be a threat, but agricultural production in Turkey must increase tremendously before the impact would be felt in the United States. The general overall direct competitive effect, therefore, is likely to be slight.

The United States has a special interest in Greece and Turkey. Ever since 1948, when the Truman Doctrine was announced, the United States has assumed the responsibility, once shouldered by Great Britain, of maintaining stability in this geographically crucial part of Europe. In practice, this has meant a large outpouring of U.S. money for economic and military aid to these countries. The United States has also maintained a military presence in Turkey for the protection of Europe and the United States from Soviet incursions. Association of these countries with the EEC has had an important effect on the economic side of this commitment. Greece was one of the first recipients of U.S. aid after the war and has had an uninterrupted record of such receipts up to recent years. Yet, after association, the U.S. economic aid program began to taper off, and by 1965 the United States was making no new economic assistance commitments to Greece. The graduation of Greece from the list

of economic aid recipients no doubt resulted primarily from the substantial amount of economic progress achieved in that country, but the
fact that the EEC had accepted responsibility for Greece did relieve the
United States from the fear that Greece would be left entirely to its own
devices. Nor is it entirely coincidential that the current economic aid program in Turkey is expected to terminate at about the time that Turkey
enters the second stage of its association agreement. This expectation may
not be realized, but the two events are likely to occur simultaneously or
not at all. The United States must, therefore, look upon the increase in
commitments by the Continental European powers to the less developed
European nations as a desirable trend.

Future Possibilities of EEC
Expansion in Europe

The fact that no other European country has joined the EEC as a full
member has not been due to a lack of effort. On August 10, 1961, after
much deliberation, the United Kingdom applied for full membership to
the Community. The other members of EFTA (except Portugal) quickly
followed suit. Denmark applied for full membership on the same day as
the United Kingdom and Norway applied somewhat later. Because of
their neutrality status, Austria, Sweden, and Switzerland applied only for
association. In addition, Ireland applied for full membership (July 31,
1961) and Spain sought association (February 9, 1962). The British
negotiations with the EEC, which were terminated by a de Gaulle veto on
January 14, 1963, have received much attention in current literature and
little can be gained for present purposes by reviewing that diplomatic history.[13] However, these abortive negotiations did lead to further EEC-
African ties, and may possibly lead to an association with Austria.

When the Rome Treaty was being negotiated in 1956-57, Austrian
government officials expressed the belief that the Austrian State Treaty
would not permit them to take part because of the degree of suprana-
tionalism involved. For its neutrality to be meaningful, a neutral must be
able to disengage its economy from that of any combatant. This was not

[13] See Nora Beloff, *The General Says No* (Penguin Books, 1963); and Miriam
Camps, *Britain and the European Community, 1955-1963* (Princeton University
Press, 1964).

TABLE 6-8

*Trade of EFTA Countries with EEC as Percentage of
Total Trade, 1959–65*

Type of Trade and Country	1959	1960	1961	1962	1963	1964	1965
Imports							
Austria	57	57	60	59	58	59	59
Denmark	37	39	40	39	37	36	37
Finland	32	34	34	35	30	30	31
Norway	35	33	32	31	30	29	29
Portugal	39	38	38	37	35	33	35
Sweden	41	40	40	41	39	37	38
Switzerland	60	61	63	63	64	62	62
United Kingdom	14	15	15	16	16	17	17
Exports							
Austria	49	50	50	50	50	48	47
Denmark	30	28	28	27	28	27	26
Finland	27	28	31	29	30	31	28
Norway	26	26	25	27	27	26	25
Portugal	23	22	22	23	22	21	21
Sweden	31	32	33	33	32	32	31
Switzerland	40	41	42	42	42	41	40
United Kingdom	15	15	17	20	21	21	20

Sources: EFTA, *EFTA Trade, 1959–64;* OECD, *Trade by Commodities.*

thought to be possible for a member of the Common Market. The Russians also seemed to be of this opinion and since the military occupation had just ended (1956) the Austrians were in no mood to upset the existing calm. Austria participated in the formation of EFTA, however, as other neutrals were also to be members, and agriculture was not to be fully integrated.

Judged by purely economic considerations, Austria belongs in the EEC and not in EFTA. As seen in Table 6-8, 60 percent of its imports and 50 percent of its exports are with the EEC. This is natural in view of Austria's landlocked geographical position bordering both Germany and Italy. None of the EFTA countries would have gained more than Austria from the enlargement of the EEC that was contemplated in 1961. When that enlargement failed, Austria decided it would attempt to negotiate its own association with the EEC and this was done with the full backing of the other EFTA countries. The Austria-EEC negotiations reached approximately the halfway point by the end of 1966. Many difficulties still exist because of the neutrality issue and because of incidents in the Alto Adigio area of Italy, but there appears to be a genuine desire on both sides to reach agreement.

Other EFTA countries have also indicated a strong desire to renew attempts to end the EEC-EFTA division of Europe. On several occasions, EFTA has made overtures to the EEC to begin some sort of direct dialogue over trade problems, but nothing has resulted. More recently, Denmark has indicated that a Scandinavian or Nordic initiative to the EEC may be in order. Referring again to Table 6-8, all of the Nordic countries conduct a third of their trade with the EEC and, therefore, have a great interest in this matter. Denmark feels particularly threatened because so many of its exports to the EEC are temperate-zone agricultural products covered by the CAP. As indicated in Chapter 3, the CAP is the most protectionist aspect of EEC policy, and Denmark is the country most directly concerned. Unlike Austria, however, Denmark could not consider a bilateral agreement with the EEC that would require it to sever its ties to EFTA. As indicated previously, the industrial sector of the Danish economy is closely linked to the rest of Scandinavia, and Danish agriculture depends on the United Kingdom as much as on the EEC for a market. Therefore Denmark's problem with the EEC will require a much more sweeping solution than in the case of Austria. In a speech before the Council of Europe in September 1966, Danish Prime Minister Otto Krag indicated that Denmark views agreement with the EEC as an urgent problem and suggested that a search for a solution should begin immediately.

In 1966 there was a renewal of speculation that Britain might make another bid for membership in the EEC and in May 1967 a formal application was submitted. The desire to join arose from the belief that Britain's economic difficulties could either be overcome or greatly reduced through membership. However, there was no indication that French objections to British entry had lessened. In fact, the French kept insisting that Britain must put its "economic house in order" before membership could even be considered. While eventual membership for Britain cannot be ruled out, there appears to be little prospect for immediate action. If previous negotiations with the EEC are any criterion, such a complicated question as British entry would take two to four years to negotiate, with success not certain until the agreement was ratified by every parliament involved.

U.S. Interest in an Enlarged EEC

The United States position on the possible enlargement of the EEC to include the EFTA countries is well-known. President Kennedy was a strong supporter of British entry into the EEC along with the other members of EFTA. American support has not wavered despite the de Gaulle veto in 1963 and the problems that have subsequently developed in the North Atlantic Treaty Organization (NATO). The reasons for this position can be traced back to the original American thinking on European integration in the early postwar period.[14] Ending the EEC-EFTA split would strengthen the economies of all countries in Europe and set the stage for a possibly enduring detente with Eastern Europe and the Soviet Union. These political objectives were thought to override the economic difficulties the United States would suffer as a result of the union (examined briefly in Chapter 7). However, if Britain were required to assume an anti-American stance in its foreign policy as a price for admission to the EEC, the United States might not obtain the political gains now anticipated.

The U.S. position concerning a partial absorption of EFTA by the EEC has not been officially presented. No doubt the special political situation of Austria and the fact that little U.S. trade is directly involved suggest that the United States would benefit indirectly by an EEC-Austria association. But even this association raises some difficulties for Switzerland and, indirectly, for other countries. If Austria became part of the EEC, Switzerland would be completely surrounded by countries discriminating against its products. If this were serious enough to cause a decline in confidence in the Swiss economy, then the ability of Switzerland to perform its unique banking function in international finance would be impaired and world capital markets would suffer. Under these circumstances, the United States would be affected directly and adversely. The EEC could, of course, make a special arrangement for Switzerland, but there seems to be no inclination to do this, nor are the Swiss likely to request it.

It would not appear to be in the interest of the United States for most of the EFTA countries, excluding Great Britain, to make separate agreements with the EEC. In that case the political gains from an enlarged

[14] See Chap. 1, pp. 25 ff.

EEC might not be forthcoming and the economic difficulties would be greater. Britain would feel the economic discrimination very severely and the United States might have to assume further burdens in its role as world banker and military protector of the free world. One might argue that, with the Scandinavian countries and Austria on the inside, the EEC would be much more receptive to a bid by Britain to join. But quick admission for the United Kingdom would have to be assured to make it worthwhile to take the risks involved.

EEC Commercial Agreements
with Other Countries

Consistent with the logic of a customs union, Chapter 3 of the Rome Treaty (Articles 110-116) directed the member countries to harmonize their existing bilateral commercial treaties with other countries so that by the end of the transition period all treaties would be entered into by the EEC as a whole.[15] A procedure was also provided by which the Community itself could negotiate new commercial agreements with nonmember countries. The EEC is limited in bilateral treaty negotiations for tariff reductions because of the GATT commitment to grant "most-favored-nation" treatment to all GATT members.[16] Requiring general rather than preferential tariff reductions would naturally inhibit the EEC from entering into tariff treaties except as part of a multilateral GATT negotiation.

Nevertheless the EEC has entered into bilateral commercial agreements with Iran, Israel, and Lebanon. After Greece became an associate and it appeared that Turkey was sure to follow, the Iranians became concerned over the prospects for some of their traditional exports which competed with goods from those countries. Informal talks began in the summer of 1962, formal talks were opened on May 6, 1963, and an agreement was initialed on September 25, 1963. The agreement is limited in scope and to two years in time, but is automatically renewable. It calls for a temporary nondiscriminatory reduction of the CXT and a reduction of tariff quotas on carpets, caviar, dried grapes, and apricots.

[15] Detailed analysis of this aspect of the EEC is found in Isaiah Frank, *The European Common Market, An Analysis of Commercial Policy* (Praeger, 1961).

[16] All of the EEC countries were members of GATT before they formed the Common Market.

Israel sought a more basic agreement with the EEC and actually suggested association, but the EEC would consider only a commercial treaty. Formal talks began on November 26, 1962 (before those with Iran), but agreement proved to be quite difficult. Israel wanted an agreement to cover most of its exports, but the EEC offered tariff and quota concessions only on bathing suits, some kinds of fertilizer, and grapefruit (but not on oranges). Final agreement was not reached until May 1964. While the agreement is broader than first proposed by the EEC, it is still very limited. The three-year agreement provides for temporary tariff reductions ranging from 10 to 40 percent of the CXT rates on twenty-one products. Furthermore, the member countries whose tariffs were above CXT rates on some 283 products of special interest to Israel immediately reduced them to the CXT level. In compensation, Israel declared its intention to increase its trade with the EEC.

The trade agreement between the EEC and Lebanon is even more limited. Talks were begun on May 13, 1964, and an agreement was initialed on March 10, 1965. It calls for the mutual granting of "most-favored-nation" treatment, made necessary by the fact that Lebanon is not a member of GATT. It provides for a coordination of technical assistance by the member countries to Lebanon and has a protocol for oranges, but no specific concessions are included.

Little can be said in appraisal of these agreements. They are very narrow in conception and international trade will not be greatly affected by them. Israel has expressed some disappointment over the results and has revived its interest in forming an association with the EEC. No immediate action on this proposal is foreseen. Probably the most important implication of these agreements comes from the fact that they were negotiated by the Commission for the entire Community, and this adds slightly to the stature of the Commission. However, the time required to reach agreements of such limited scope underlines the difficulties involved in negotiating with the EEC.

Of greater concern are the trading relations between member countries and Eastern European countries, which have been regulated by bilateral agreements since the end of the war. According to the Rome Treaty, these must become Community-wide agreements by the end of the transition phase, but little progress has been made. The Commission has shown particular interest in harmonizing these bilateral agreements not only to protect the integrity of the Rome Treaty, but also to gain recognition of the EEC as an entity by the Communist bloc. Practically all countries except

those of the Communist bloc and some Arab countries have recognized the
EEC and set up diplomatic missions in Brussels. Nikita Khrushchev, when
Premier, denounced the EEC, and official Russian policy has never been
reversed. The EEC even offered to reduce the CXT on vodka, caviar, and
canned crab in return for Soviet recognition, but the offer was not accepted.

Nor have the member countries been in any hurry to coordinate their
own bilateral trade agreements. A great deal of diplomatic negotiation is
required to draft a commercial treaty with a communist country, and the
member countries have been unwilling to give up national sovereignty
over this aspect of their foreign policies. Until early 1967, Germany had
no diplomatic representation, other than commercial missions, in Eastern
Europe (except in the Soviet Union and Rumania). Shortly after the start
of the EEC, the member countries were encouraged to include a safeguard
clause in their treaties to the effect that the bilateral arrangements could
be superseded by an agreement with the Community as a whole, and some
were negotiated. In April 1964, the Council of Ministers approved a program to coordinate the bilateral agreements, but little forward progress
has been made, and some backsliding may have occurred when the safeguard clause was dropped.

The economic pressures for coordination that were anticipated when
the Rome Treaty was drafted have been building up. As a result of the agricultural decisions of January 1963, the EEC has been forced to regulate
agricultural imports from the Eastern bloc countries. Since many bilateral
agreements provide quotas for the sale of bloc farm products in member
countries, the effect was to give these products a guaranteed market,
something that is denied imports from other member countries, to say
nothing of imports from other nonmembers. The problem with farm products has its counterpart in imports of iron and steel from the Soviet bloc
which have been of major concern to the High Authority of the European
Coal and Steel Community. In this same connection, crude petroleum imports from the USSR are another potential source of difficulty. While ad
hoc solutions can always be found if a problem becomes serious enough, a
more general solution would be greatly preferred to avert the difficulties
between the member countries and the bloc that could arise under bilateral treaties. As seen in Table 6-9 (and Appendix Tables A-5 and A-6 for
country detail), EEC trade with Eastern Europe has been growing—in the
aggregate it amounts to about $1.5 billion in each direction. This trade,
however, amounts to less than 5 percent of EEC imports and exports

TABLE 6-9

EEC Trade with Soviet Area and China, 1958-65[a]

(Dollar amounts in millions)

Type of Trade and Area	1958	1959	1960	1961	1962	1963	1964	1965
Exports								
To Soviet area and Albania	$ 697	$ 786	$1,039	$1,136	$1,188	$1,101	$1,287	$1,459
To China	304	250	233	111	105	118	107	231
Total Sino-Soviet countries	1,001	1,036	1,272	1,247	1,293	1,219	1,394	1,690
Total as percent of all exports	*4.4*	*4.1*	*4.3*	*3.9*	*3.8*	*3.2*	*3.3*	*3.5*
Imports								
From Soviet area and Albania	$ 735	$ 858	$1,039	$1,143	$1,237	$1,470	$1,462	$1,670
From China	107	127	126	86	89	105	140	194
Total Sino-Soviet countries	841	985	1,165	1,229	1,326	1,575	1,602	1,864
Total as percent of all imports	*3.7*	*4.1*	*3.9*	*3.8*	*3.7*	*3.9*	*3.6*	*3.8*

Source: IMF-IBRD, *Direction of Trade, Annual 1958-62* and *Annual 1961-65.*
[a] Soviet area includes USSR, Bulgaria, Czechoslovakia, East Germany, Hungary, Poland, Rumania, North Korea, Outer Mongolia, Cuba, and North Vietnam. Detail may not add to totals because of rounding.

since 1958, and the relative share of this trade has been declining. Nor is Eastern European trade of particular importance to any single member country, although it is somewhat more important to Italy and Germany than to France and Benelux.[17] Nevertheless, the trade is not inconsequential and could cause some economic disturbances through trade deflection if the bilateral agreements of the member countries are not coordinated.

Tariff Negotiations with the United States

While the United States has an indirect interest in the commercial treaties the EEC has signed with nonmember countries, it is most concerned with its own direct negotiations with the EEC and EFTA countries. All parties concerned have ties to GATT, and negotiations are naturally carried out under GATT auspices. The mere forming of the common external tariff (CXT) by the EEC necessitated a round of GATT negotiations because, under GATT rules, consultations are required whenever a country raises its tariffs above previously negotiated rates, even if this comes about by joining a customs union. The countries (Germany and the Benelux) that

[17] It should be noted that trade between West Germany and East Germany is not counted in the aggregate figures or in the percentage calculations.

were required to raise their rates in order to reach the level of the CXT were in technical violation of GATT. The prospect of a general tariff reduction was another reason for a GATT negotiation. Under the terms of the U.S. congressional renewal of the Trade Agreements Act in 1958, the President was authorized to reduce United States tariffs by a maximum of 20 percent. The Congress, when granting this authority, clearly had a negotiation with the Common Market in mind. Therefore a twofold GATT conference was called. The first part was to be devoted to negotiations with the EEC to compensate for the formation of the CXT; this was expected to take three months. The second purpose was a general multilateral negotiation which came to be called the Dillon Round.[18]

The compensation round began in Geneva on September 1, 1960, but it soon became evident that the original timetable was wholly unrealistic. The EEC adopted the very natural position that little or no compensation was required since increases in the German and Benelux tariffs were matched by reductions by France and Italy. To support this position, painstakingly detailed comparisons were required between national tariff lists and the CXT, and these were repeated for each major trading partner of the EEC. In addition, the agricultural issue plagued the negotiations and prevented early agreement. While little, if any, of the Common Agricultural Policy was then in force, the EEC was negotiating on the basis of a variable levy system (Mansholt Plan) and this in itself caused grave concern among agricultural exporters. To no avail, the United States made strong representation to the EEC that the system itself was wholly protective and gave even the most efficient producer no assurance of access. The EEC insisted that the variable levy system was the only conceivable way to integrate the agricultural markets of the member countries— an essential element in a successful customs union—and that its protective effects would not be known until as yet undetermined prices were set. In the end, an agreement was reached whereby the United States reserved its right to compensation in agriculture, pending the completion of the CAP. Only relatively minor adjustments of a few industrial tariffs in the CXT resulted from these negotiations, which took nine months.

The Dillon Round was finally launched on May 29, 1961, on an optimistic note. The EEC made a public offer to reduce the CXT by 20 percent if it could obtain reciprocity from its trading partners. The EEC offered in

[18] Named after C. Douglas Dillon, Under Secretary of State during the Eisenhower Administration, who proposed the talks. He later became Secretary of the Treasury in the Kennedy Administration.

addition to reduce the CXT provisionally by 20 percent in the expectation that reciprocity would be forthcoming, even if not assured during current negotiations. Jean Rey, the EEC Commissioner then in charge of external relations, suggested that a 20 percent reduction across the board on all tariffs by all countries (the linear method) would be the best way to handle the negotiations, but the EEC was prepared to go through the traditional item-by-item examination of offers if other countries were unable to use the more rational technique.

The United States negotiators could not contemplate across-the-board tariff reductions and, in fact, had very little bargaining authority whatsoever. The 1958 United States trade legislation contained both an escape and a peril point clause which severely limited its usefulness for tariff bargaining. The escape clause was included to allow the reinstatement of a tariff cut if the resulting imports caused or threatened to cause injury to competing United States producing interests. This had long been part of U.S. legislation and, since it had not been abused in practice, was not in itself a major barrier to negotiations. The peril point clause, however, was a barrier because it was designed to prevent a tariff cut if it threatened to injure a U.S. producer. The peril point was determined through interagency deliberations and set limits on the tariff reductions that the United States could offer. While a peril point clause had occasionally appeared in U.S. legislation in the past, this was the first time that the peril points had been set so high that they effectively emasculated most of the negotiating authority.

Given the United States position, a disappointing result was almost foreordained. Yet the Dillon Round was completed on March 7, 1962, and produced a better agreement than might have been expected. The EEC reduced some tariffs and provisionally reduced most of the remaining items by 20 percent. The United States, for its part, made a few significant reductions. Despite the competitive pressures being felt by the American automobile industry (imports zoomed in 1958 and 1959 to reach 10 percent of domestic registrations compared to 4 percent in 1957), automobile tariffs were subjected to the 20 percent reduction, along with certain classes of machinery, electrical apparatus, steel, and glassware plus some other items. Most of the other GATT members made correspondingly small tariff reductions.

Even in these negotiations, however, the difficulty of bargaining with the EEC was apparent. Having no real authority, the EEC representative in Geneva was hamstrung in the give-and-take of bargaining. All decisions were made in the Council of Ministers by unanimous vote and there was no assurance that the Council would back up a promise of an EEC negotiator if it went beyond the previously determined mandate in any respect. At one point a tentative agreement was reached between EEC and U.S. negotiators, only to be refused by the Council. In the end, the Council of Ministers agreed to the negotiated package, but only after strenuous efforts by M. Rey in which he put his personal integrity at stake. Needless to say, M. Rey's position in Brussels was not improved by the official U.S. announcement of the Dillon Round which boastfully proclaimed that the United States obtained the best part of the bargain at the expense of the EEC.[19]

The "era of good feeling" between the United States and the EEC which resulted from the successful Dillon Round lasted exactly ten days. On March 17, 1962, President Kennedy announced that he had concurred with a Tariff Commission finding that imported carpets and sheet glass were injuring U.S. producers, and that the previous tariff cuts on these items should be rescinded according to the escape clause procedure. For both products, the EEC was the principal supplier to the United States.[20] The United States, in recognition of its GATT commitments, offered to negotiate with all countries suffering injury as a result of the escape clause action. It drew up a list of products whose tariffs were offered for reduction to replace the concessions withdrawn. While some countries took up this offer, the EEC rather perfunctorily rejected the U.S. initiative and in-

[19] The announcement was all the more foolish because the "bargaining coup" was measured by the meaningless statistic of the amount of current annual U.S. exports to the EEC covered by tariff reductions ($1.6 billion) compared to corresponding U.S. imports from the EEC ($1.2 billion). The announcement, of course, was meant for domestic consumption to prepare the way for the introduction of new trade legislation in the Congress.

[20] The EEC was obviously aware, before the conclusion of the Dillon Round, that the President had such a recommendation before him. It is possible that a misunderstanding occurred over this matter. M. Rey apparently thought that the President was going to reject the recommendation. This belief was reportedly transmitted to him by a person 'very close' to the President. The American side of this story suggests that a promise was made to recommend to the President that he reject the Tariff Commission finding; however, it was clear that the decision rested solely with the President. The matter was all the more painful for M. Rey because these products are important to Belgium and he is himself Belgian. Furthermore, the increases were very great. The U.S. tariff rate on carpets was raised from 21 percent to 40 percent and on glass the increases varied from 73 percent to 150 percent depending on dimensions, but some of these increases were subsequently reduced. In 1967 M. Rey became President of the expanded Commission that serves all three European Communities.

stead retaliated against U.S. exports. GATT rules permit a retaliatory increase in tariffs to be applied exclusively to the exports of the erring country. This procedure was used by the EEC against U.S. exports of polyethylene, polystyrene, synthetic cloth, artificial cloth, and varnishes and paints. Furthermore, the tariff increases of the EEC were comparable in magnitude to the U.S. move and were to be applied immediately rather than approached in stages as with the rest of the CXT. Through this action, the EEC very dramatically made the point that the days were ended when the United States could dictate its will in GATT.

The actions of the United States during this period, which appear inimical to expanding international trade, are more understandable when it is recognized that President Kennedy was attempting to garner domestic support for the most liberal negotiating authority ever granted by Congress. In January 1962 he recommended legislation that ultimately became the Trade Expansion Act.[21]

The Trade Expansion Act attempted to equip U.S. negotiators with the tools needed to reach commercial agreements in the changed world of common markets. The United States could offer substantial tariff reductions and use the linear technique in bargaining. The peril point straitjacket was discarded and the escape clause softened. In addition, the United States tried to anticipate future needs with the dominant supplier authority which would be meaningful only if Britain joined the Common Market. Some observers believed rather naively that this authority might encourage the EEC to accept British membership. Events proved otherwise and the authority became useless, but the mere attempt to legislate for an evolving situation rather than for just current conditions is a noteworthy achievement.[22] On the basis of this legislation, the United States

---

[21] This Act had many features, some of which were radical departures from previous legislation. First, the President was authorized to reduce U. S. tariffs by 50 percent. Second, he was permitted to transfer certain items from the dutiable to the free list, something never before allowed. The products included under this authority were: (a) manufactured products for which the United States and the EEC are together the world's dominant suppliers; (b) some tropical agricultural products generally not produced in the United States; (c) items whose tariffs are already so low as to be only of nuisance value; (d) certain temperate agricultural products. Third, the peril point procedure was eliminated. Fourth, the escape clause was redefined to make the concept of injury more reasonable and to give the President the alternative of giving adjustment assistance to an injured industry rather than raising tariffs. Finally, the legislation was enacted for a five-year period—the longest ever granted.

[22] The whole effort may have been misguided in view of the reluctance of European supporters of the Common Market to consider any measure that would blur

sought another GATT negotiation and this suggestion was generally well received in Europe.

Even before the Kennedy Round was officially opened, difficulties were apparent between the two major participants, the United States and the Common Market. American fears about the evolving agricultural policy of the EEC came to a head following the application of the CAP to poultry in July 1962. The result of the CAP was to raise the total levy on American chickens entering the principal market, Germany, from 4.9 cents per pound to 13.4 cents per pound, or the equivalent of an *ad valorem* tariff of at least 50 percent. The move converted a rapidly growing export market into a declining one. United States objections to the policy were communicated to the EEC and, in March 1963, the Commission recommended to the Council of Ministers that the EEC reduce the burden on U. S. exporters of chickens. But no action was taken. Under rights resulting from previous GATT agreements, the United States asked for formal negotiations with the Common Market to discuss this problem. The United States proposed some modifications of the levy system, but these were rejected by the EEC on the ground that they were in basic contradiction to the principles of the CAP. The EEC Commission showed sympathy for the U. S. position, but could not act without a mandate from the Council. When the Council continued to procrastinate, the United States finally decided to take retaliatory action.[23]

Two remedies were open to the United States under GATT. One approach, using the general retaliatory procedure, would call for a discriminatory tariff increase by the United States on EEC products similar to the EEC action in regard to carpets and glass. The alternative was to blame the infringement of U.S. rights on the formation of the customs union itself, in which case GATT rules provide for a nondiscriminatory tariff increase by the United States on products for which the EEC is the principal supplier. In order not to escalate the "chicken war" further, the United States chose the second alternative. The disputed amount of U.S. injury was settled via GATT arbitration and the United States withdrew trade concessions on an equivalent value of goods.

The whole episode brought out in bold relief some difficulties underly-

the distinction between members and nonmembers. Clearly the CXT is the most important such distinction.

[23] The last straw, as far as the United States was concerned, may have been the technical adjustment made by the agricultural ministers of the member countries which raised the protectiveness of the external levy on chickens at the very time when efforts were being made to reduce it.

ing the commercial relations between the United States and the EEC. The sensitivity of the United States to trade barriers against its agricultural exports was made abundantly clear. The inability of the EEC to override agricultural producer interests for its own general well-being was also illustrated. Together, these suggest a collision course which in fact came into the open during the Kennedy Round. The conflict also showed excessive EEC and U.S. reliance on the legalistic approach of GATT in governing the commercial relations between them. In the "chicken war," as well as the carpets-glass conflict, the use of GATT rules led the parties to retaliation despite the fact that the producer interests originally injured were not benefited and further injury was caused. Finally, it showed that commercial differences can be exaggerated out of proportion to their importance if prompt attention is not given to them. Unfortunately, the United States has not always acted in a prompt and reasonable manner, and the Common Market has almost never done so. Against this background, the Kennedy Round began.

As the Kennedy Round progressed, the dimensions of possible trade liberalization narrowed. The breakthrough to free trade for advanced manufactured products was rejected, along with Britain's bid to join the Common Market. The goal of an across-the-board tariff reduction of 50 percent with a bare minimum of exceptions was undermined by the refusal of some countries to adopt the linear method and the fact that other countries offered less than 50 percent reductions on some products, and no reductions on too many others. The hope that the Kennedy Round would solve most of the economic difficulties resulting from the European split between EEC and EFTA was extinguished. The possibility that agricultural trade might be liberalized to the same degree as industrial products evaporated with the EEC insistence that agricultural trade accommodate itself to the CAP and not the converse. The desire of many to see nontariff barriers to trade eliminated along with tariffs was frustrated, in part by the very complexity of the issues involved, and in part by the fact that many of the negotiators, including those of the United States, did not have the authority to make commitments about such barriers.

Despite these limitations, enough scope remained for the Kennedy Round to achieve a notable amount of trade liberalization. Intra-European trade difficulties could be eased. Agricultural trade could be elevated in status so that it was no longer automatically eliminated from discussions of tariff reductions. The less developed countries could still be assured that barriers to the entrance of their products into the channels of international trade need not remain intact despite their inability to bargain in the same way as the developed nations. And most important from the point of view of this study, the opportunity remained for the Common Market to demonstrate that it could reach an agreement to liberalize trade and that the long claimed outward-looking policy was a reality. Most of these objectives were in fact achieved in the Kennedy Round (Chapter 7).

This chapter has reviewed some of the many external relations of the EEC and EFTA and has tried to identify the U.S. interests involved. The development of a tie between EFTA and Finland was recognized as being in the interest of the United States, as was the association of Greece and Turkey with the EEC. The association of the former French, Belgian, Dutch, and Italian dependencies to the EEC has not been harmful to the United States, but possibly is not the best possible arrangement. The extension of that association to Nigeria, however, raises more objections and the interests of the United States may well be injured by it. The commercial treaties already concluded by the EEC are not important.

As to the future relations between the two groups, no fundamental reason was found for the United States to reverse its support for the absorption of EFTA by the Common Market. If that is not possible, then the association of Austria alone is desirable, even though it raises some difficult questions. The scales would be tipped the other way, however, if the EEC accepted most of EFTA but continued to exclude Great Britain. As to the direct commercial relations between the EEC and the United States, the Kennedy Round stood as the test which will set the tone of the relationship for many years to come.

CHAPTER SEVEN

Summary and Conclusions

THIS STUDY HAS ATTEMPTED to appraise the economic consequences of European integration for the United States. The importance of membership in the European Economic Community and the European Free Trade Association has been documented. It has been assumed that the United States as a nonmember is also affected by these organizations, and this impact has been documented as well. The documentation, however, is more akin to circumstantial evidence than to proof. Because of the nature of the question, cause-and-effect relationships have been inferred rather than observed. This should serve as a warning to those who would take the numerical estimates in this study too literally.

Europe and European Economic Integration

The substantial changes in the patterns of international trade since 1958-59 have led investigators to conclude that European economic integration has had an impact upon member countries. Whether one considers the distribution of total trade of member countries, or manufactured products or agricultural products separately, the observation is the same. Since joining the EEC or EFTA, members have established much closer commercial ties with each other, and this appears to be primarily due to economic integration. While the observation differs in degree between the EEC and EFTA, and among the various members of both groups, it is in substance valid.

An attempt was made to go beyond the trade effects of economic integration to investigate the impact on levels of income in the member countries. Income changes can be expected if economic integration stimulates business investment, and if a country's international trade expands enough to increase the share of the foreign sector in the domestic economy. Both of these stimuli did occur in the EEC and EFTA, and their effects upon the income levels of the member countries were evaluated by the methods employed by Edward Denison.[1] This analysis showed that the EEC has had a somewhat greater impact on the income levels of its members than EFTA has had upon its members. Italy and Belgium-Luxembourg received the greatest stimulation from the EEC, while Denmark benefited the most from EFTA.

Chapter 5 considered additional ways in which the EEC was affecting or potentially could affect the economies of member and nonmember countries. Specifically, the consequences of a common antitrust policy, a common patent system, a common energy policy, and a harmonized tax system were discussed. These consequences are not easily summarized, but they are all of great potential importance. Furthermore, the implications of EEC membership for aggregate economic problems such as imbalances in international payments were examined. Membership in a customs union changes the solutions for a balance-of-payments problem of a member country, but not so fundamentally as to require a radical change in the approach to the problem.

Integration has had some effect on the economic ties of member countries to nonmembers. EFTA has forged an institutional link with Finland that is especially important for the Scandinavian countries. The EEC has been instrumental in the development of new institutional ties between its members and the former colonial dependencies of France, Belgium, Italy, and the Netherlands. It has formed an association with Nigeria which may prove to be important and may be a forerunner of other associations with African members of the Commonwealth. Greece and Turkey have become associated with the EEC, with the intention of eventually becoming full members. The most important unsettled issue remains the relationship between the EFTA countries and the EEC. Many inferences were drawn throughout this study concerning the economic split in Europe. If Britain were to join the Common Market with most of the other members of EFTA, the economic situation in Europe would be fundamentally changed.

[1] Edward F. Denison, assisted by Jean-Pierre Poullier, *Why Growth Rates Differ: Postwar Experience in Nine Western Countries* (Brookings Institution, 1967).

British Membership in the Common Market

On May 2, 1967, British Prime Minister Harold Wilson notified the EEC Council of Ministers and announced in Parliament that the United Kingdom intended to renew its application for membership in the EEC under Article 237 of the Rome Treaty. Even if this action does not lead to membership, it indicates that the British government recognizes that the future of Britain depends on its relationship with the continent of Europe. With the conversion of the Labour Party from opposition to support of EEC membership, all major parties in Britain support entry, and, although it is not universally approved, it no longer appears to be a partisan issue.

The prospects for British entry are far from certain. Some of the difficult problems uncovered in the 1961-63 negotiations seem to have been resolved with the passage of time, but others have remained, and new obstacles have appeared. The "Commonwealth problem" has receded in importance as the older dominions have reduced their dependence on U.K. markets and the tropical African countries have evidenced greater willingness to become associated with the EEC. The opposition of British farmers has been reduced as they have become aware of the advantages of operating under the Common Agricultural Policy (CAP). However, the inflationary consequences and balance-of-payments costs to Britain of adopting the CAP remain problems, the other EFTA countries still need to be accommodated, and a number of other vexing problems remain. Furthermore, the fundamental French objection to British membership, based on Britain's alleged lack of a European consciousness and its historic ties to the United States, has not been removed, as indicated in President de Gaulle's news conference of May 16, 1967. In addition, the Six have questioned whether Britain's economy is strong enough to adjust to membership without imposing burdens on existing members, and whether the reserve currency status of sterling might impose a barrier to membership. Thus, there are many issues over which negotiations could founder. Nevertheless, with determined British effort, membership could conceivably be obtained, even if not in the near future.

Given this possibility, it is worth speculating on some of the major consequences of British membership for the United States, despite the obvious hazards of such an attempt. The analysis requires assumptions concerning the terms under which new countries would be accepted into EEC membership, the number of countries admitted, their entry as full or associate members, and the time required for negotiations and transitional arrangements. The most reasonable assumption concerning terms of membership is that all new members will be required to accept the Rome Treaty as it stands, with possibly a few modifying changes. Thus, the existing level of the common external tariff would be extended to all countries, the CAP would cover all countries (perhaps with some adjustment of specific regulations), and freedom of movement of labor and capital and all the regulations concerning such issues as antitrust policy would prevail throughout the area. Membership could be restricted to just a few additional countries, but it is more likely that the EEC would eventually be extended to include the United Kingdom, Denmark, and Norway as full members; Ireland, Portugal, and Spain as associate members in the process of development (like Greece and Turkey); and Sweden, Finland, Switzerland, and Austria as permanent associate members (because of neutrality). One can imagine a sequential chain in which first the United Kingdom, then Denmark, then Norway, and others are accepted into the EEC.[2] Thus the EEC would eventually encompass all of Western Europe. Much time would be required to bring this about. The negotiations for British membership alone would require two to three years and the whole of the arrangement might require the better part of ten years to negotiate. Adding the time needed for the transition, the adjustment might be spread over two decades. Thus, even without a single substantive change in the Rome Treaty, the EEC could become a much different organization. The size, the continental scope, and the diversity of resources (both natural and human) of the new entity would create an economic power of primary dimensions. An expanded EEC would obviously be overwhelmingly important in international commerce.

Because of the great length of time required to complete an expanded EEC, only the probable effects of British entry are now worth examining. These would be in any case the most important for the United States.

---

[2] This presumption is based on the belief that the EEC will find it very difficult to refuse membership to a country wishing to join once most of its major trading partners are included, for example, to refuse Sweden after Britain, Denmark, and Norway are included. If there were a general movement toward free trade among industrial countries, some EFTA countries such as Switzerland and Finland might not desire to join the EEC. But under this assumption, it would not be fruitful to speculate on the effects of an expanded EEC for the United States, since the consequences of the general freeing of trade would then be dominant.

Both Britain and the Common Market could look forward to a renewed stimulus to income. Business investment would be encouraged in both areas to meet the competitive challenge, and for Britain an expansion of exports and imports relative to gross domestic product could be expected. This means that exports from the United States would be encouraged by higher real income in Europe. However, an extension of tariff discrimination against U.S. goods would also occur as tariffs between Britain and the EEC were dismantled. The trade-pattern effect of this tariff change would be much less deleterious to U.S. exports of manufactured goods than the original consequences of the EEC and EFTA. First, British tariffs are generally above the common external tariff (and it would presumably not be increased upon British entry) and thus the tariff wall surrounding the new entity would be, on average, less than that previously existing. Second, the CXT itself is below its 1959 level because of the Kennedy Round, and would cause proportionately less trade diversion. Third, under GATT rules, the United States would have a right to some compensation because of the tariff discrimination, and the EEC (including Britain) might be more willing to grant tariff reductions than it was in 1959-60. It would thus appear that U.S. exports of manufactured products might not be too seriously affected by British entry.

The agricultural situation could be more serious from the point of view of the United States. The United Kingdom is still one of the largest markets for U.S. agricultural products—approximately one-half billion dollars per year—but little growth has occurred since the mid-1950's. U.S. agricultural sales to Britain have been inhibited by the rapid increase in British domestic production, by the preferred access given to Commonwealth commodities, and possibly by the special access given to other EFTA countries. Entry into the EEC would tend to reduce the aggregate of British imports of agricultural products, since local production would be stimulated and consumption discouraged. Prices paid to British farmers would be, on the average, higher under the CAP than under the existing deficiency payments arrangement, and prices to consumers would be sharply higher.[3] In addition, other EEC suppliers would have preferred access to the market. The degree to which this would be at the expense of the United States rather than the Commonwealth would depend very much on the terms of the agreement. If the Commonwealth maintained its privileged position, then the United States would take the brunt of the

[3] The usual assumption that demand for agricultural products in the aggregate is price-inelastic would get a "clinical" test.

EEC competition. Other results are possible, but it does not appear to be worthwhile to examine all conceivable possibilities.

Some notion of the magnitude of the possible loss of U.S. agricultural exports to the United Kingdom can be obtained by examining the product structure of these exports. There would be no additional threat to U.S. exports of those products in which the EEC and the United Kingdom are both deficient in supply and unlikely to produce surpluses. In this category fall soybeans, cotton, flue-cured tobacco, and some less important products. Together these amount to about 45 percent of U.S. exports. The next category includes products in deficit in both the EEC and the United Kingdom but for which surpluses could be induced if agricultural policies were drawn for this purpose. This category includes feed grains, fats and oils, and specialty meats, which make up another 45 percent of U.S. exports. The remaining 10 percent of U.S. agricultural exports to the United Kingdom includes products in which EEC suppliers have already developed surpluses, for example, wheat, rice, poultry, and dairy products. None of the U.S. exports in the first category, some in the second category, and most of the products in the third category would be threatened, depending on the arrangements made for Commonwealth trade. The direct loss of U.S. exports to the United Kingdom could be as little as $20 million per year (mainly wheat), or possibly as much as $100 million. Some indirect offsets would occur, as the EEC would be forced to give up selling in some of its export markets because of lack of supplies, but the effect upon U.S. trade would be too difficult to estimate.

In the area of direct investment, British entry would probably have little effect upon American direct investment outflows to Europe, but would have a significant effect upon the way in which American firms conduct their businesses. Most internationally minded American firms already own substantial facilities in both the United Kingdom and the EEC, so one would not expect much aggregate expansion. However, these firms would rationalize their production by eliminating duplicate facilities and reaching a greater degree of specialization. Thus, the profitability of American firms might increase with very little additional investment. American firms would demonstrate again that they know how to operate efficiently in a continent-wide market.

Even if the economic effects on the United States of British entry into the EEC were many times greater than those implied above, they would still be small compared to the political effects. The discussion of a U.S. partnership with a federalized Europe would be ended by British opposition to federalism. But by healing the trading split in Europe and the divisive issues accompanying it, the EEC might be able to develop a meaningful European consciousness even without much institutional development. It might then be possible to get an answer to the question, "What do Europeans think about an issue?" Such an EEC would be a third force in the world requiring recognition and adaptation by the United States. Western Europe would then return as a focal point of U.S. foreign policy. But this will occur only if and when Britain is well integrated into the Common Market.

The United States and European Economic Integration

Because of the close ties between the European and American economies, every important result of economic integration in member countries has an effect upon the United States. Some of these effects are measurable. The most direct impact is on EEC and EFTA imports from the United States. The estimated aggregate loss of U.S. export sales between 1958-59 and 1970 is $2.3 billion, as summarized in Table 7-1. The loss was derived as the difference between the value of manufactured and agricultural products that the EEC and EFTA countries would have been expected to import from the United States without economic integration and the expected value of these imports with integration. A net loss resulted because the negative consequences of the trade-diverting effects of economic inte-

TABLE 7-1

*Summary of Estimated Trade Loss of the United States
Caused by EEC and EFTA for the Period 1958–70*

(Millions of dollars, 1958 prices)

Area Causing Loss	Total, All Products	Manufactured Products[a]	Agricultural Products[b]
EEC	2,211	161	2,050
EFTA	77	77	—
Total	2,288	238	2,050

[a] From Chap. 2, Table 2-20.
[b] From Chap. 3, sum of estimated annual losses.

gration were estimated to be greater than the positive consequences of the higher levels of income coming from economic integration. Virtually all of the loss is attributed to the EEC. Most of it occurs in agricultural trade, and only the EEC noticeably affects this trade. The EEC also has a greater effect upon the imports of manufactured goods of its members.

Direct investments of American firms in the EEC and EFTA have been affected by economic integration. A lack of data severely limited the analysis, but an attempt was made to arrive at an empirical measurement of this effect. Between 1958 and 1965, new American investment in the EEC and EFTA was estimated to have been $1 to 2 billion greater than it would have been without economic integration. About three-quarters of this stimulus was attributed to the EEC and one-quarter to EFTA. Thus, without integration, American investment in the EEC and EFTA might have risen from $4.3 billion in 1958 to $11-12 billion in 1965 rather than to $13 billion, as actually occurred (measured in book value). All of these measurements, however, are very tentative.

Some other aspects of economic integration, particularly with respect to the EEC, will also affect the international trading, investing, and banking interests of the United States. Tax harmonization, for example, might have serious repercussions on international trade, and antitrust developments could affect investment. Also, the role of the dollar as an international currency could be affected by economic policy decisions of the EEC. But none of these consequences can be discussed with precision, because the Common Market's policies dealing with these matters have not been completed. In addition, the United States could be affected by the association agreements of the EEC and EFTA with other countries, but little actual effect has been discerned.

All things considered, what is the meaning of European economic integration for the United States? When the EEC and EFTA began operations in 1958 and 1959, the United States had a sizable deficit in its international balance of payments. This deficit was frustrating because it occurred during a period of recession and slow growth in the U.S. domestic economy. Since an external solution—a change in the dollar exchange rate—was ruled out, the internal adjustment required to correct the deficit had to be substantial, and it was painful. The EEC and EFTA added to the burden of this adjustment by causing a loss of U.S. exports, which, although probably amounting to no more than $200 million in any single year, made the adjustment that much harder. Thus, one answer to the question posed above is that European economic integration has meant that the United States has had to run in order to stand still in its balance of payments.

But European economic integration has meant more than this. It has created two entities that, in terms of international commercial strength, are equal to the United States. Imports of both the EEC and EFTA from nonmembers are now greater than the imports of the United States. Furthermore, the European capital market has grown substantially so that, in the first half of 1966, for the first time in many years, more foreign long-term securities were floated in European markets than in the United States.[4] Certainly the U.S. Interest Equalization Tax had much to do with this, but the fact remains that a high value of securities was successfully placed in Europe. This size creates economic power, and the EEC has demonstrated that on occasion it is prepared to exercise that power.

The importance of this for the United States might best be illustrated by returning to the balance-of-payments problem. The U.S. deficit has been matched by a European surplus, primarily earned by the Common Market. Unless the Europeans are prepared to allow their surpluses to be reduced, the United States will not be able to end its deficit. Every policy measure that the United States might employ could be countered by the Europeans with policy moves of their own. Suppose that the United States considered its balance of payments to be in deficit, but that the Europeans did not consider themselves to be in surplus. If the United States raised its interest rates to attract capital, the Europeans could increase their own rates, offset the differential, and prevent the capital flow—in the name of protecting their balance of payments. If the United States restrained its domestic economy to reduce imports, the Europeans could do the same thing, and probably much more easily. Needless to say, any trade restrictions imposed on imports by the United States could, and probably would, lead to immediate retaliation by the Europeans. Even if the United States wanted to take the extreme step of devaluing the dollar, it could not do so unless the Europeans were willing to let their own currencies appreciate relative to the dollar. While this dilemma for the United States has a simple solution—to stop worrying about the balance of payments—the principle of relative power that it illustrates is very important.

An example of the change in relative power is found in the area of commercial policy. The dominant position of the United States in GATT evaporated with the implementation of the Rome Treaty. The United

[4] Lawrence A. Veit, *Handbook of International Finance 1958-1966* (National Industrial Conference Board, 1967).

States once could have forced its trading partners to accept a compensating U.S. tariff reduction in return for the U.S. withdrawal of a previously negotiated concession. However, when the United States withdrew its concession on carpets and glass in 1962, the Common Market refused compensation, and instead retaliated against American goods. This was a sobering experience. The U.S. Congress can no longer legislate a round of tariff reductions for all GATT members as it had done for most of the postwar period (even though vestiges of this thinking appeared as late as 1962 in the Trade Expansion Act). The Common Market is now the most important member of GATT, and can determine in large measure the success or failure of any attempt to liberalize trade. When Europeans instruct Americans in the realities of the new international economic situation they are demonstrating the change in relative power that has taken place.

The Kennedy Round

Because of economic developments in Europe, the Kennedy Round of tariff negotiations in GATT took on special meaning. The most sweeping move toward trade liberalization in the postwar period was contemplated. For the first time when major issues were at stake, the Common Market bargained as a single unit rather than as separate countries. Also, the negotiating of the EFTA countries was coordinated, although not required by the Stockholm Convention. Thus, the Kennedy Round was the acid test of whether the EEC and EFTA were outward-looking or inward-looking. Beyond the commercial questions involved, the Kennedy Round was to be the first step in forming a partnership between Europe and the United States.

The tariff reductions negotiated during the Kennedy Round have particular interest for this study because they have reduced the tariff discrimination faced by nonmembers in the EEC and EFTA. In particular, the trade-diverting effects estimated here for manufactured products reflect the tariff rates of the Common Market's CXT and the rates of the individual EFTA countries. The consequences of the Kennedy Round were determined by estimating the effects of a full 50 percent across-the-board reduction in tariffs (according to the formula originally employed in Chapter 2) and then adjusting the estimate for those items not given the full reduction. Since some of the trade-diverting effects of integration have

TABLE 7-2

Adjustment of Estimated Loss in Trade in Manufactured Products of Nonmembers from Tariff Reductions in the Kennedy Round

(Dollar amounts in millions, 1958 prices)

Nonmember Area	Estimated Trade Loss Without Adjustment for Kennedy Round[a]	Reduction If Full 50 Percent Cut in Tariffs	*Actual Kennedy Round Coverage*[b] *(Percent)*	Reduction After Adjustment for Coverage	*Reversible Loss (Percent)*	Total Adjustment for Kennedy Round	Net Estimated Trade Loss with Adjustment for Kennedy Round
United States	$238	$119	—	$ 94	—	$ 56	$182
Loss from EEC	161	80	72.0	58	50	29	132
Loss from EFTA	77	39	93.2	36	75	27	50
EEC	378	189	77.3	146	75	110	268
EFTA	279	140	74.4	104	50	52	227
Other	250	125	—	100	—	66	184
Loss from EEC	108	54	67.2	36	50	18	90
Loss from EFTA	142	71	89.9	64	75	48	94

[a] From Chap. 2, Table 2-20.
[b] Partly estimated.

already occurred and are nonreversible, a further adjustment was made. The results are shown in Table 7-2.

According to these rough calculations, the United States will gain about $30 million of additional exports of manufactured goods to the EEC as a result of the reduction of tariff discrimination coming from the Kennedy Round. This represents an offset of 18 percent to the loss of manufactured goods estimated to have resulted from the formation of the EEC. The United States will gain almost $30 million of additional exports from the EFTA reductions of tariff discrimination. The increase to EFTA is an offset of 35 percent to the estimated loss of U.S. exports of manufactured products. The difference in the percentage of offsets is a result of the greater trade coverage by EFTA in the Kennedy Round and the fact that more of the estimated EFTA loss is thought to be reversible. Taken together, almost one-quarter of the trade-diverting consequences of European integration for the United States was offset.

A more important result of the Kennedy Round—in terms of value of trade—will be a diminution of the consequences of the trade split within Europe. Because of the reduction of tariff discrimination by the EEC, exports of manufactured goods by EFTA are expected to increase by about $50 million, or an offset of 19 percent to its originally estimated trade loss. Likewise, the reduction of EFTA tariff discrimination is expected to increase EEC exports of manufactured products by $110 million, or 29 percent of its estimated trade loss. Thus, the Kennedy Round will apparently achieve one of its major objectives. If a more fundamental solution to the trade split is not found, at least the commercial consequences for manufactured products will not be as great as once feared.

Unfortunately, similar results have not been obtained for agricultural products. The U.S. desire to see the Kennedy Round liberalize agricultural trade as much as trade of manufactured products has been frustrated. In truth it was always more of a hope than a realistic expectation. One must conclude that the Kennedy Round, like all previous GATT negotiations, has hardly scratched the surface of protection of temperate agricultural products. Since most of the trade loss attributable to the formation of the EEC is concentrated in temperate agricultural products, the Kennedy Round has done relatively little to offset these consequences for the United States.

The extensive Kennedy Round bargaining over temperate agriculture did lead to a World Grains Agreement, but, as with all commodity agreements, the results are not what they may seem. The United States has been assured of a somewhat higher price for wheat exports, but there is no guarantee of the amount of wheat to be bought at the higher price. A conclusion of this study is, however, that substantial amounts of U.S. grain will be purchased by the EEC, even with a highly protective agricultural policy. What has been missed is the opportunity to redirect this policy and that of other countries to a more rational market-oriented path.

A new departure in agricultural policy, growing out of the Kennedy Round, could lead to some important results in the future. It was agreed that the advanced countries who are not exporters of temperate agricultural products should share the financial burden of supplying these products to less developed countries under concessionary terms, even though the actual exporters are other advanced countries. The amount of such aid agreed to was 4.5 million tons of grain by all developed countries. The Common Market's contribution is to provide 23 percent of this total or roughly $100 million. If the Common Market were to pay for some of the food now being provided as a gift by the United States to the less developed countries, then the loss of U.S. agricultural sales to the EEC could be offset. To make an equivalent economic offset, the EEC contribution could be much less than the $200 million annual agricultural trade loss estimated in this study, because a trade loss would be compensated for by an outright grant.[5] If the agricultural payment by the EEC were not wholly at the expense of aid it otherwise would grant to less developed countries, and if the United States did not utilize the payment to increase its own aid above what it otherwise would grant, then the payment need only be large enough to cover the additional cost to the United States of producing domestically the imports it must forego as a result of its lower agricultural exports. Using the average level of U.S. import tariffs of 10 percent as a rough measure of the marginal inefficiency of U.S. import-competing industries, the EEC incremental payment needed to offset completely the $200 million U.S. trade loss would be $20 million annually. Such a result is a conceivable outcome from the $100 million EEC contribution.

Beyond Economics

Integration is of political as well as economic importance to Europe. Within recent years, diplomatic relations between France and Germany, for instance, have been dominated by issues and contacts related to their integrated economies, and this is true of all other EEC countries. The relations between Great Britain and the Continent have likewise been dominated by the issue of membership (or nonmembership) in the Common Market. Even the internal politics of European countries have felt the impact of economic integration. That issue has been important in the national elections of many countries, especially in Denmark, Britain, and France. All this has occurred despite the lack of movement toward political integration in Europe.

The importance of integration to the United States is also not confined to the economic sphere. Europe will remain politically very important to the United States for all the old reasons, even if less so than in the past.[6] Europe is the only stable and prosperous region capable of sharing the burdens of providing security and furthering the economic development of noncommunist countries. Because the European countries do have sub-

[5] The same distinction exists between the value of increased aid and increased international trade for a less developed country. See Harry G. Johnson, *Economic Policies Toward Less Developed Countries* (Brookings Institution, 1967).

[6] J. Robert Schaetzel, "The Necessary Partnership," *Foreign Affairs,* Vol. 44 (April 1966), pp. 417-33.

stantial resources, the balance of power in the world would swing very unfavorably against the United States in the unlikely event that they became aligned with the Communist countries. Furthermore, the possibility that internecine European warfare could once again involve the United States cannot be overlooked.

Because the reasons for U.S. interest in Europe have not changed, U.S. goals in Europe have not changed. The United States still desires a politically stable and economically expanding Europe that is both able and willing to contribute to its own security and to that of the rest of the Atlantic Alliance. Recognizing that "the future of Germany remains the central problem for Europe's future,"[7] the United States continues to seek a consolidation of Germany's role in Western Europe. A further increase in Europe's contribution to the economic development of less developed countries also continues to be a U.S. objective. Finally, the United States wishes to cooperate with Western Europe in establishing contacts with Eastern Europe in an added effort to bury the cold war.

In the context of these objectives, what is the political meaning of European economic integration for the United States? What has happened to the prospects of forming an Atlantic partnership—the preferred approach toward these objectives? Progress so far is not very comforting for the United States. Economic integration has certainly increased the economic prosperity of Europe and may have added to its political stability, but it has not led to a greater European contribution to the security of the Alliance. The European contribution to NATO has been reduced, despite the success of the EEC (and EFTA), graphically illustrating the difference between ability and willingness.

There is also little evidence that economic integration has led to a greater European contribution to the economic development of less developed countries. While members of the EEC have given more aid to some African countries than they would have done otherwise, in part this multilateral aid has merely replaced the bilateral aid previously given by France. Another part of the increased aid to African countries reflects a redirection of aid from other less developed countries and not an increase in the total amount.

Western European countries have been interested in increasing their peaceful contacts with Eastern European countries and economic integration may have made this easier, but the United States may not have

[7] Kenneth Younger, *Listener,* Nov. 25, 1965, as quoted by Schaetzel in *Foreign Affairs,* p. 423.

benefited to the degree that was expected. The expansion of markets induced by the EEC and EFTA has led many Eastern bloc countries to seek
commercial accommodations with them. These commercial ties have been
particularly important in helping Germany reestablish normal relations
with some of its Eastern neighbors. However, this development has been
completely independent of the United States. No cooperative efforts have
evolved between the United States and Western Europe in dealing with
Eastern Europe. In fact, Western Europe has shown a desire to be more
independent of the United States in order to have more flexibility in dealing with the East. Economic integration has probably increased the desire
for independence rather than reduced it.

It is only with respect to Germany that economic integration has furthered American political objectives in Europe as originally anticipated.
German political development has progressed and reached a stage of maturity that could scarcely have been hoped for twenty years ago. A great
deal of credit must be given to those postwar European institutions, especially the EEC, which have given Germany an honorable role in the West.
But even here there are some grounds for American concern. It is not necessarily in the U.S. interest to have German economic resources become
an instrument for supporting French foreign policy, and there is some
possibility of this developing through the EEC. To the degree that the
EEC has had political leadership, it has come from France. The French
have dominated the Community without controlling it. Germany, on the
other hand, has been reluctant to exercise its power within the EEC and
the French have been only too willing to fill this vacuum. While this may
be only a transitional development, it is of some importance.

As to Atlantic partnership, recent developments have been discouraging. There has been very little progress in European political integration—
and it is only political integration that would make feasible a partnership
between Europe and the United States. The system of nation states seems
to have been strengthened. While the policies of President de Gaulle have
been most important in advancing the old kind of nationalism, it would be
incorrect to think that his departure from the scene will alter this course.
De Gaulle's policies are popular in France, and French-style nationalism
strikes a responsive chord in the rest of Europe. Political integration, if it
is to come to Europe, will require a herculean effort. Nor has the success
of the Kennedy Round brought the partnership any closer. While a failure
of the Kennedy Round would have had substantial political consequences,
its success merely reinforces the political status quo. No new political link

has been forged between the United States and Europe. No unified position has been reached with respect to the communist East or the less developed South. The first real step toward partnership is yet to be taken.

Finally, it is necessary to judge progress by the past so as not to lose perspective. The failure to reach a better economic or political position does not imply that the present position is a bad one. The postwar record of economic and political cooperation between Europe and the United States has been outstanding when compared with any other period of history. Economic growth has been rapid and the expansion of international trade has been even more so. This would not have been possible if, in the 1950's and 1960's, the industrialized countries had followed the policies of the 1930's. The knowledge that today is better than yesterday leads one to hope and even to expect that tomorrow will be better than today.

≫≫APPENDIXES≪≪

APPENDIXES

Tables on Imports and Exports
of EEC and EFTA Countries

FOR THE EEC, 1958 divides the periods before and after integration, since it was the last year before internal tariff reductions were begun. Unfortunately, 1958 was a year of economic weakness in Europe, and comparisons which use this year tend to pick up cyclical phenomena. The normal statistical procedure for avoiding this difficulty is to use an average of several years as a base period. However, trade data for 1957 reflect in part the effects of the Suez Crisis, and 1959 is a postintegration year; thus the average is suspect. Therefore an eclectic approach has been used: when a particular measure is unlikely to be greatly influenced by cyclical variation, for example, shares of imports, the year 1958 alone is used; when cyclical variations are important, an average of either two or three years is employed.

For EFTA, 1959 was the last full year before internal tariff reductions were begun and is employed in many comparisons. For some measures, however, comparability with the EEC is required, necessitating the use of the same historical period. In those cases, a 1958-1959 or a 1957-1959 average is used.

TABLE A-1

*Growth of Imports of EEC Countries from Members
and Nonmembers, Selected Years, 1953–65*

(Dollar amounts in millions)

Source of Imports and Importing Country	1953	1958–1959	1965	Compound Annual Rate of Increase (Percent)	
				1953 to 1958–59	*1958–59 to 1965*
Imports from members	$ 3,969	$ 7,436	$20,435	*12.2*	*17.0*
Belgium-Luxembourg	934	1,539	3,473	*9.6*	*13.4*
France	667	1,296	4,081	*13.0*	*19.4*
Germany	957	2,180	6,663	*16.3*	*18.7*
Italy	529	788	2,295	*7.6*	*18.0*
Netherlands	882	1,634	3,986	*12.0*	*14.8*
Imports from nonmembers	11,178	16,237	28,569	*7.1*	*9.2*
Belgium-Luxembourg	1,489	1,746	2,901	*3.0*	*8.2*
France	3,499	4,058	6,323	*2.8*	*7.1*
Germany	2,852	5,795	10,819	*13.9*	*10.2*
Italy	1,866	2,491	5,052	*5.4*	*11.6*
Netherlands	1,472	2,148	3,474	*7.2*	*7.7*
Total imports	15,147	23,673	49,004	*8.5*	*12.0*
Belgium-Luxembourg	2,423	3,285	6,374	*5.8*	*10.8*
France	4,166	5,354	10,341	*4.8*	*10.6*
Germany	3,809	7,975	17,482	*14.5*	*13.0*
Italy	2,395	3,279	7,347	*6.0*	*13.3*
Netherlands	2,354	3,782	7,460	*9.1*	*11.1*

Sources: United Nations, *Commodity Trade Statistics*, Series D, Vol. III, No. 4 (New York, June 1954); International Monetary Fund—International Bank for Reconstruction and Development, *Direction of Trade, Annual 1958–62* (Washington, D. C., 1963) and *Annual 1961–65.*

236

Growth of Exports of EEC Countries to Members and Nonmembers, Selected Years, 1953–65

(Dollar amounts in millions)

Destination of Exports and Exporting Country	1953	1958–1959	1965	Compound Annual Rate of Increase (Percent)	
				1953 to 1958–59	1958–59 to 1965
Exports to members	$ 3,993	$ 7,517	$20,836	12.3	17.1
Belgium-Luxembourg	867	1,449	3,957	9.9	16.8
France	747	1,332	4,117	11.2	19.8
Germany	1,317	2,570	6,310	13.1	14.9
Italy	297	701	2,891	17.1	24.5
Netherlands	765	1,467	3,561	12.7	14.7
Exports to nonmembers	10,311	16,484	27,080	9.0	8.0
Belgium-Luxembourg	1,392	1,721	2,425	4.0	5.4
France	3,272	4,043	5,936	4.0	6.1
Germany	3,100	6,739	11,591	15.3	8.8
Italy	1,191	2,035	4,297	10.3	12.3
Netherlands	1,356	1,945	2,831	6.9	6.0
Total exports	14,304	24,001	47,916	10.0	11.3
Belgium-Luxembourg	2,259	3,170	6,382	6.4	11.5
France	4,019	5,375	10,053	5.5	10.2
Germany	4,417	9,309	17,901	14.7	10.7
Italy	1,488	2,736	7,188	11.8	16.2
Netherlands	2,121	3,412	6,392	9.1	10.2

Sources: *U. N.*, *Commodity Trade Statistics;* IMF-IBRD, *Direction of Trade, Annual 1958–62* and *Annual 1961–65.*

TABLE A-3

Growth of Imports of EFTA Countries from Members and Nonmembers, Selected Years, 1953–65

(Dollar amounts in millions)

Source of Imports and Importing Country	1953	1958–1959	1965	Compound Annual Rate of Increase (Percent)	
				1953 to 1958–59	1958–59 to 1965
Imports from members	$ 2,681	$ 3,592	$ 7,178	5.5	11.3
Austria	72	129	313	11.3	14.7
Denmark	401	542	1,020	5.7	10.3
Finland	119	219	561	11.9	15.7
Norway	364	492	925	5.7	10.3
Portugal	76	102	194	5.5	10.5
Sweden	430	606	1,424	6.5	14.2
Switzerland	150	220	548	7.3	15.2
United Kingdom	1,069	1,284	2,194	3.5	8.7
Imports from nonmembers	12,755	16,627	26,668	4.9	7.6
Austria	474	980	1,788	14.3	9.8
Denmark	599	930	1,791	8.4	10.7
Finland	411	565	1,075	6.1	10.5
Norway	547	821	1,281	7.8	7.2
Portugal	255	376	702	7.4	10.2
Sweden	1,146	1,779	2,955	8.4	8.2
Switzerland	1,033	1,591	3,133	8.3	11.1
United Kingdom	8,291	9,587	13,944	2.7	6.0
Total imports	15,436	20,219	33,846	5.2	8.3
Austria	546	1,109	2,101	13.9	10.4
Denmark	1,000	1,472	2,811	7.4	10.6
Finland	530	783	1,636	7.4	12.1
Norway	911	1,313	2,206	6.9	8.4
Portugal	331	477	896	6.9	10.3
Sweden	1,576	2,385	4,379	7.9	9.9
Switzerland	1,183	1,810	3,681	8.2	11.7
United Kingdom	9,360	10,871	16,138	2.8	6.3

Sources: European Free Trade Association, *EFTA Trade 1959–64* (Geneva, February 1966); IMF-IBRD, *Direction of Trade, Annual 1961–65;* U. N., *Commodity Trade Statistics.*

Growth of Exports of EFTA Countries to Members and Nonmembers, Selected Years, 1953–65

(Dollar amounts in millions)

Destination of Exports and Exporting Country	1953	1958–1959	1965	Compound Annual Rate of Increase (Percent)	
				1953 to 1958–59	*1958–59 to 1965*
Exports to members	$ 2,543	$ 3,385	$ 6,831	*5.4*	*11.5*
Austria	82	109	294	*5.4*	*16.7*
Denmark	464	543	1,059	*3.0*	*10.9*
Finland	165	240	470	*7.1*	*11.0*
Norway	198	303	646	*8.2*	*12.5*
Portugal	39	51	156	*5.1*	*18.7*
Sweden	540	804	1,692	*7.6*	*12.2*
Switzerland	174	265	590	*8.1*	*13.2*
United Kingdom	882	1,066	1,924	*3.5*	*9.6*
Exports to nonmembers	10,397	14,046	21,129	*5.7*	*6.6*
Austria	456	834	1,306	*11.7*	*7.2*
Denmark	431	778	1,214	*11.4*	*7.2*
Finland	407	566	948	*6.3*	*8.3*
Norway	310	469	797	*7.9*	*8.6*
Portugal	180	238	413	*5.3*	*8.9*
Sweden	938	1,343	2,281	*6.9*	*8.6*
Switzerland	1,031	1,350	2,383	*5.1*	*9.2*
United Kingdom	6,643	8,469	11,786	*4.6*	*5.3*
Total exports	12,940	17,430	27,960	*5.6*	*7.6*
Austria	538	943	1,600	*10.9*	*8.6*
Denmark	895	1,321	2,273	*7.4*	*8.8*
Finland	572	805	1,418	*6.5*	*9.2*
Norway	508	776	1,443	*8.1*	*10.1*
Portugal	219	289	569	*5.2*	*11.1*
Sweden	1,478	2,146	3,973	*7.1*	*10.0*
Switzerland	1,205	1,615	2,973	*5.6*	*9.9*
United Kingdom	7,525	9,535	13,710	*4.4*	*5.8*

Sources: EFTA, *EFTA Trade 1959–64;* IMF-IBRD, *Direction of Trade, Annual 1961–65.*

240

TABLE A-5

Imports of EEC Members from Soviet Area and China, 1958–65[a]

(Dollar amounts in millions)

Importing Country and Source of Imports	1958	1959	1960	1961	1962	1963	1964	1965
Belgium-Luxembourg								
Soviet area and Albania	$ 61.3	$ 77.6	$ 82.7	$ 88.0	$103.2	$118.5	$119.2	$124.2
China	6.0	8.7	9.9	3.4	4.8	8.2	13.6	14.2
Total Sino-Soviet countries	67.3	86.3	92.6	91.4	108.7	126.7	132.8	138.4
Total as percent of all imports	*2.2*	*2.5*	*2.3*	*2.2*	*2.4*	*2.5*	*2.3*	*2.2*
France								
Soviet area and Albania	$181.4	$168.9	$167.7	$167.7	$199.6	$255.2	$266.7	$287.0
China	11.4	16.2	22.7	15.9	16.9	21.1	30.8	43.7
Total Sino-Soviet countries	192.8	185.1	190.4	183.6	216.5	276.3	297.5	330.7
Total as percent of all imports	*3.4*	*3.6*	*3.0*	*2.7*	*2.9*	*3.2*	*3.0*	*3.2*
Germany								
Soviet area and Albania	$292.3	$337.8	$413.7	$469.2	$505.9	$500.2	$552.1	$655.4
China	58.5	66.3	69.4	39.7	39.3	40.8	51.8	72.7
Total Sino-Soviet countries	350.8	404.1	483.1	508.9	545.2	541.0	603.9	728.1
Total as percent of all imports	*4.7*	*4.7*	*4.7*	*4.6*	*4.4*	*4.1*	*4.1*	*4.1*
Italy								
Soviet area and Albania	$105.4	$155.4	$265.8	$309.6	$325.8	$457.8	$389.3	$445.9
China	13.7	13.2	24.1	12.3	14.1	19.1	23.7	38.4
Total Sino-Soviet countries	119.1	168.6	289.9	321.9	339.9	476.9	413.0	484.3
Total as percent of all imports	*3.7*	*5.0*	*6.1*	*6.2*	*5.6*	*6.3*	*5.7*	*6.6*
Netherlands								
Soviet area and Albania	$ 94.1	$118.7	$109.2	$108.0	$102.6	$138.0	$134.4	$157.0
China	17.1	22.1	—	15.1	13.9	15.7	20.0	25.4
Total Sino-Soviet countries	111.2	140.8	109.2	123.1	116.5	153.7	154.4	182.4
Total as percent of all imports	*3.1*	*3.6*	*2.4*	*2.4*	*2.2*	*2.6*	*2.2*	*2.4*

Source: IMF-IBRD, *Direction of Trade, Annual 1958–62* and *Annual 1961–65.*
[a] Soviet area includes USSR, Bulgaria, Czechoslovakia, East Germany, Hungary, Poland, Rumania, North Korea, Outer Mongolia, Cuba, and North Vietnam.

TABLE A-6

Exports of EEC Members to Soviet Area and China, 1958–65[a]

(Dollar amounts in millions)

Exporting Country and Destination of Exports	1958	1959	1960	1961	1962	1963	1964	1965
Belgium-Luxembourg								
Soviet area and Albania	$ 75.7	$ 74.9	$105.3	$ 97.3	$ 87.9	$ 77.1	$ 83.0	$ 99.5
China	52.1	33.5	44.6	10.2	8.0	9.5	7.4	16.6
Total Sino-Soviet countries	127.8	108.4	149.9	107.5	95.9	86.6	90.4	116.1
Total as percent of all exports	*4.2*	*3.3*	*4.0*	*2.7*	*2.2*	*1.8*	*1.6*	*1.8*
France								
Soviet area and Albania	$155.0	$172.6	$231.2	$241.0	$268.9	$230.4	$258.4	$320.9
China	44.4	39.8	52.8	36.4	43.3	58.4	49.6	60.1
Total Sino-Soviet countries	199.4	212.4	284.0	277.4	312.2	288.8	308.0	381.0
Total as percent of all exports	*3.9*	*3.8*	*4.1*	*3.8*	*4.2*	*3.6*	*3.4*	*3.8*
Germany								
Soviet area and Albania	$308.7	$343.9	$455.3	$489.3	$510.4	$445.1	$565.1	$591.4
China	162.4	128.7	95.4	30.5	31.1	15.4	25.4	79.0
Total Sino-Soviet countries	471.1	472.6	550.7	519.8	541.5	460.5	590.5	670.4
Total as percent of all exports	*5.3*	*4.8*	*4.8*	*4.1*	*4.1*	*3.1*	*3.6*	*3.7*
Italy								
Soviet area and Albania	$ 99.7	$127.9	$177.2	$220.0	$236.6	$265.9	$280.9	$334.4
China	32.7	36.4	39.7	29.7	18.9	21.4	18.4	56.4
Total Sino-Soviet countries	132.4	164.3	216.9	249.7	255.5	287.3	299.3	390.8
Total as percent of all exports	*5.1*	*5.7*	*5.9*	*6.0*	*5.5*	*5.7*	*5.0*	*5.4*
Netherlands								
Soviet area and Albania	$ 57.9	$ 66.6	$ 70.2	$ 88.5	$ 84.5	$ 82.8	$ 99.4	$112.9
China	11.9	11.2	—	4.1	3.6	12.9	5.9	18.9
Total Sino-Soviet countries	69.8	77.8	70.2	92.6	88.1	95.7	105.3	131.8
Total as percent of all exports	*2.2*	*2.2*	*1.7*	*2.2*	*1.9*	*1.9*	*1.8*	*2.1*

Source: IMF-IBRD, *Direction of Trade, Annual 1958–62* and *Annual 1961–65*.

[a] Soviet area includes USSR, Bulgaria, Czechoslovakia, East Germany, Hungary, Poland, Rumania, North Korea, Outer Mongolia, Cuba, and North Vietnam.

APPENDIX B

Measurement of Income Effects:
The Denison Method

THE MEASUREMENT of integration-induced income effects follows the methods employed by Edward Denison.[1] The method examines the growth of national income from the supply side. The contribution of a factor to growth is evaluated by measuring the increase in the quantity of the factor used over time and weighting that increase by the contribution to national income attributable to it during the period.

Increase in Business Investment

According to the Denison method, the contribution to the growth rate of an increase in business investment (measured by nonresidential construction plus machinery and equipment, including government enterprises) comes through increasing the capital stock. Denison, in Chapter 12 of *Why Growth Rates Differ,* demonstrates that the ratios of investment to gross domestic product (GDP) and capital stock growth are not correlated in an intercountry comparison, but they are related within a single country. The lack of correlation results primarily from the differing age of the capital stock in different countries. From the Denison work, a conversion factor for changing the ratios of investment to GDP into capital stock growth can be estimated for each country by calculating the effect that the actual ratios of investment to GDP had in increasing capital stocks from 1955 to 1962. Unfortunately for this purpose, Denison did not examine in detail four EFTA countries: Austria, Portugal,

[1] Edward F. Denison, *The Sources of Economic Growth in the United States,* Supplementary Paper No. 13 (Committee for Economic Development, January 1962), and, for current references, Edward F. Denison, assisted by Jean-Pierre Poullier, *Why Growth Rates Differ: Postwar Experience in Nine Western Countries* (Brookings Institution, 1967).

TABLE B-1

Derivation of Estimates of Annual Income Effects from
Business Investment, EEC and EFTA Countries

Country	Increment in Ratios of Investment to Gross Domestic Product[a] (Percent) (1)	Capital Stock Investment Conversion Factor[b] (2)	Growth in Capital Stock[e] (3)	Capital Stock Share of National Income[d] (Percent) (4)	Annual Income Effect[e] (Percent) (5)
EEC					
Belgium-Luxembourg	1.4	.224	.314	13.0	0.0408
France	2.1	.276	.580	13.1	.0759
Germany	2.8	.342	.958	15.8	.1513
Italy	2.8	.247	.692	13.6	.0941
Netherlands	1.3	.247	.321	13.7	.0440
EFTA					
Austria	3.1	.250[f]	.775	12.0[f]	.0930
Denmark	4.9	.318	1.558	12.0	.1870
Norway	0.2	.163	.033	14.0	.0046
Portugal	3.8	.250[f]	.950	13.0[f]	.1235
Sweden	2.7	.300[f]	.810	12.0[f]	.0972
Switzerland	3.4[g]	.150[f]	.510	13.0[f]	.0660
United Kingdom	2.9	.254	.737	11.2	.0825

[a] Table 2-4, col. 3.
[b] From Denison, *Why Growth Rates Differ*, Chap. 12, Table 12-1. Figures are for gross stock.
[c] Col. 1 multiplied by col. 2.
[d] *Ibid*, Table 12-4. Share of nonresidential construction plus machinery and equipment in national income in 1960–62.
[e] Col. 3 multiplied by col. 4.
[f] Estimated.
[g] Includes residential construction.

Sweden, and Switzerland. Rough estimates were made for these countries and are, therefore, subject to greater error. Switzerland in particular was difficult to estimate because data for residential construction could not be removed from the gross investment figures, and the conversion factor had to be adjusted accordingly. The derived figures for growth in capital stock were related to income growth by multiplying them by the share of national income attributable to business investment. These calculations are shown in Table B-1.

Increase in Efficiency

Economic integration increases economic efficiency by encouraging the expansion of efficient export industries and discouraging import-competing industries. This transfer of resources leads to cost savings, which can be measured and evaluated in terms of income growth. The Denison method for measuring this effect involves (a) measuring the increase of exports and imports in relation to gross domestic product attributable to trade liberalization, (b) measuring the cost savings from trade expansion, and (c) converting the cost savings into income-growth equivalents.

Since trade is to be related to income growth, only real changes should be measured, excluding price variations. Price indexes of exports and imports of manufactured products are notoriously poor, and at best give only a rough indication of price changes. Indexes of unit values of exports for all the EEC and EFTA countries are available, and these data were utilized, but with some misgivings. The import unit value indexes are derived from the average of export unit values of manufactured goods of all industrial countries, weighted by their shares in international trade of manufactured products. The same import unit value index was used for every country.

As noted in Chapter 2, total imports (and exports) must grow in relation to gross domestic product in order to obtain greater efficiency; a mere redirection of trade from nonmembers to member countries is not enough. However, to justify attribution of increases in trade to economic integration, trade with member countries must be increasing at a faster rate than trade with nonmembers. In order to examine this question, ratios of exports and imports to gross domestic product were calculated for trade with members and nonmembers. Ratios of current values were used, since price indexes properly broken down were not available. The ratios were converted to an index on a 1957-59 base, and are shown in Tables B-2 and B-3. Since economic integration influences growth by affecting trade with member countries, a difference should be noticeable in the ratios of exports and imports to gross domestic product that refer to intra-Community trade in comparison with those relating to nonmember countries. If no difference can be found, then economic integration cannot be credited with stimulating growth.

The difference between member and nonmember trade is very marked for all the EEC countries. Ratios of exports and imports to gross domestic product all rose substantially between 1957-59 and 1964, while the corresponding nonmember ratios either increased much less or declined.

For the EFTA countries the comparison of ratios of exports and imports to GDP for members with the corresponding nonmember ratios yields a very mixed picture, which appears to be influenced by the major shifts in competitiveness. The expected effects of economic integration appear in the ratios of exports to GDP, since the member ratios exceed those for nonmembers for all countries. However, for some EFTA countries (Denmark, Portugal, and Switzerland) very little difference is seen in the import ratios between member and nonmember countries. This can be explained by the loss of competitiveness of the major Community suppliers of manufactured products, which prevented them from taking full advantage of the EFTA trading preferences. This has considerable impact on the growth stimulus coming from

Indexes of Ratios of Imports and Exports to Gross Domestic Product for EEC Countries, 1953-64[a]

(1957–59 = 100)

Country and Index	1953	1954	1955	1956	1957	1958	1959	1960	1961	1962	1963	1964
Ratios of Exports to Gross Domestic Product												
Belgium-Luxembourg												
Member	70	80	96	104	101	96	104	122	136	151	168	178
Nonmember	99	89	99	108	100	96	103	99	94	89	82	81
France												
Member	61	67	83	78	89	94	117	144	161	167	172	174
Nonmember	87	87	88	78	96	103	103	108	97	85	82	83
Germany												
Member	76	83	88	100	105	93	100	102	110	117	134	134
Nonmember	73	82	85	91	99	99	101	95	89	82	80	82
Netherlands												
Member	75	78	84	86	90	100	110	120	123	138	151	165
Nonmember	109	106	105	99	96	98	106	101	96	81	93	86
Italy												
Member	47	59	71	82	94	88	112	147	171	153	165	234
Nonmember	77	75	82	91	98	100	104	123	126	130	116	119
Ratios of Imports to Gross Domestic Product												
Belgium-Luxembourg												
Member	71	76	83	92	96	97	107	122	140	144	159	165
Nonmember	96	94	105	116	104	91	105	114	116	121	121	117
France												
Member	42	53	68	84	100	95	95	126	147	163	184	208
Nonmember	85	80	95	100	110	110	85	110	115	120	130	138
Germany												
Member	61	70	87	83	84	96	122	130	126	139	135	149
Nonmember	48	63	80	80	88	100	114	123	108	106	106	111
Netherlands												
Member	81	88	95	107	107	92	101	108	110	111	127	134
Nonmember	95	101	109	112	110	94	97	109	119	115	104	104
Italy												
Member	86	95	90	95	105	90	110	148	171	195	229	192
Nonmember	112	104	104	112	112	96	96	144	156	168	172	139

Sources: Organization for Economic Cooperation and Development, *National Accounts Statistics, 1955–64* (Paris, March 1966); and United Nations, *Commodity Trade Statistics, Series D*, Vol. III (New York, June 1954) and subsequent years.
[a] Ratios of current values.

TABLE B-3

Indexes of Ratios of Exports and Imports to Gross Domestic Product for EFTA Countries, 1953-64[a]

(1957–59 = 100)

Country and Index	1953	1954	1955	1956	1957	1958	1959	1960	1961	1962	1963	1964
Ratios of Exports to Gross Domestic Product												
Austria												
Member	137	105	105	116	110	89	105	116	132	137	142	172
Nonmember	82	84	86	97	107	96	96	102	96	96	94	94
Denmark												
Member	60	70	93	90	100	103	97	117	120	113	140	145
Nonmember	66	70	80	93	92	102	108	114	103	104	110	115
Norway												
Member	77	81	90	96	100	94	106	131	121	110	115	135
Nonmember	74	78	83	101	103	96	101	95	96	95	104	109
Portugal												
Member	45	109	118	109	118	91	91	136	136	145	191	249
Nonmember	84	98	97	105	100	102	100	105	95	115	123	128
Sweden												
Member	76	91	93	89	100	100	100	107	118	118	131	135
Nonmember	79	80	82	94	98	100	103	112	112	118	116	116
Switzerland[b]												
Member	94	—	—	—	—	110	100	110	110	113	110	122
Nonmember	57	—	—	—	—	62	100	100	97	93	93	91
United Kingdom												
Member	127	127	118	109	100	100	109	109	127	127	127	137
Nonmember	102	101	104	106	106	97	98	97	91	90	91	88
Ratios of Imports to Gross Domestic Product												
Austria												
Member	67	81	95	105	105	95	100	119	124	128	138	143
Nonmember	53	69	89	89	98	97	105	119	121	116	117	122
Denmark												
Member	104	101	90	96	98	98	104	107	106	113	108	124
Nonmember	75	88	87	91	97	93	110	121	116	114	104	117
Norway												
Member	102	114	114	97	101	104	95	101	107	103	116	104
Nonmember	82	87	80	89	92	105	103	103	94	88	85	89
Portugal												
Member	87	91	91	96	102	104	91	87	122	104	98	98
Nonmember	79	82	95	91	102	102	96	100	109	92	98	102
Sweden												
Member	102	109	98	100	104	100	95	109	111	114	123	125
Nonmember	76	86	94	94	101	100	99	114	103	104	103	105
Switzerland[b]												
Member	65	65	69	81	85	77	100	92	108	115	115	130
Nonmember	63	70	80	92	99	87	100	112	127	128	123	126
United Kingdom												
Member	86	88	105	98	102	93	105	125	125	125	132	166
Nonmember	90	90	112	105	100	94	105	136	119	119	121	147

Sources: OECD, *National Accounts Statistics;* U. N. *Commodity Trade Statistics.*
[a] Ratios of current values.
[b] 1959 base.

246

TABLE B-4

Derivation of Estimates of Annual Income Effects from Greater Efficiency, EEC and EFTA Countries, 1957-59 to 1964

(In percentages)

Country	Increment in Ratios of Imports to Gross Domestic Product[a] (1)	Import Tariffs[b] (2)	Cost Savings[c] (3)	Annual Income Effect[d] (4)
EEC				
Belgium-Luxembourg	10.5	9.9	1.040	0.173
France	3.9	17.2	.671	.112
Germany	2.1	8.3	.173	.029
Italy	5.3	14.5	.768	.127
Netherlands	9.3	9.9	.921	.152
EFTA				
Austria	5.6	14.9	.834	.139
Denmark	6.3	6.1	.384	.064
Norway	0.9	12.5	.112	.019
Portugal	0.5	30.6[e]	.153	.025
Sweden	3.2	7.8	.250	.042
Switzerland	5.7	9.4	.536	.089
United Kingdom	2.7	17.2	.464	.077

[a] From Table 2-6, col. 3.
[b] J. A. Warta, "Import Duties Inside and Outside the European Economic Community," *Statistical Information*, No. 2, Statistical Office of the European Communities (Brussels, 1966).
[c] Col. 1 multiplied by col. 2.
[d] Col. 3 at compound annual rate from 1957-59 to 1964.
[e] Reduced by 50 percent for excess protection.

EFTA. While EFTA has provided the growth stimulus of larger markets via internal tariff reductions, it has not led to increases in competition and efficiency which are major parts of the growth stimulus. While the results suggest that some adjustment of the EFTA data might be made, this was not done, in view of the small increase in the overall ratios and the relatively slight amount of growth stimulation indicated by the unadjusted figures.

The inputs required for calculations of increased economic efficiency are shown in Table B-4. The changes in ratios of imports to GDP are taken from Table 2-6. The measure of resource savings from greater trade is the average of import tariffs of consumer durables, other consumer goods, and fixed assets, excluding food, beverages, and tobacco. The calculations to obtain cost-savings figures are shown, with the conversion into equivalent compound annual growth rates.

TABLE B-5

Derivation of Estimates of Integration-Induced Imports from Nonmember Countries During Transition Periods

Country	Annual Income Increment[a] (1)	Total Income Increment[b] (2)	1958 Gross Domestic Product (3)	Increment to Gross Domestic Product[c] (4)	Ratios of Imports to Gross Domestic Product				Increments of Imports			
					All Nonmembers (5)	United States (6)	EFTA (7)	EEC (8)	All Nonmembers[d] (9)	United States[e] (10)	EFTA[f] (11)	EEC[g] (12)
			(Billions of dollars)						(Millions of dollars)			
EEC												
Belgium-Luxembourg	0.21%	10.50%	9.784	1.027	7.0%	1.5%	3.4%	—	72	15	35	—
France	0.19	9.50	49.857	4.736	1.8	0.7	0.7	—	85	33	34	—
Germany	0.18	9.00	55.338	4.980	3.0	0.6	1.4	—	149	30	70	—
Italy	0.22	11.00	24.059	2.646	2.3	0.7	1.2	—	61	19	31	—
Netherlands	0.19	9.50	8.633	0.820	7.4	1.7	4.2	—	61	14	36	—
EFTA												
Austria	0.23	5.64	4.628	.261	11.1	0.6	—	9.7%	29	2	—	25
Denmark	0.25	6.13	4.400	.270	10.4	0.8	—	8.1	28	2	—	22
Norway	0.03	0.74	3.642	.027	14.9	1.3	—	10.8	4	[h]	—	3
Portugal	0.15	3.68	1.901	.070	10.7	2.0	—	8.9	7	1	—	6
Sweden	0.14	3.43	9.718	.333	10.8	1.7	—	8.0	36	6	—	27
Switzerland	0.16	3.92	7.232	.283	13.8	1.7	—	10.8	39	5	—	31
United Kingdom	0.16	3.92	56.238	2.205	4.0	0.7	—	1.4	88	15	—	31

a From Table 2-8.
b Compounding annual increment for length of transition period (for EEC countries, 9½ years; for EFTA, 6½ years).
c Col. 2 multiplied by col. 3.
d Col. 4 multiplied by col. 5.
e Col. 4 multiplied by col. 6.
f Col. 4 multiplied by col. 7.
g Col. 4 multiplied by col. 8.
h Less than $0.5 million.

Despite the fact that the cost savings were calculated from the import side alone, this does not imply that exports are unimportant. Without a parallel expansion of exports, a balance-of-payments crisis would ensue, requiring an adjustment process which would absorb some or all of the cost savings of larger imports. Tariff reductions by a country's trading partners permit it to expand exports without difficulty, and thus benefit from the full cost savings of larger imports stimulated by its own tariff reductions. Alternatively, one could measure the cost savings from liberalized commercial policy from the export side alone by assuming that imports would rise by an amount permitted by export expansion, or by a combination of export and import effects (as done by Denison).

The calculation also assumes that the economy of a country gains from the full amount of the resources released from the inefficient import-competing industries, that is, that the export industries will not suffer increases in unit costs as they expand output. A constant-cost assumption may appear to be extreme for fully employed economies. However, it must be remembered that the process of trade liberalization is a gradual one which, for the EEC, will last a decade. Supply in the long run is clearly more elastic than in the short run as gradual expansion of facilities is encouraged. Also, economies of scale are available in the longer run, to offset an increase in unit costs that might otherwise occur. For these reasons, no adjustment for higher unit costs of exports was thought necessary.

APPENDIX C

Measurement of the Trade-Pattern Effects of Integration

Direct Approach

The trade-pattern effects of economic integration were calculated by making empirical estimates of an equation adapted from the work of Harry G. Johnson.[1] The equation is stipulated as follows:

$$
(1) \qquad \dot{x}_{ij} = \eta_{xi} \frac{t_{ij} - T_i}{1 + t_{ij}} + \eta_{xi} \frac{T_i(1 - S_{ij})}{1 + t_{ij}} - E_{S_{ij}} T_i,
$$

$$
(2) \qquad Y = \sum_{ij} X_{ij} \dot{x}_{ij},
$$

where X_{ij} is the 1958 value of imports from nonmember countries of product i by member country j;

$\dot{x}_{ij}$ is the proportional change of X_{ij} due to economic integration;

η_{xi} is the elasticity of import demand for product i from all sources;

t_{ij} is the old national tariff on product i by country j;

T_i is the common external tariff on product i;

S_{ij} is the nonmember country share of product i imports by country j; and

$E_{S_{ij}}$ is the share elasticity of nonmember country imports of product i by country j.

Y is the total value of the trade-pattern loss of nonmember countries.

The products used are the three-digit Standard International Trade Classification groups 5, 6, 7, and 8, excluding nonferrous metals. The 1958 SITC

[1] Harry G. Johnson, "The International Competitive Position of the United States and the Balance of Payments Prospect for 1968," *Review of Economics and Statistics,* Vol. 46 (February 1964), pp. 14-32.

250

was used in preference to the 1960 classification for greater comparability. The SITC groups used are listed in Table C-1.

The parameters η_{xi} and $E_{S_{ij}}$ were assumed to be equal to 0.5 and 2.0, respectively, and constant for all products. This is the so-called "Dutch" convention, having been calculated by Verdoon from Benelux experience. Elasticity measurements do not exist for individual products, and these parameters correspond to average measures obtained from European experience. The value of these parameters may be somewhat low as the Benelux experience

TABLE C-1

Three-Digit Standard International Trade Classification Codes
Used in Calculation of Trade-Pattern Effects of Integration

Product Name	SITC Code	Product Name	SITC Code
Inorganic chemicals	511	Glassware	665
Organic chemicals	512	Pottery	666
Tar-coal chemicals	521	Gems	667 (672)
Coal-tar dyes	531	Iron and steel	670 (681)
Dye tanning extract	532	Silver and metal	681
Paints	533	Ordnance	691
Drugs	541	Metal manufactures, n.e.s.	699
Essential oils	551	Power machinery, n.e.s.	711
Soap, cosmetics	552	Agricultural machinery	712
Fertilizer manufactured	561	Tractors, non steam	713
Explosives	571 (591)	Office machinery	714
Chemicals, n.e.s.	599	Metalworking machinery	715
Leather	611	Machinery, n.e.s.	716
Manufactures of leather	612	Electric machinery	721
Furs, dressed	613	Railway vehicles	731
Rubber, semi-finished	621	Road motor vehicles	732
Rubber, manuf. n.e.s.	629	Aircraft	734
Boards, plywood	631	Ships and boats	735
Wood manufactures, n.e.s.	632	Prefab buildings	811
Cork manufactures	633	Furniture	821
Paper, paperboard	641	Handbags	831
Paper, manufactures	642	Clothes	841
Yarn, thread	651	Fur clothes, n.e.s.	842
Cotton fabrics	652	Footwear	851
Ribbons	654	Instruments	861
Special fabrics	655	Photogoods	862
Made-up textiles	656	Watches, clocks	864
Rugs	657	Musical instruments	891
Lime, cement	661	Printed matter	892
Mineral manufactures, n.e.s.	663	Manufactures, n.e.s.	899
Glass	664		

Source: United Nations, *Commodity Trade Statistics* ,Series D .Vol. III .No. 4 (New York .1954).
n.e.s. Not elsewhere specified

may not be fully representative of the EEC as a whole nor of EFTA. It would be reasonable to expect that if one of the parameters were larger, the other one would also be larger. In the accompanying tabular presentation, estimates of the EEC trade-pattern effect for nomember countries are shown for different combinations of η_{xi} and Es_{ij} values.

Es_{ij} / η_{xi}	2.0	3.0	4.0
0.5	975	1,105	1,235
1.0	900	1,030	1,160
1.5	825	955	1,085
2.0	750	880	1,010

It is clear that taking higher values for the elasticity parameters makes little difference to the overall loss estimate as long as both parameters are increased together, since larger η_{xi} values reduce the loss estimate while larger Es_{ij} values increase it by somewhat comparable amounts. In fact, the diagonal elements in the tabulation should be considered to be identical.

The old national tariff was obtained from a study on tariffs by Political and Economic Planning,[2] in which the three-digit SITC averages were obtained by weighting product codes by 1958 imports. The common external tariff was also obtained from this source. Nonmember country shares of trade were calculated from 1958 data.

The potential trade loss for all nonmember countries was calculated as specified in the equation. The total loss was distributed among the United States, EFTA (EEC), and others according to their respective shares of 1958 imports.

This calculation assumes an infinitely elastic supply curve, that is, constant costs over a great range of output. This assumption is reasonable for the EEC countries, considering the relevant range of change, the scale of production, and the gradualness of internal tariff reductions. However, this assumption could not easily be made for EFTA countries other than the United Kingdom. An adjustment was made for possible inelasticity of supply by reducing by half all potential trade diversion to EFTA countries other than the United Kingdom.

[2] *Atlantic Tariffs and Trade* (London: Allen and Unwin, Ltd., 1962).

Indirect Approach

The indirect approach to measuring the trade-pattern effect of economic integration estimates the changes in market shares of manufactured products indicated by changes in competitive conditions, assuming no change in trade barriers. The effect of the change in trade barriers is then measured indirectly as the difference between actual changes in shares and competitively determined changes in shares. The time period chosen for the analysis was 1958 to 1963. Most of the data were taken from the Junz-Rhomberg study.[3] Estimates for more recent years were not undertaken. The change in shares due to changes in competitive conditions was estimated by multiplying the change in price relatives by an elasticity of substitution coefficient. A constant elasticity of substitution of −2.0 was used. This figure, taken from the Junz-Rhomberg study, was the mean (and median) value of the parameter that was found among the statistically significant estimates in larger markets (Tables 3 and 4 of the Junz-Rhomberg study).

Because of the dispersion of the estimates of this parameter, a test was made of the sensitivity of this analysis to alternative values of the elasticity of substitution. For the EEC, with $E = -2.0$, estimated intra-EEC shares in 1963 were 49.5 percent, and with $E = -1.0$ and $E = -3.0$, intra-EEC shares were estimated at 49.8 percent and 49.3 percent, respectively. The lack of sensitivity of the EEC estimate to different parameter values comes from the almost equal division between competitive improvement and deterioration of EEC countries.

For the EFTA countries, somewhat greater sensitivity is indicated. With $E = -2.0$, estimated intra-EFTA shares in 1963 were 21.7 percent. With $E = -1.0$ and $E = -3.0$, the estimated intra-EFTA shares were 22.5 percent and 20.9 percent, respectively. The greater sensitivity comes from the general deterioration of competitive positions of the EFTA countries. The larger the elasticity of substitution, the smaller will be the estimated intra-EFTA shares because the many losses are offset by very few gains.

[3] Helen B. Junz and Rudolf R. Rhomberg, "Prices and Export Performance of Industrial Countries, 1953-63," International Monetary Fund, *Staff Papers* (Washington, D.C., July 1965).

APPENDIX D

Select Bibliography

Balassa, Bela. *The Theory of Economic Integration*. Homewood, Ill.: Richard D. Irwin, 1961.

Benoit, Emile. *Europe at Sixes and Sevens*. New York: Columbia University Press, 1961.

Camps, Miriam. *European Unification in the Sixties: From the Veto to the Crisis*. New York: McGraw-Hill Book Company for the Council on Foreign Relations, 1966.

————. *What Kind of Europe? The Community Since De Gaulle's Veto*. London: Oxford University Press, 1965.

Cleveland, Harold Van B., and Cleveland, Joan B. *The Atlantic Alliance: Problems and Prospects*. New York: Foreign Policy Association, 1966.

Coppock, John O. *Atlantic Agricultural Unity: Is It Possible?* New York: McGraw-Hill Book Company for the Council on Foreign Relations in cooperation with the Food Research Institute, Stanford University, 1966.

Cottrell, Alvin J., and Dougherty, James E. *The Politics of the Atlantic Alliance*. New York: Frederick A. Praeger, 1964.

Curzon, Gerard. *Multilateral Commercial Diplomacy*. London: Michael Joseph Ltd., 1965.

Deniau, J. F. *The Common Market*. London: Barrie and Rockcliff, 1961.

Diebold, William. *The Schuman Plan*. New York: Frederick A. Praeger for the Council on Foreign Relations, 1959.

Frank, Isaiah. *The European Common Market*. New York: Frederick A. Praeger, 1961.

Hallstein, Walter. *United Europe, Challenge and Opportunity*. Cambridge: Harvard University Press, 1962.

Haviland, H. Field, Jr., ed. *The United States and the Western Community*. Haverford: Haverford College Press, 1957.

Hinshaw, Randall. *The European Community and American Trade: A Study in Atlantic Economics and Policy*. New York: Frederick A. Praeger for the Council on Foreign Relations, 1964.

Humphrey, Don D. *The United States and the Common Market: A Background Study.* New York: Frederick A. Praeger, 1962.

Kitzinger, U. W. *The Politics and Economics of European Integration.* New York: Frederick A. Praeger, 1963.

Kleiman, Robert. *Atlantic Crisis: American Diplomacy Confronts a Resurgent Europe.* New York: W. W. Norton & Company, Inc., 1964.

Kraft, Joseph. *The Grand Design: From Common Market to Atlantic Partnership.* New York: Harper & Brothers, 1962.

Kravis, Irving. *Domestic Interests and International Obligations.* Philadelphia: University of Pennsylvania Press, 1963.

Lichtheim, George. *The New Europe: Today—and Tomorrow.* New York: Frederick A. Praeger, 1963.

Lindberg, Leon N. *The Political Dynamics of European Economic Integration.* Stanford: Stanford University Press, 1963.

Liska, George. *Europe Ascendant: The International Politics of Unification.* Baltimore: Johns Hopkins Press, 1964.

Meyer, F. V. *The Seven.* London: Barrie and Rockcliff, 1960.

Uri, Pierre. *Partnership for Progress.* New York: Harper and Row, 1963.

INDEX

Index

Africa: EEC aid to, 229; EEC trade with nonassociated countries of, 183-85; proposed associations of EEC with, 193-95

Agricultural products: EEC imports of, 101-02; EEC marketing procedure for, 90-91; EEC trade in, 98-99; effect of Kennedy Round on, 227; EFTA imports of, 113-15; European consumption of, 82-84, 96; imports of, from Eastern Europe, 207; net imports, 84-85; prices, 82, 82n. See also Agriculture

Agriculture, 10; growth of Common Market countries and, 22; EEC conflicts over, 75; export subsidies, 79; employment, 108; migration of workers from, 107-08; output, 80-81, 88; policy based on resource allocation, 107; producer prices, 79-81, 88, 111-12; real costs of protecting, 78; restrictive policies following World War II, 77, 77n; self-sufficiency in, 77-78, 84-85, 87, 88, 96; technical developments in, 81; as welfare problem, 76, 116-18. See also Agricultural products

Antitrust policy, 10, 11, 12, 223; EEC, 149-52; EEC implementation of, 152-53; European business and, 150; European consumer groups and, 150; European governments and, 150-51; lack of, 149; proposed European liberalization of, 144-45

AOC. See Associated Overseas Countries

Ashton, David, 121, 121n

Associated Overseas Countries (AOC): EEC imports of tropical products from, 189; German opposition to association with, 195; relations with EEC, 182-85, 193-95

Association Council for Administration, 191-92

Atlantic Alliance, 6, 26, 28, 229

Austria: in formation of EFTA, 15; negotiations with EEC, 202-03, 204; reaction to formation of EEC, 13-14; tariffs, 43. See also European Free Trade Association

Austrian State Treaty, 14, 201

Bakker, J. A., 146n

Balance of payments, 24; CAP and, 116; conditions for equilibrium of, 168, 170-71; postwar problems in, 77; United Kingdom and, 77n; U.S. and, 74, 119, 140, 174, 223-24

Balassa, Bela, 32n, 122, 122n

Ball, George W., 119n

Barlow, E. R., 123n

Belgium: agricultural price supports, 79. See also Benelux customs union; European Economic Community

Beloff, Nora, 201n

Benelux customs union, 21, 67

Benoit, Emile, 143n

Business investment: effect on growth of national income, 37-40; ratio to gross domestic product, 38, 39

Camps, Miriam, 201n

CAP. See Common Agricultural Policy

Cartels: involvement of American subsidiaries with, 154; lack of regulation of, 151. See also Antitrust policy

"Chicken war," 75, 102, 213

China, relations with U.S. and Western Europe, 27-28

Coal, 158; EEC production, 159-60; European imports, 159-60

Cold war, 5, 229

Commission, EEC, 7, 24; agricultural proposal, 89; executive function, 9; initiation of studies by, 9

Common Agricultural Policy (CAP), 12, 13, 89, 209; effect on agricultural prices, 94-95; effect on agricultural production, 95; effect on balance of payments, 116; evaluation of, 116-17; financing of, 93

Common Energy Policy, 161

Common external tariff (CXT), 32, 49, 71n, 195; changes in, from Dillon

259

264   *European Economic Integration and the United States*

Patents: diversity of laws for, 156; EEC policy for, 156-57; EFTA policy for, 157; U.S. interest in European policy, 157-58

Petroleum: control of, 159; U.S. foreign investment in, 134-35; USSR imports, 207

Pfaltzgraff, Robert L., Jr., 145n

Philips, Claude S., Jr., 191n

Plant and equipment, U.S. direct foreign investment in, 126-27

Political integration, 5, 6, 7, 23-25, 228-31

Polk, Judd, 140n

Population: EEC and EFTA countries, 83; effect on food consumption, 82-84, 109; projected to *1970*, 105

Portugal: in formation of EFTA, 15; tariffs, 42. *See also* European Free Trade Association

Poullier, Jean-Pierre, 36n, 107n, 217n

Price supports, agricultural, 79-81, 82, 82n, 87, 88

Prices: effect of CAP on agricultural, 94-95; EFTA agricultural producer, 111-12. *See also* Target prices

Production: in agriculture, 80-81, 88, 95; in manufacturing industries, EEC and U.S., 129-30

Protocol on Energy Policy, 160

Resnick, Stephen, 167n

Resource allocation, 41, 107, 171

Rey, Jean, 210, 211, 211n

Rhomberg, Rudolph R., 63n, 67n

Rome Treaty, 2, 11, 15, 36, 108n; agricultural policy, 89n; antitrust provisions, 149, 151-52; AOC specified in, 182n; emphasis on agriculture, 88-89; omission of political provisions, 7; proposed treaty negotiations in, 205-06; provisions for formation of customs union, 10; provisions for majority voting, 8-9; provisions for special relationships with other countries, 176. *See also* European Economic Community

Salant, Walter S., 52n, 170n

Schaetzel, J. Robert, 228n

Schroeder, Gerhard, 25, 195

Scitovsky, Tibor, 119n

Self-sufficiency, in agriculture: effect on net imports, 84-85; and government purchase of surplus, 87; for

national defense, 77-78; real costs of, 88; stimulated by Common Market, 96

SITC. *See* Standard International Trade Classification

Soviet bloc, trade with EEC, 207-08

Spenale, George, 184n

Standard International Trade Classification (SITC), 50n

Static effects of tariff changes. *See* Trade

Stockholm Convention, 16, 36, 109; agricultural policies, 110; provisions for new members, 176-77. *See also* European Free Trade Association

Sweden: in formation of EFTA, 15; reaction to formation of EEC, 13. *See also* European Free Trade Association

Switzerland: in formation of EFTA, 15; proposed entry into EEC, 204; reaction to formation of EEC, 13. *See also* European Free Trade Association

Target prices, for agricultural products, 91; difficulty in determining, 93; estimated for *1970*, 102-05; grains, 92, 93, 103

Tariffs: discrimination under EEC, 120, 121; and EEC bilateral treaties, 205; increased efficiency from reduction of, 40; negotiations between EEC and U.S., 208-15; time-path for reduction in, 57-60. *See also* Common External Tariff; Dillon Round; General Agreement on Tariffs and Trade; Kennedy Round

Taxes: border, 162, 163, 166, 166n; for control of inflation, 169; harmonization of, 162-67, 223; indirect, 162; proposed changes in, 164-65; treatment of indirect versus direct, 166n; turnover system of, 164-65

Tinbergen, Jan, 164, 168n

Tinbergen Committee, 164

Trade: agricultural commodities, EEC, 97-98; between EEC and AOC, 183-85; EEC, 20-22; effect of common external tariff on, 49-50; effect of tariff changes on, 32, 49-70; EFTA, 17-20; Finland, 179-81; Greece, 198-99; losses to nonmembers of EEC and EFTA, 70-73; Nigeria, 190; and removal of all tariffs, 49; Turkey, 198-99; of U.S. with EEC and EFTA,